10

AFRICAN HISTORICAL DICTIONARIES
Edited by Jon Woronoff

Historical Dictionary
of
THE REPUBLICS OF
GUINEA-BISSAU
AND
CAPE VERDE

Richard Lobban

African Historical Dictionaries, No. 22

The Scarecrow Press, Inc.

Metuchen, N.J., & London

1979

Library of Congress Cataloging in Publication Data

Lobban, Richard.
   Historical dictionary of the Republics of Guinea-
Bissau and Cape Verde.

   (African historical dictionaries ; no. 22)
   Bibliography: p.
   1. Guinea-Bissau--History--Dictionaries.
2. Cape Verde Islands--History--Dictionaries. I. Ti-
tle. II. Series.
DT613.5.L62   966'.57'003   79-18227
ISBN 0-8108-1240-1

To those men, women, and
children who gave their
lives in the pursuit of
freedom from colonialism
in Guinea-Bissau and Cape Verde.

ACKNOWLEDGMENTS

It is something of an embarrassment to put my own name as the author on a work of history to which so many individuals have contributed by their acts: the generations of Africans, the Portuguese explorers and settlers, thousands of slaves, and those colonial and anti-colonial forces in the recent wars. Of course, this collective process of history making gives me the material for history writing. In more concrete terms I would like to thank the leadership of the PAIGC for permitting my travels in 1973 and 1975 to Guinea-Bissau and in 1975 to Cape Verde for the independence celebrations.

Typing, library work, and bibliographic compilation for this book were aided by the faithful and accurate research of Linda Zangari. Shirley Chouinard also assisted with careful typing. A faculty research grant from the Rhode Island College Research Fund helped to support some of the costs of typing and duplication.

Particular thanks must also be directed to Jose Aica, Professor of Portuguese at the University of Rhode Island for his continual willingness to answer my detailed questions about translation. The Cape Verdean community of New England also contributed by supplying inspiration and answers to questions which just are not found in books. Raymond Almeida, of the American Committee for Cape Verde, was kind enough to review some of the material and to give it a trial run in the "Tchuba" newsletter.

Although usually common in Acknowledgments of others, I can't thank my wife for typing or staying home with our daughter, Josina. My wife is a busy productive scholar in her own right and we equally share the child-raising responsibilities. However, Carolyn Fluehr-Lobban offered the on-going concern and interest that keeps alive the patience to complete this effort and the challenge to make it meaningful and accurate.

iv

CONTENTS

EDITOR'S FOREWORD

Although small in size and population, Guinea-Bissau and Cape Verde have acquired unusual significance and prestige in Africa. This was largely due to the nationalist party, PAIGC, and its founder Amílcar Cabral, who managed to carry on one of the longest and hardest armed struggles against colonialism. Just a corner of Portugal's colonial empire, of scant value compared to Angola or Mozambique, it was realized that if Guinea obtained independence the others were bound to follow. PAIGC and Cabral won even broader acceptance due to ideas that were radical but also realistic and an ideology that did not lose contact with what was possible. Now that both states are free and sovereign, it is important to see how they have gone about the tasks of nation building and what their future contributions will be.

It is thus fortunate that this book was written by Dr. Richard Lobban, an American anthropologist who regards himself as an "activist-scholar." Otherwise he would not have visited Guinea-Bissau in 1973, in the midst of the war, and crossed the whole country by foot with the nationalists in an effort to know the people and their struggle. He also visited Guinea-Bissau and Cape Verde after independence. This has permitted him to compare the situation and see what improvements have been made and what remains to be done. During this period, he has also written very broadly on Portuguese Africa and especially the subjects of this dictionary.

But this African Dictionary is not restricted to recent history. Its entries reach back to trace the pre-colonial and colonial past, to present the indigenous groups and describe the explorers and conquerors, before concluding with the liberators. Considerable attention is devoted to the economy and politics, domestic and foreign, as well as important cultural, linguistic, sociological, and geographical aspects. Its list of acronyms, entries giving definitions of Portuguese expressions and a very comprehensive bibliography further enhance its value.

Jon Woronoff
Series Editor

ABBREVIATIONS AND ACRONYMS

ALNG	Armée de Libération Nationale Guinéene
ANP	Assembleia Nacional Popular
BDG	Bloc Démocratique de Guinée-Bissao
BNU	Banco Nacional Ultramarino
CEI	Casa dos Estudantes do Império
CEL	Comité Executivo da Luta
CONCP	Conferência das Organisações Nacionalistas das Colónias Portuguesas
CSL	Conselho Superior da Luta
CUF	Companhia União Fabril
DGS	Direção Geral Segurança
FARP	Forças Armadas Revolutionárias do Povo
FLG	Frente de Libertação da Guiné
FLGC	Frente de Libertação da Guiné Portuguesa e Cabo Verde
FLING	Frente de Luta Pela Independência Nacional da Guiné-Bissau
FRAIN	Frente Revolucionária Africana para a Independência Nacional das Colónias Portuguesas
FRELIMO	Frente de Liberação de Moçambique
FUL	Front Uni de Libération
JAAC	Juventude Africana Amilcar Cabral
MAC	Movimento Anti-Colonialista
MING	Movimento para Independência Nacional da Guiné Portuguesa
MLG	Movimento de Libertação da Guiné
MLGCV	Mouvement de Libération de la Guinée "Portugaise" et des Iles du Cap Vert
MLGP	Movimento de Libertação da Guiné Portuguesa
MLICV	Mouvement de Libération des Iles du Cap Vert
MPLA	Movimento Popular de Libertação de Angola
NATO	North Atlantic Treaty Organization
OAU	Organization of African Unity
PAIGC	Partido Africano da Independência da Guiné e Cabo Verde
PIDE	Policia International e de Defesa do Estado

RDAG	Rassemblement Démocratique Africain de la Guinée
UDC (UDCV)	União Democrática de Cabo Verde
UDEMU	União Democrática das Mulheres
UDG	União Democrática da Guiné
UGEAN	União Geral dos Estudantes da Africa Negra
UGTGB	União Geral dos Trabalhadores da Guiné-Bissau
UN	United Nations
UNGP	União dos Naturais da Guiné Portuguesa
UNTG	União Nacional dos Trabalhadores da Guiné
UPG	União das Populações da Guiné
UPICV	União das Populações das Islas do Cabo Verde
UPLG	União Popular Para Libertação da Guiné
URGP	Union de Ressortissants de La Guinée Portugaise

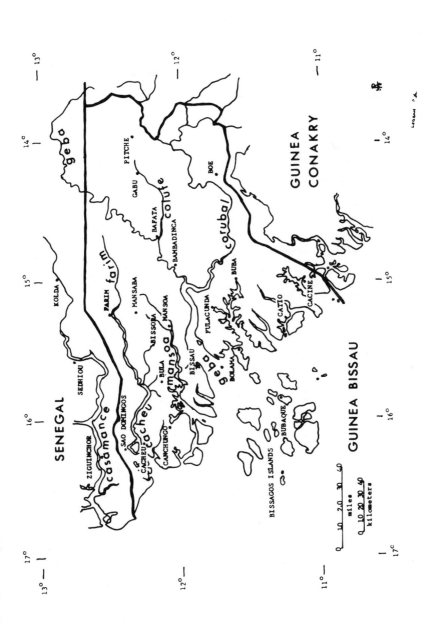

SENEGAL

ZIGUINCHOR

KOLDA

SEDHIOU

casamance

SAO DOMINGOS

CACHEU

cacheu

CANCHUNGO

BULA

mansoa

BISSAU

BISSORA

MANSOA

MANSABA

FARIM

farim

geba

BAFATA

GABU

PITCHE

colufe

BAMBADINCA

corubal

BOE

geba

BOLAMA

PULACUNDA

BUBA

corubal

CATIO

CACINE

BUBAQUE

BISSAGOS ISLANDS

GUINEA BISSAU

GUINEA
CONAKRY

0 10 20 30 40
miles
0 10 20 30 40
kilometers

13° —

17° —
16° —
15° —
14° —
13° —

12° —

11° —

— 17°
— 16°
— 15°
— 14°

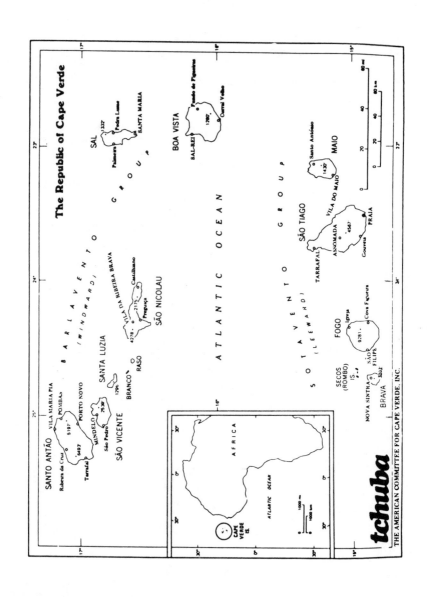

The Republic of Cape Verde

B A R L A V E N T O (WINDWARD)

G R O U P

S O T A V E N T O (LEEWARD)

G R O U P

ATLANTIC OCEAN

SANTO ANTÃO
VILA MARIA PIA
Ribeira da Cruz
POMBAS
5191'
PORTO NOVO
Tarrafal
6493'
MINDELO
75.36'
São Pedro
SÃO VICENTE

SANTA LUZIA
1796'
BRANCO'
RASO

VILA DA RIBEIRA BRAVA
Casilhiano
4278'
2172'
Preguiça
SÃO NICOLAU

SAL
1337
Palmeira
Pedra Lume
SANTA MARIA

BOA VISTA
Fundo de Figueiras
1280'
Curral Velho
SAL-REI

Santo Antônio
MAIO
1430'
VILA DO MAIO

SÃO TIAGO
ASNOMADA
4567'
Gouveia
PRAIA
TARRAFAL

FOGO
Igreja
9281'
Cova Figueira
SECOS
(ROMBO)
IS.
SÃO
FILIPE
NOVA SINTRA
3102'
BRAVA

AFRICA
ATLANTIC OCEAN
1000 mi
1000 km
CAPE
VERDE
IS.

0   20   40   60 mi
0   20   40   60   80 km

tchuba

THE AMERICAN COMMITTEE FOR CAPE VERDE, INC.

HISTORICAL CHRONOLOGY FOR
GUINEA-BISSAU AND CAPE VERDE

4000 BC (?)	Independent development of agriculture in the West African savanna.
3000 BC	Berbers initiate trans-Saharan trade.
2000 BC	Rise of small states in the savanna.
1000 BC	Southeast Asian crops arrive on the West African coast.
500 BC	Agriculture penetrates the West African forest; coastal peoples diversify.
250 BC	Iron-working in Nigeria.
100 BC	Camels in trans-Saharan trade.
ca 300 AD	Formation of Ghana and Tekrur.
900 AD	Savanna peoples enter forest zones.
990 AD	Tekrur falls.
1076	Ghana conquered by Almoravids.
1143	Portugal becomes an independent monarchy.
1230	Formation of Mali.
ca 1250	Formation of Gabu.
1384	Rise of Portuguese Royal house of Avis.
1420-1470	Epoch of Portuguese coastal exploration.
1441	First slaves captured by Portugal.

1446	Portuguese reach coast of Guinea-Bissau.
1460	Portuguese discover Cape Verde archipelago and settlement begins.
1469	Songhai becomes dominant on the Niger.
1490	Formation of Futa Toro.
1514	Expansion of slave trade to and from Cape Verde.
1546	Fall of the Mali Empire.
1562	English begin slaving on Guinea coast.
1580-1640	Portugal is ruled by the Spanish crown.
1587	Direct royal administration of Cape Verde replaces captaincy system.
1588	Cacheu captaincy formed.
1591	Collapse of Songhai.
1600's	Intensification of the slave trade.
1775	End of Denianke dynasty in Futa Toro.
1788	Formation of Futa Jallon as Fula state.
1800's	European nations abolish slavery.
1836	Creation of governor general of Cape Verde to govern Guinea-Bissau as well.
1867	Fall of Kansala, capital of Gabu.
1868	Grant arbitrates in favor of Portugal at Bolama.
1878	End of Futa Jallon, Portuguese initiate military campaigns of "pacification" (1878-1936).
1879	Guinea-Bissau gains separate administrative status from Cape Verde.
1884-5	Berlin Congress.

1910-20	Portuguese monarchy overthrown.
1926	Rise of Portuguese fascism.
1941	Bissau replaces Bolama as the capital of Guinea-Bissau.
1956	PAIGC formed and leads successful nationalist war (1963-74).
1974	Fall of fascist Portugal, Guinea-Bissau becomes independent.
1975	Cape Verde becomes independent.

INTRODUCTION

This book is unusual in this series of Historical Dictionaries in that it includes two African nations within its covers. The Republic of Cape Verde, since its settlement in the 15th century, has been closely linked with the Republic of Guinea-Bissau through the trade in African slaves and products and through their common Portuguese colonial administration. In fact the trade on the Guinea coast was long under the influence of Cape Verdean lancados serving their own interests and those of the Portuguese Crown. It was only late in the 19th century that two separate colonial administrations began for the two territories.

During the centuries of slavery these peoples and others living along the coast went to plantations in Cape Verde and to the New World. Thus the unity between the two republics has a long history and deep roots. It is symbolic that many of the leaders of the PAIGC were from Cape Verde and risked their lives to fight for the independence of Guinea-Bissau as a stepping stone for the independence of their own archipelago.

The name "Guinea" appears to be derived from the Berber word "aguinaou, " meaning "black, " which was applied by the early Portuguese in West Africa. The Guinea coast is sometimes divided into Lower and Upper sections stretching fron Senegal to the Congo River. Gold from this region has given the term "guinea" to British currency. Portuguese sources refer to Guiné Portuguesa, French sources identify Guinée Portugaise and the new government uses the name Guiné-Bissão. For simplicity and consistency I have used Guinea-Bissau throughout this book as this is the correct English translation of the name of the new republic. The hyphenated name distinguishes it from its neighbor to the south, Guinea-Conakry. The terminology for the Republic of Cape Verde may also have its confusions with Cap Vert on the coast of Senegal for which the archipelago is named.

1

There is also the false implication that there is much "green" in the Cape Verde Islands.

Physical Features

The Republic of Guinea-Bissau lies between 12° 40'N and 10° 52'N latitude and between 13° 38'W and 16° 43'W longitude. Generally the climate is hot and tropical although there are two seasons. From June to November is the hot and rainy season during which the bulk of the annual 78" rainfall occurs. From December to May is the cool, dry season. Usually the temperatures vary only between 77° F (January) to 86° F (May), 25-30° C. The 13,947.9 square miles (36,125 square kilometers) of the territory lie on a very broad coastal plain which results in labyrinthine coastal creeks and mangrove swamps. Aside from shallow river valleys and the slightly uplifted Boe hills in the southeast, the terrain is rather undifferentiated and rises only to a maximum altitude of 985 feet. Areas between the coastal swamps have considerable tropical brush and hardwood forests. Further to the interior the scrub bush gives way to semi-grassland zones. The soil is tropical lateritic or of clay depending upon region; this requires shifting agricultural land use as the soil is exhausted. Along the coastal areas extensive rice paddies are well developed.

The Cape Verde Islands lie about 370 miles off the coast of Senegal between latitudes 14° 48'N and 17° 12'N and longitudes 22° 41'W and 25° 22'W. The archipelago consists of ten major islands and five minor islets. The climate is tropical, but it is extremely dry with less than 10" of rain falling on São Tiago annually. The strong prevailing winds and the maritime location result in a temperature fluctuation between 72-80° F (22-27° C) and a notable lack of seasonality. The land is 1,557 square miles (4,033.3 sq. kms.) and is particularly rocky and mountainous owing to the volcanic origin of the islands. Only 1.65 percent (52,688 hectares) of the land area may be cultivated and much of this is fallow at any one point in time. What little vegetation there was has been destroyed by early farmers and grazing animals. Aside from mountain tops which draw water from passing clouds the terrain is exceptionally bleak and moon-like with sharp crags, deep valleys and pronounced erosion. Some islands are very low and rise only a few hundred feet above sea level while another rises immediately from the sea bed to soar to 9,281 feet. This high point on Fogo represents a sometimes active volcano.

Peoples

The 640,000 people who inhabit Guinea-Bissau are essentially derived from the Niger-Congo or Congo-Kordofanian language stock. This group is represented by the West Atlantic and Manding families. Those people of Fula ethnic extraction are descended from an admixture of West Atlantic peoples and from the Berber language family. Except for the Fulas and their sub-groups, the other West Atlantic cultures of Guinea-Bissau are known collectively as Senegambians or Semi-Bantu Littoral peoples. Some of the more numerous Senegambians include the Balantas, Papeis, Beafadas and Nalus. The Manding or Nuclear Mande are best represented by the Mandingos, Susus, and Dyulas. In general the coastal Senegambians have acephalous or slightly centralized political organization. The Manding have inherited a somewhat more complex system of political organization and were the members of the autonomous state of Gabu for many centuries. At the time of independence the Fulas were the most hierarchical in their political organization, but this relates, in part, to their function in the system of Portuguese colonial rule. While there is some debate about the term "peasants" in African ethnography, one may say that these people were locked into rural modes of subsistence and cash cropping which have numerous peasant-like qualities. Such production met domestic needs and yielded agricultural goods for a world market.

In the context of the relationship between the local people and foreign commerce, various special groups of traders and intermediaries have also been found. Examples of African traders include the Manding Dyulas descended from a similar role in the trade nexus of early Sudanic states.

The centuries of slavery brought many Guineans, and Senegambians in general, to the Cape Verde Islands to work on slave plantations producing subsistence goods and other market commodities. The small Portuguese population mixed extensively with the slaves to produce the rich and varied cultural heritage which typifies Cape Verdeans. Settlers from Algarve and the Madeira islands as well as Iberian political exiles (such as those of Jewish extraction, adventurers, and criminals) made up a large portion of the earliest Portuguese population in the Cape Verde islands in addition to the Portuguese administrators and clergy. Trading and slaving activities on the coast created unique groups of Luso-Africans (e.g. Ladinos, Mestiços, and Tangomaus) and Afro-Portuguese

(e. g. , Degredados, Feitors, and Lançados); these groups were also represented on the islands.

Of course, the largest portion of the Cape Verdean population traces its roots mainly to Africa, but specific ethnic identification has been eroded with Crioulo culture and language acting as a strong unifying theme in the islands and among Cape Verdeans wherever they may be found. Racist ideology supporting Portuguese colonialism denigrated African culture and history so that some Cape Verdeans may be reluctant to accept their full heritage. In Cape Verde virtually everyone communicates in Crioulo or in Portuguese, however literacy is not high, with about 73 percent of the population not able to read even at the elementary level. By comparison, the illiteracy rate in Guinea-Bissau was far worse at 98 percent, although the PAIGC educational program has now reduced this considerably. In the mainland republic there are many who do not communicate in Crioulo, but speak in the various representative languages of the Fula, Senegambian, and Manding stocks. Some effort is being made to standardize Crioulo as the language of elementary instruction, but all formal and official communication is carried out in Portuguese.

Populations

The sizes of the populations of the two republics are difficult to determine with accuracy. A reasonable estimate for Guinea-Bissau is in the vicinity of 640, 000 persons. Throughout this century there has been a rather steady, but relatively low, rate of natural increase. The actual loss of life during the war, while tragic, was relatively low on a national basis and the main demographic effect was in the significant population of refugees from the contested areas. The greatest portion of these refugees have now returned to their original territory.

The population of Cape Verde is most likely to be in the neighborhood of 285, 000 thus making for a joint population of almost 1 million between the sister republics. The health conditions in Cape Verde are generally more favorable than for Guinea-Bissau but the recurrent droughts in the archipelago have a negative effect on nutrition. The acute limitations on agriculture and farm labor have resulted in a long history of out migration which has been a significant brake to population growth.

History

          The earliest human occupation of the West African
savanna dates back to Acheulian times of Homo erectus about
600, 000 years ago or perhaps even much earlier.   However,
the forested regions closer to the coast may not have been
occupied until about 9000 BC by small groups of hunters and
fishermen.   The possibility of the independent development
of agriculture in the Upper Nile between 5000-4000 BC and
its spread to the east and other directions was, no doubt,
responsible for the first permanent occupation of the northeastern regions of Guinea-Bissau.   Cultural development was
slow since the territory of today's Guinea-Bissau was at the
periphery of the Sudanic states and the trans-Saharan trade
routes.   The demographic transformation of the interior
brought about by new and improved crops, camel transport
and iron-working had the effect of initiating population pressure on the adjacent territories.

          The arrival and spread of southeast Asian tropical
crops was slow at first in the centuries before Christ but
later became significant in supporting the diversification of
the pioneer peoples in the Senegambian forest littoral.   The
expansion of trade of the Empire of Ghana and the introduction of Islam to the savanna in about the 9th century lay the
basis for the penetration of the forest on a greater scale by
people from the interior at the expense of the coastal hunters
and gatherers.   By the 11th century the ancestors of Guinea-
Bissau's Fula population were forming in Senegal as the result of the mixture of Berber and Atlantic peoples.   By the
end of the 11th century the Almoravids had briefly conquered
Ghana only to have it re-established in 1205 by the Susu
(Soninke) of whom modern descendants are found in southern
coastal Guinea-Bissau.   The Susu reconquest was maintained
only for thirty years when the Keita dynasty of Mali founded
its powerful military and trade structure in 1235.   The 13th-
century influence of Mali was felt directly and profoundly in
Guinea-Bissau with the creation of the secondary, semi-autonomous kingdom of Gabu.   The Senegambians living in
Guinea-Bissau and even further to the interior were pushed
toward the coast by the growing kingdom and sub-states of
the Mande-based Gabu.   In this way the Senegambians who
displaced the hunters and gatherers were themselves displaced
by the more dominant local representatives of Mali.

          A developing interest in Africa and its valuable re-
sources, and a desire to push Moorish influence out of Iberia

led to the early 15th-century moves by the Portuguese to explore, conquer, and claim portions of northwest Africa such
as the 1415 conquest of Ceuta by Prince Henry "The Navigator." Throughout the 15th century Portuguese barks and
caravels pushed further and further down West Africa's coast
reaching Cape Bojador in 1434, the Senegal River mouth in
1445 and exploration of the estuaries and islands of Guinea-
Bissau in 1446 particularly by Captains Gil Eanes and Nuño
Tristão. By 1456 the Cape Verde Islands were first noted
for the Portuguese by Captain Cadamosto. Possibly Phoeni-
cian or Malian sailors or Lebou fishermen from Senegal had
visited the islands before the Portuguese but the record is
unclear. By 1460 Antonio da Noli and Diogo Gomes claimed
official discovery of the Cape Verde Islands for King Afonso
V of Portugal. Almost immediately Portuguese settlers began to arrive on São Tiago, Fogo, and other islands. From
the very earliest days of exploration one may also date the
earliest examples of Portuguese slaving and African resistance. At first there were only dozens of slaves captured but
by the mid 15th century there were already hundreds of Africans kidnapped annually and sent to work in Europe. The
settlement of the Cape Verde Islands gave rise to the slave
plantation system with 500-1,000 slaves reaching the islands
annually in the second half of the 15th century; many of these
slaves were exported to Europe from the islands. The discovery and settlement of the New World triggered a great intensification of the slave trade in the 16th century in which
European competition grew and Portugal was no longer able
to meet the demand. The Portuguese Crown issued slave
trade monopolies on the coast but European marauders and
African and Luso-African middlemen sought their own private
gains. By 1580 Portugal came under the rule of the Spanish
Crown and English, Dutch, and Spanish slavers and pirates
eroded Portuguese control and influence on the West African
coast by attacking and looting Portuguese forts and trading
"factories." The penetration and knowledge of the interior
was extremely superficial at this time as Africans were encouraged to war against each other to produce slaves and acquire firearms. For example, when asked by Mali in 1534
to help them defend against attacks by Songhai, the Portuguese declined both because their influence was weak and because slaves would be generated with either side being victorious. Slaves were brought to the coast on foot or in light
river craft and were then exchanged by middlemen for various merchandise. Aside from the "captaincy" system in
Cape Verde and at such places as Cacheu and Bissau, the
Portuguese hold on the African continent was very marginal

although the economic stimulus for slave wars was penetrating and extensive.

The 17th century saw even greater build up of the slave trade, but the portion of slaves transported on Portuguese ships steadily declined and one of Portugal's main goals in Guinea-Bissau and Cape Verde was defense against the frequent attacks and encroachments of other European powers. Although attempts at administrative reform and military consolidation were made in Guinea-Bissau, Portugal's rule on the coast was rather undisciplined and precarious and generally dependent upon their good relations with Gabu in the interior. Except for slaving, the economy was in a state of overall stagnation in both of the Portuguese West African territories at this point.

These themes continued into the 18th century although the centers of the slave trade had moved considerably to other parts of west and central Africa. Cape Verdeans often escaped the drought and economic uncertainty by joining the crews of whaling and packet ships. The Portuguese Crown reasserted its monopoly over Cape Verdean trade and it made some short-lived endeavors to revitalize slavery in Guinea-Bissau by granting trade rights to a Brazilian company. French attacks continued in the islands and the British began a protracted campaign to wrest Bolama from Portuguese rule.

The early 19th century saw the widespread abolition of the European slave trade but the Portuguese were especially slow to respond fully. American merchant ships continued to acquire slaves on the coast and in the islands, and indeed, commerce with Americans sometimes exceeded that with Portugal. The salt and slave trade went on, but, as before, a central Portuguese concern was not administrative or commercial reform, but simply the defense of their territories from British and French expansion. As the slave system drew to a close the production of palm and coconut export increased, indeed, the cash market economy offered the stagnant slave trade competition which it could not resist. Earlier centuries had shown Portuguese encouragement of wars between African peoples however the second half of the 19th century saw numerous treaties drawn between the Portuguese and the Banhun, Cobianas, Dyulas, Balantas, Papeis, and other coastal groups as the Portuguese began to venture towards the interior from the comparative security of their fortified posts. Those Africans who refused to make treaties became targets for open colonial warfare during the last

quarter of the 19th century, especially after the Berlin Congress of 1884-5 which effectively created the contemporary
territorial delineation between the holdings of Portugal and
France. In order to make the colonial rule more responsive,
the administration of Guinea-Bissau was separated from Cape
Verde in 1879 for the first time in the centuries of Portuguese presence.

The main barrier to the full colonial conquest of
Guinea-Bissau was the large state of Gabu occupying approximately the eastern half of the territory. Unfortunately much
of Gabu's strength lay upon its role in the slave trade and
when the trade was curtailed the state it supported entered a
period of sharp decline so that it fell victim to local Fula uprisings and a major incursion of Fulas from Futa Jallon's
Labé province. The new Fula rulers never really established
their own genuine sovereignty but soon functioned as indirect
colonial rulers for the region in the northeast. Less centralized peoples than the Manding of Gabu, especially the
Papeis, Balantas, and Bissagos waged sporadic tax revolts
and manifested persistent resistance until as late as 1936
despite the brutal "pacification" campaigns of 1912-1915.

The overthrow of the Portuguese monarchy in 1910 and
the establishment of fascist rule in 1926 brought greater colonial exploitation of peanuts and palm oil but Guinea-Bissau
was seldom run efficiently and usually incurred a debt unlike
Cape Verde which was virtually self-sustaining except at times
of drought. The period between 1936 and 1956 was particularly repressive and finally resulted in the formation of the
PAIGC nationalist movement.

Following a program of peaceful appeals to the Portuguese and to international bodies, the PAIGC was set back in
a brutal massacre in 1959 which forced it to elect a path
of armed struggle to national independence. The nationalist
war was fought from 1963 to 1974 when, in association with
battles in Mozambique and Angola, the fascist colonial structure was toppled on April 25, 1974, and soon led to the total
independence of Guinea-Bissau on September 24, 1974, and
July 5, 1975, for Cape Verde. Both republics are now ruled
by the PAIGC although other aspects of unity are still to be
developed. Frequently it is said that these dates acknowledg-
ing independence show the symbolic end to 500 years of colonialism, but this brief account demonstrates that Portugal's
effective colonial rule was mainly concentrated at the end of
the 19th century lasting only until the victories of the inde-

pendence movements in the 20th century. Moreover, even
this period is punctuated with numerous examples of opposition, revolt, and resistance.

Development and Economics

        Both nations are remarkably poor and underdeveloped.
Under colonial rule both the human and relatively few natural
resources were sadly neglected or ruthlessly exploited. The
main source of subsistence or wealth was generated by agricultural production. In Cape Verde this required large numbers of slaves for sugar cane or contract workers for banana
or coffee cultivation. After formal slavery ended, backward
systems of land tenure provided only a small minority with
adequate quality land. Recurrent droughts and massive erosion also provided sharp limitations to agricultural productivity. The very low cost of labor in the islands retarded
and resisted any innovations which might be capital expensive
thus maintaining a generally stagnant economy. Over the
years attempts were made to introduce cash crops such as
peanuts, cotton, coffee and plant dyes but unreliable climato-
logical conditions made these efforts quite unpredictable.
Other products of Cape Verde have included livestock, fruits,
puzzolane (a cement additive) and significant amounts of salt.

        The main areas for future growth obviously include:
an end to the backward systems of land tenure, a variety of
soil and water conservation programs, and a strong commit-
ment to the development of fishing and fish processing industries. One of the leading exports of the islands has been
laborers, originally as slaves, later as contract laborers and
sailors, and today as low-paid workers in Europe, North and
South America. While the emigration of workers reduces
population pressure and results in remittances to the islands,
it denies the islands their most basic human resource. Pro-
posals have been made to utilize Cape Verdeans in light manufacture in such areas as textiles, and ceramics, and in oil
refining to create wealth in the islands and to diversify the
economy. The sunny and warm climate may also offer the
possibility of solar or wind energy and a potential of developing tourist facilities, although the later represents a ques-
tionable path to economic independence. The development of
Cape Verde will also include a role in bunkering, transport,
warehousing, and communication given its strategic location
hundreds of miles in the Atlantic Ocean. The degree of im-
poverishment is, however, so extreme that the islands are

still distantly far from self sufficiency in even food production and a notable portion of the national budget is consumed
on basic foodstuffs.

The specifics of underdevelopment for Guinea-Bissau
differ from those in Cape Verde except that the general short-
term outlook is similarly backward as a result of colonial indifference and exploitation. The involvement with a cash
economy and limited land in Cape Verde have blocked large-
scale subsistence cultivation while in Guinea-Bissau a large
portion of the population is heavily oriented toward subsistence
crops and land is generally plentiful even with a system of
land fallowing. In addition, settler colonialism and backward
social relations to land were barely developed in Guinea-Bissau, quite to the contrary of Cape Verde.

The chief exports of Guinea-Bissau from the 15th to
the 19th centuries were slaves, ivory, hides, some gold, and
African spices and woods. The late arrival of cash cropping
undermined slavery and stimulated production of peanuts,
rice, and palm oil. The end of the disruptions of the long
nationalist war has seen a return of thousands of farmers
and land has relatively quickly been restored to productivity.
The nation is virtually self sufficient in basic food stuffs and
has begun to resume agricultural exports to earlier levels.
Unfortunately, peanuts, peanut products, coconuts, palm oil
and palm products are the chief cash crops and changeable
market and weather conditions pose serious challenges to
systematic economic development of agriculture. New rice
production and an expanded role for livestock will help to
broaden the spectrum of agricultural exports. The economic
infrastructure of roads, bridges, ferries, transport, communications, and port facilities is required for significant
expansion of the orderly flow of goods and services. The
course of the war saw the creation of the Peoples' Stores
system which has, following independence, been greatly expanded and provides for a grass roots structure for distribution and collection of various commodities.

Other unmeasured potentials of Guinea-Bissau may be
reserves of bauxite ore in the Boe hills area and the possi-
bilities of oil in the river estuaries and in off-shore loca-
tions. Rubber, tropical fruits and hardwoods could be much
more fully developed in addition to the production of meat
and hides. Given the large number of rivers in Guinea-Bissau there is some potential for hydroelectric power generation unlike the barren mountains of Cape Verde. Industrial

development is extremely meager and amounts mainly to processing industries for agricultural goods except for such light
industries as bottling and soap factories.   Guinea-Bissau's
development will require maximum scientific use of its agricultural potentials and its relatively limited natural resources
while diversifying into a large range of manufacture and import replacement and seeking to avoid the dangers of mono-
crop production.

Some important advances have been made in the fishing and fish-processing industries with joint ownership between Guinea-Bissau and Algeria, Libya, and the Soviet
Union, in which capital expenses are jointly shared at first,
with percentage profits declining regularly for the guest nation for a proscribed period until full ownership is in the
hands of Guineans as well as providing for training for Guinean fishermen.   The fishing industry helps to stimulate
growth in canning and refrigeration industries which, in turn,
can be incorporated into other sectors of the economy.

For either nation one may not expect rapid economic
growth, but the elimination of colonial taxes and the market
and trade monopolies opens the possibility of Guinea-Bissau's
own capital accumulation for the public sector.   The nation-
alization of Portuguese banking and the cancellation of some
outstanding colonial debts also serves to enhance the genuine
economic independence of the two nations.

The following table gives a brief statistical image of
some other dimensions of economic development of Cape
Verde and Guinea-Bissau.

Economic Development

	GUINEA-BISSAU	CAPE VERDE
Electricity production	7. 7 million kwh (1968) 13. 0 million kwh (1973)	6. 0 million kwh (1972)
Roads	3, 000 km (1965) 3, 500 km (1970)	986 km (1976)
Gross National Product	$130 million (U. S. , 1972)	$55 million (1975)

	GUINEA-BISSAU	CAPE VERDE
GNP/Capita	$230 (1975)	$150 (1972) $240 (1975)
Annual Income/ Capita	$65 (1963) $300 (1977)	$167 (1975)
1960-72, Popula- tion Growth Rate	0. 8%/year	2. 5%/year
1960-72, GNP Growth Rate	1. 9%/year	5. 3%/year
Population, 1978 est.	640, 000	285, 000

AFONSO, DIOGO. Head of one of the two first captaincies
on São Tiago Island in 1462. Afonso was a nephew of
Prince Henry the Navigator. See HENRY, NOLI.

AGRICULTURE.
    Guinea-Bissau: Agriculture in Guinea-Bissau may be
conveniently divided into subsistence and cash spheres,
although some may be found in both sectors. Accurate
statistics do not exist for subsistence crops under nor-
mal conditions, but particularly during the period of the
nationalist war. Subsistence crops include rice, maize,
millet, manioc, sorghum, and assorted legumes, squashes,
and fruits. The leading cash crops are peanuts, rice,
palm oil, and other palm products. Approximately 60-
75 percent of the total value of exports is derived from
peanuts. Palm products represented about 25-30 percent
of exports by value. Unlike other Portuguese colonies,
Guinea-Bissau had only a very few large plantations;
these were placed under state authority after independence.
Some 11,000 small peasant holdings were the more significant units of agricultural production under a land extensive slash-and-burn system of crop rotation.
    Agricultural productivity fluctuated markedly during
the war, but generally went into a decline, particularly
in peanut and rice cultivation. While some 90 percent
of the total export value was derived from agriculture,
the Portuguese Third Development Plan (1968-1973) only
provided 3-4 percent of the budget for agriculture and
livestock.
    A small effort to harvest rubber on a commercial
basis was initiated in 1957 with the Companhia da Bor-
racha de Guiné (CABORNEL) but this was never properly
developed. Some timbering has been done but in the
early 1970's this represented only about 10,000 tons per
year. Coconut export for 1967 was reported at 12,000
tons with some possibility for future expansion. Off-
shore and river fishing in the early 1970's resulted in a

13

fish catch of about 1, 500 tons per year.   Since independence, state run fishing companies have expanded considerably including a number of jointly owned Soviet and Guinean fishing boats which will become Guinean property after a period of five years.   The increased catch has added some to export revenues and to the protein deficient diet of Guineans.

Approximately 12 percent of the territory of Guinea-Bissau is cultivated or, in other terms, there are 1. 2 acres cultivated per person.   Thirty-two percent of the arable land is devoted to rice cultivation and 22 percent is alloted for peanuts.   The following table provides additional data:

Crops	Acres	% of arable land	production (in tons)
hulled rice	308, 170	25. 86	90, 247
dry rice	69, 815	5. 86	10, 630
peanuts	259, 394	21. 78	63, 975
millet	189, 958	15. 95	23, 968
sugar cane	130, 678	10. 97	17, 834
maize	61, 278	5. 15	7, 994
manioc	36, 591	3. 07	24, 171

(Source: Chaliand 1969: p. 6.)

With the exception of some palm oil and peanut by-products, virtually all exports went to Portugal or, in some cases, to other Portuguese African colonies.   The almost complete colonial monopoly locked Guinea-Bissau into stagnant relations of extreme underdevelopment.

Cape Verde: The situation of agricultural production in Cape Verde is even more bleak than that of Guinea-Bissau.   First, the colonial monopoly on trade had a similar stagnating effect, but secondly the arable land is far more restricted, with only 0. 3 acres available per capita.   A third negative factor is the savage effect of the prolonged drought and soil degradation.   Lastly, the system of land tenure was extremely backward.   As a result of these factors, the level of agricultural production is very low and uncertain.

The only significant exports have been cane sugar and bananas, but other cash crops include coffee, citrus fruits, and castor beans.   Valuable land was taken up by these cash crops at a time when the production of basic subsistence crops was declining.   In recent years, for example, maize production only equaled 4 percent of the total need with the balance being imported.

crop	Agricultural Production in Cape Verde (tons)					
	1967	1968	1969	1970	1973	hectares
bananas	6, 470	6, 889	9, 291	8, 323	4, 690	2, 365
sugar cane	9, 919	11, 223	14, 377	8, 072	9, 742	?
maize	11, 057	678	3, 354	910	713	16, 900
sweet potato	5, 937	3, 172	3, 895	2, 306	1, 055	7, 000
beans	5, 073	392	983	339	144	14, 300
peanuts	?	72	164	14	?	215
coffee	?	82	94	113	?	339
manioc	?	2, 934	3, 008	2, 095	?	?
TOTAL*		25, 442	35, 166	22, 172		

*Total production from 1971 was 18, 381 tons, and for 1972, 11, 429
tons. (Sources: compiled from United Nations and official Portuguese documents.)

While banana cultivation has fluctuated quite markedly
in recent years, overall production has remained very
high relative to other crops. For example, bananas
were produced at 3. 92 tons/hectare while the next highest productivity was recorded for peanuts at 0. 76 tons/
hectare. Moreover some of the land used for bananas
is some of the best watered in the archipelago including
rather large privately owned plantations. The 30-hectare
banana plantation of Fazenda Santa Cruz on São Tiago
once employed about 1, 000 workers. This plantation was
taken over by the workers after April 1974. About 90
percent of the Cape Verdean working population (some
77, 000 workers) lives by agricultural production, thus,
when production falls drastically one may understand just
how devastating and extensive the impact has been. In
figures for the early 1960's it was calculated that only
1. 65 percent (or 52, 688 hectares) of the total land area
of Cape Verde was being cultivated or only 0. 32 acres/
person. This is in sharp contrast with the 12 percent
of Guinea-Bissau which is being farmed. The limitations
on agriculture are even more obvious when it is considered that about 30 percent of the farmland of Cape Verde
is being fallowed and only 50 percent is for permanent
regular crops. This harsh picture is worsened by the
exploitative systems of land tenure under which 69. 4
percent of the 36, 309 farms are operated by share-crop-
ping or tenant farming and are not owned by those who
work the land. For those farmers who own their own
land the holdings are usually small. Aside from private
capitalists, the Catholic Church was a large land owner.
Colonialism in Guinea-Bissau did not significantly disrupt
traditional patterns of land use. Some narrow coastal
areas of Fogo are particularly good for peanut and coffee cultivation, but most agriculture is concentrated on
São Tiago, Santo Antão, and São Nicolau, all of which
have more regular sources of water.

Agricultural labor is generated also through frentes de trabalho (labor pools) which were compensated at the following levels: men, 30 escudos per day, women 22.5 /day, and children 18/day.   These rates were similar to those paid to the brigadas da estrada (road building crews) which have built, mainly by hand, endless cobblestone roadways throughout the islands.   Other Cape Verdean produce would include fish from the off-shore waters, but fishing and fish processing has not expanded in a systematic fashion and it suffers from a notable shortage of capital and scientific equipment.

Traditionally Cape Verde has had more diversified exports such as rum (grog) produced from sugar cane, salted meat, beads, livestock (especially horses), cotton, and the unique Cape Verdean textiles known as paños. Paños are woven from cotton fibre on a narrow loom and the strips are sewn together to make a wider cloth of typically white and blue designs.   The blue plant dye has sometimes been a Cape Verdean export.   Many of these traditional exports (from as early as the 15th century) were used in the trade on the African coast for slaves, ivory, plant dyes, hides and beeswax.   See also RICE; PEANUTS; ECONOMICS (TRADE); MINERALS; MILLET; FONIO; OIL PALM; WEST AFRICAN CROPS.

ALDEAMENTO.   Fortified village system used by the Portuguese in Guinea-Bissau to concentrate rural populations behind barbed wire to deny access of the PAIGC to the people.

ALFA MOLO OF JIMARA (?-1881).   An elephant hunter of the Bande family of Futa Jallon who led the successful movement against King Janke Walli of the Mandingo state of Gabu in 1867, thus creating the first Fula state in Guinea-Bissau.   The conquest of Gabu was achieved in association with the general military efforts of Al-Haj Umaru of Futa Jallon.   Alfa Molo was the son of the Almami of Timbu, a Fula province of Futa Jallon.   The Almami had married a Gabu princess named Kumancho Saane.   Around the time of Alfa Molo's conquest of Gabu, he also had married into the Gabu royal family of Kumba Wude, but this may have taken place as a result of the conquest.   This marriage resulted in at least two sons, Dikori and Musa Molo.   Upon the death of Alfa Molo he was replaced by his brother Bakari Demba until he was overthrown in 1893 by Alfa Molo's son Musa Molo who continued the line of Fula dominance of Gabu.

In establishing the hegemony of the new Fula state
Alfa Molo came into conflict with other Fulas occupying
regions north of the Gambia River.   After his death by
disease in 1881 in Guinea-Bissau, Fulas in Guinea-Bissau
led by Alfa Mbukku also staged local revolts.   Strong
measures taken by Musa Molo temporarily renewed the
Fula state, but after 1931 there was no effective, legitimate king.   See also FUTA JALLON; GABU; MUSA MOLA.

ALFA YAYA OF LABE.   Alfa Yaya was the chief representative of Fula power in Futa Jallon whose rise in power
was simultaneous with French penetration from the coast.
Although Alfa Yaya had a nominally pro-French position
it appears that he sought to use French rule to consolidate
his own position especially between 1891-1896.   Alfa
Yaya's opportunism led to a revolt by his son, resulting
in a decisive battle in which Alfa Yaya crushed his opposition.   In 1897 he served French interests by the reconquest of other regions in Futa Jallon including Timbu.
In 1904 the relationship between Alfa Yaya and the French
had soured in a series of jurisdictional disputes including
the severance of a portion of Labé province to be transferred to Portuguese control in Guinea-Bissau.   Seeing
his power being eroded Alfa Yaya planned an armed revolt against the French, but a spy revealed the plans
leading to Alfa Yaya's arrest and deportation to Dahomey.
After his release in 1910 he made another attempt to organize resistance in 1911 but this too was blocked by arrest and deportation.

AL-HAJ AL-MAMI UMARU   see   FULA; ALFA MOLO

AMERICAN CROPS.   Many of the important crops in West
Africa today are, in fact, native to the Americans and
were only introduced in the 16th century.   Chief among
these is maize or corn (Zea mays) which is well suited
to the rainy areas in West Africa.   In other areas maize
is found in river valleys or is farmed with irrigation.
The lima and haricot beans are common American legumes now found in West Africa.   The American root crop
manioc plays a basic role as a starchy foodstuff while
peanuts (Arachis hypogaea, in Portuguese, mancarra) are
a vital source of foreign exchange as a leading commercial export.   Many West African diets include pineapples,
pumpkins, squash and tomatoes, and the papaya is a popular fruit.   American condiments are red pepper, tobacco
and cacao, which is another big export earner in some
West African nations.   See also PEANUTS.

ARAUJO, JOSE EDUARDO. PAIGC militant who has served
in various high-ranking capacities including political com-
missar of the permanent commission of the southern national committee in Guinea-Bissau. Araujo has also been
head of the PAIGC information section in Conakry and was
a member of the Executive Committee for the struggle in
charge of production. After the reorganization of CEL
Araujo became a Minister of the General Secretariat.
Following independence he became the organizational secretary for the PAIGC and a trouble-shooting Minister
without portfolio. See also CEL; CONCP; PAIGC.

ARMAZENS DO POVO [Peoples' Stores]. During the period
of the nationalist war, the PAIGC had two main points
in its economic program. On the one hand, it sought
to halt the Portuguese use of the Guinean exports and to
force a heavier reliance on imports thereby raising the
economic costs of continuing colonialism. On the other
hand the PAIGC had the goal of launching a small scale
export and import economy for the liberated zones. The
system of Peoples' Stores operated to address these two
points and improve the quality of life in the liberated
zones. Imported items included textiles, machetes, hoe
blades, blankets, salt, sugar, cigarettes, tobacco, bicy-
cles, pots, sewing machines, string, matches, flash lights,
soap, needles, thread, paper, sandals, buttons, and fish
nets, to name a number of the more popular items. By
1973 about 32 Peoples' Stores were in operation throughout the country and in the frontier regions.
    This integrated economic system strictly excluded cash
but determined fixed exchange equivalents for agricultural
produce and other items generated in Guinea-Bissau. For
example, 1 kg. of rice could be exchanged for 1 kg. of
sugar or for clothing which could be tailor-made at the
larger Peoples' Stores. Three kgs. of rice would be
worth a pair of trousers. A pair of woman's shoes was
equivalent to 15 kgs. of rice, or 1 meter of crocodile
skin could be converted to 2 kgs. of rice. Although rice
was the main staple exchanged, exports of the Peoples'
Stores also included peanuts, palm oil, ivory, hides,
honey, beeswax, kola nuts, palm nuts, sesame seeds,
and corn. The export of kola nuts was the greatest export earner by value but rice was the major export by
volume, which, in 1971, represented 668,511 kgs. In
the late 1960's and early 1970's exports generally increased with the export high in 1971 put at 34.4 million
Guinean (C) francs or about 4.25 million escudos ($145,000

U. S.). While this sum is not large in absolute terms,
the bulk of trade through the Peoples' Stores was by barter with no cash flow. The degree to which the needs of
the people of Guinea-Bissau could be met through the
Peoples' Stores denied an additional market to the colonial
economy.
    The embryonic Peoples' Stores system, developed dur-
ing the struggle, underwent major expansion in the post-
independence period to provide for the state distribution
and regulation of basic commodities. Currently there are
more than 125 Peoples' Stores and the system has incorporated the former Casa Gouveia commercial chain operated for Portuguese interests. See also AGRICULTURE;
ECONOMICS (TRADE); LIVESTOCK; PEANUTS; RICE.

ARMEE DE LIBERATION NACIONALE GUINEENE (ALNG).
    The armed branch of FLING, formed shortly after 1962.
    There is little evidence about the strength of the ALNG,
    but it saw combat only on the rarest of occasions and
    exclusively in the area of Guinea-Bissau near the western
    Casamance.

ARRENDAMENTO. The system leasing land by the morgados
    to peasant farmers in turn for payment; practiced in
    Cape Verde.

ASKIA MOHAMMAD. Ruler of Songhai (1493-1528). See
    SONGHAI.

ASSEMBLEIA NACIONAL POPULAR (ANP) [Peoples National
    Assembly]. The governmental structure of Guinea-Bissau
    and Cape Verde distinguishes between the ruling party,
    the PAIGC and the supreme legislative body of the state,
    the ANP. While there is overlap in membership, the
    functions and meetings of the bodies are quite distinct.
    The ANP empowers the Council of State Commissioners,
    passes laws, ratifies decrees, and can revise the consti-
    tution. In turn, the Council of State Commissioners acts
    as the executive organ of the ANP when it is not in ses-
    sion. The ANP meets annually for several weeks at a
    time. At the first meeting of the ANP in the liberated
    zones during the war it adopted the Constitution and
    elected officers and ministers for the Council of State
    which had fifteen members in 1973. The first meeting
    had 125 delegates representing various party organs and
    various regional councils. In April 1975 held its first
    meeting after liberation. Since this time the membership

has been expanded to 150 delegates from an original 125
and the structure of the ANP has become more formal-
ized.   The ANP still elects the officers of the Council
of State (i. e. , cabinet), but these officers may appoint
the various Commissioners (Ministers) with the ultimate
approval granted by the ANP.

ASSIMILADO.   One who has "assimilated" Portuguese cultural
standards of literacy, education, financial status or other
criteria in order to gain fuller rights of a Portuguese
citizen.   A status reserved for Africans although only a
tiny percentage were in this culturo-racial, political category.

AZAMBUJA, DIEGO DA.   Portuguese knight under the reign
of Dom Joao II (1477, 1481-95) who was charged with the
rapid construction of El Mina on the Gold Coast.   Materials and specialist craftsmen were brought from Portugal in 1480 and the project was completed in 1482 to
guard the Portuguese trade in slaves and gold.

AZURARA, GOMES EANES DE.   A well-known 15th-century
chronicler for Prince Henry.   He wrote of the 1415 Ceuta
campaign in "Key to Mediterranean. "   In 1453 he wrote
"Cronica de Guiné" which described some of the earliest
kidnapping of Africans and their resistance to the preda-
tions of the early slavers.   See also HENRY.

-B-

BAIOTES.   A numerically small group of the Diolá cluster
of the Senegambian littoral people.   Their concentration
is in the Casamance area in northwestern Guinea-Bissau
around the town of Suzanna.   The Baiotes are related to
the Felupes, the other member of the Diolá cluster.   The
Baiotes depend on rice cultivation and have acephalous
political organization although there are instances of local
petty chiefs.   See also DIOLAS; FELUPES.

BALANTAS (Balantes).   The largest single ethnic group of
Guinea-Bissau.   The Balantas are members of the Senegambian cultural stock, Atlantic sub-family of the Niger-
Congo language stock.   The Balanta people are generally
egalitarian in socio-political organization but some areas
have local chiefs.   Today they are found mainly in areas
nearer the coast although they once occupied the interior

in such areas as Gabu until the Mandingo expansion. Major Balanta concentrations are in the central northern area
west of Farim and in coastal southern areas around Catio.
They are, in short, located both north and south of the
River Geba.   Virtually all Balanta are non-Islamic rice
cultivators who are most closely related to the Mancanha
ethnic group.
    Numerous campaigns of subjugation were directed a-
gainst the Balanta in 1883-5, 1891-1910 and in 1912-1915
until they were brought under nominal Portuguese control.
As one of the more oppressed groups in Guinea-Bissau,
the Balanta were particularly heavily involved in the nationalist struggle 1963-1974.   The 1950 census counted
146,300 people as identifying as Balanta, or 29.1 percent
of the total population.   In 1960 the population was estimated at 250,000.

BAMBARAS.   A relatively large member of the Mande group
    concentrated on the Upper Niger in Mali where they are
    often occupied as slightly Islamized fishing people.   In
    the third quarter of the 17th century the Bambaras re-
    volted against the rule of Mali and created the two inde-
    pendent states of Segou and Kaarta which absorbed the
    local remnants of the Malian empire.   Between 1670 and
    1810 the Bambaras controlled Djenne and they briefly held
    Timbuktu.   The Bambara influence declined after this
    period and from 1854 to 1861 Fulani jihads destroyed the
    Bambara states.   In Guinea-Bissau there are very small
    concentrations of these animistic peoples in the vicinity
    of Gabu (Nova Lamego).

BANCO NACIONAL ULTRAMARINO (BNU) [Overseas National
    Bank].   The BNU is a major Portuguese banking organ-
    ization, established in Lisbon in 1864 and in Cape Verde
    in 1868, which monopolized banking in Guinea-Bissau dur-
    ing colonialism.   In 1963 the BNU held more than $50
    million in capital and stocks with 52 bank branches in
    Portugal.   The BNU Board of Directors has been in in-
    timate association with the colonial and fascist adminis-
    tration including two former colonial secretaries as well
    as major shareholders associated with CUF and its over-
    seas linkages.   In addition, the BNU has significant as-
    sociation with finance capital in Paris, Madrid and Lon-
    don.   A net profit during a typical year (1963) was al-
    most $3 million (U.S.) with dividends commonly at 9 per-
    cent.   The BNU is associated with the major insurance
    firm, Companhia de Seguios a Mundial.   In Guinea-Bissau

the BNU is also represented in the Sociedade Comercial
Ultramarina, which was second only to the Antonio Silva
Corporation, the affiliate of CUF which dominated trade
and commerce in Guinea.   The relatively small Sociedade
Algodoeira da Guiné (Guinea Cotton Corporation) was also
tied to the BNU.   With such extensive connections the
BNU had an important influence in agriculture, transport,
petro-chemicals, oil-processing and rice-processing in
Guinea-Bissau and Cape Verde.   After independence there
was deep divisions between Lisbon and Bissau over the
terms of repatriating BNU capital.   Guinea-Bissau nationalized the BNU in February 1975 and ended the escudo
currency to be replaced by the new peso of Guinea.   See
also COMPANHIA UNIAO FABRIL.

BANYUNS (Banhuns).   This very small Senegambian group is
closely related to the Cassangas and the Cobianas and may
be found in the southern Casamance area.   During the
period of Mandingo expansion the Banyuns were pushed
toward the coast and were largely absorbed by the Diolás,
Manjacos and Balantes.   While the Banyuns are acephalous, agricultural animists, the related Cassangas developed a secondary kingship structure with its capital at
Birkama.   The term Casamance is said to be derived
from Kassa-Mansa, the Cassanga ruler at Birkama.   The
Banyuns and Cassangas are known as skilled weavers and
dyers.   In the late 16th century the Cassangas became
active slave hunters and expanded into Banyun territory
assimilating many of these people.

BARBOSA, RAFAEL (1924-).   Barbosa was born in the Safim
section of Bissau of a Guinean mother and Cape Verdean
father.   He was employed in Bissau as a public works
foreman when he and Amílcar Cabral and several others
joined to form the PAIGC in 1956.   Barbosa operated under the nom de guerre of Zain Lopes as the President of
the Central Committee of the PAIGC until his March 13,
1962, arrest by the Portuguese in Bissau where he carried out clandestine preparatory work and in the Oio and
Bafata regions to organize cadres.   Barbosa was initially
tortured and then released by the Portuguese on August
3, 1969, after seven years of imprisonment.   His confinement led him to compromising and, finally, treason-
ous positions (from the viewpoint of the PAIGC) which ex-
pelled him from the party in April 1970.   He had still
been considered as the President of the PAIGC until February 1964.

After winning state power, Barbosa was charged with
high crimes against the state and party having been directly implicated in the assassination of Amílcar Cabral.
At the conclusion of his trial on October 18, 1976, he
was sentenced to death for his anti-PAIGC and pro-Spin-
ola statements and activities. On March 4, 1977, the
death sentence was commuted to 15 years hard labor.
See also A. CABRAL; PAIGC; SPINOLA.

BARRETO, COLONEL HONORIO PEREIRA (1813?-1859).
Barreto is believed to be the first Cape Verdean Governor
of Guinea-Bissau. This ambitious representative of Crioulo culture was appointed superintendent of the Portuguese
fortress at Cacheu in 1834 and was the Governor of Cacheu and Bissau in 1837. Barreto's importance also lies
in the defense of Portuguese colonial interests against the
intrusions of the French and British.

BAUXITE see COMPANHIA LUSITANA DO ALUMINIO DA
GUINE E ANGOLA

BEAFADAS (Biafadas). This non-Islamic Senegambian group
once occupied the Gabu area until their 14th- or 15th-
century expulsion by the Mandingo. The Beafadas acquired many Mandingo characteristics including the system of secondary kingship, especially in the 16th century
when they were tributaries to the Empire of Mali.   In
the 19th century the Beafadas resisted the incursions of
the Futa Jallon Fulani under Coli Tenquella and forced
him to divert to the northeast of the Beafada territory.
Today the major concentrations of the Beafadas are in the
region just north of Bambadinca and mainly in the area
in the vicinity of a Fulacunda-Buba axis.   The period of
Portuguese colonial penetration was met by numerous instances of Beafada resistance in 1880-2, 1886, 1900, and
in 1907-8 before they were considered "pacified."

BERLIN CONGRESS. Between 1884 and 1885 the major European powers met in Berlin to organize the colonial partition of Africa.   The Congress was dominated by France
and England, but claims in Africa were established by
Portugal, Belgium, Spain, Germany and Italy. This meeting launched the "scramble for Africa" which triggered
an era of military conquest and subjugation by European
powers in order to support their claims of effective occupation and control.
The basic configuration of modern African national

boundaries is descended from the Berlin Congress with
various local adjustments throughout the colonial era.
Before the Congress the European ruling classes had, in
general, neglected Africa as too expensive for permanent
settlement and there was remarkably little knowledge of
the people and resources of the interior at the time of
the Congress which resulted in artificial and controversial
borders of today.

BIKER, JUDICE. Early 20th-century Governor of Guinea-
Bissau, best known for his 1903 documentation of the
slave labor conditions of São Tomé. Biker's article un-
leashed a major political scandal showing that 2,000-4,000
"contract laborers" went to São Tomé each year but few
ever returned to Angola where they originated.

BISSAGOS (Bujagos, Bojagos, Bijagos). This ethnic stock is
the principal group which occupies the Bissagos Archipelago (11° 15'N, 16° 05'W) off the coast of Guinea-Bissau.
They are animists with petty chiefdoms and are likely derived from the adjacent mainland. They show ethnic af-
finities to the Diolas, Cocolis, Nalus, Padjadincas, and
Papeis. Their economy is largely based on fishing and
palm products at the present time.
     The fiercely independent Bissagos peoples were not
"pacified" by the Portuguese until as late as 1936 and
were distinguished among the peoples of Guinea-Bissau
for the persistence of their opposition to foreign penetration and colonial rule. The earliest resistance dates to
the very first Portuguese explorer, Nuño Tristão, who
reached the islands in 1447 and was killed in his attacks
on the Bissagos people. A Portuguese attack on Ilha
Roxa in the Bissagos likewise failed in 1550. The Bissagos people are famed for their large, ocean-going canoes holding up to 70 people. These fast-moving canoes
enabled them to conduct liberal slave raids on the coast
with little fear of retaliation.
     In the period between 1840-50 the Bissagos again
mounted a stiff resistance against European intrusion and
were certainly not under effective Portuguese control.
The British and French called on the Portuguese to suppress these people, but the Portuguese were unable to
meet this request. In 1849 the British and French organized a joint "punitive" raid on the islands with three
ships and more than 50 soldiers. After meeting with
strong opposition they too withdrew. Additional recorded
instances of attempts to suppress the Bissagos "tax re-

volts" occurred in 1900, 1906, during the Pinto campaign
of 1913-15, in 1917, 1918, 1924, and in 1936.   See also
PINTO, T. ; TRISTAO, N.

BISSAU.   Capital city of the Republic of Guinea-Bissau at the
broad estuary of the Geba River on the north shore (11°
51', 15° 35'W).   The area has been occupied by a concentration of the Papel people.   The first European to
reach the area was the Portuguese explorer Nuño Tristão
in 1446, who was killed in the following year in the Bissagos Islands.   In the 16th century Bissau became a modest coastal base for slave-trading lançados and other Luso-
Africans who continued in this capacity through the late
19th century.   Following attacks by European powers and
virtually anarchy in the slave trade Bissau was appointed
as a captaincy-general in 1692 in order to strengthen the
Portuguese monopoly and establish a more meaningful
coastal presence between Cacheu to the north and Bolama
to the south.   By 1696 Bissau town held a fort, church and
hospital and controlled the trade on the Geba and Corubal
Rivers.   The trade remained largely in the hands of unreliable lançados.   About a dozen settlers were assigned
there each year in the early 18th century; later this number was raised to 40 per year.   A high death rate from
tropical diseases and frequent attacks by Africans on ports
and forts strongly discouraged expanded colonization.   In
1869 Bissau became one of four administrative comunas
in order to establish a more effective local administration, although the governor's residence was at Geba, a
small town much further east in the interior.   When the
administration of Guinea Bissau was fully separated from
Cape Verde in 1879 the capital was transferred to Bolama.
The first three decades of the 20th century saw almost
continuous resistance by the Papeis in the Bissau area
but in 1941 the capital was moved to Bissau from Bolama.
In 1956 the Pijiguiti dockyards in Bissau were the
scene of bloody repression against the rising nationalist
movement, and the nation's international airport near
Bissau came under attack in 1968 and June 1971 during
the war of national liberation (1963-1974).   The population statistics for Bissau are notoriously poor but it appears that in the 1960's about 26,000 people lived in the
city, but by 1973 the population may have reached as
many as 60,000 as a result of dislocation from military
activities in the interior.   An extreme population estimate
for Bissau in 1975 was 80,000 including Portuguese troops.
Today Bissau is facing major problems of adequate hous-

ing and employment. However, progress is already being made on the expansion of the port facilities and other
dimensions of urban planning including expansion of elec-
tric power and piped water systems. See also BARRETO;
BOLAMA; CACHEU; LANÇADOS; PIJIGUITI.

BLOC DEMOCRATIQUE DE GUINEE BISSAO (BDG). The
BDG was formed in 1967 with civil servants proposing
the creation of a government in exile. As with other
nationalist organizations of the period, the BDG was never
much more than a paper movement.

BOA VISTA (16° 10'N, 23° 50'W). Third largest (239.3 sq. mi.)
island in the Cape Verde archipelago, and easternmost
member of the Barlavento (windward, northern) islands.
Boa Vista was among the islands "discovered" by da Noli
and D. Gomes in 1460. It was first known as São Cris-
tóvão. No serious settlement took place until the 16th
century when it was used for animal grazing. Unlike
other Cape Verde Islands, Boa Vista is low (maximum altitude 1280 feet) and sandy. The animals were
used in the Islands and in the slave trade. However,
the periodic droughts in the islands have sometimes
decimated the livestock. During the last years of Portuguese colonialism a West German company, AIP, had
planned to develop three hotels having 6,000 beds but this
did not materialize. Since independence the PAIGC has
built a number of catchment dams thus creating 170 badly
needed public works jobs. The main town of Boa Vista
is Sal-Rei, other villages are Gata, Fundo de Fiqueiras,
and Curral Velho. The 1960 population of Boa Vista was
3,309.

BOLAMA (Bulama). Island and important town (11° 35'N,
15° 28'W) in Guinea-Bissau facing the estuary of the Fulacunda tidal flood basin. The Portuguese navigator Nuño
Tristão reached the vicinity of Bolama in 1446 when he
explored the Geba River. Throughout the period of slavery but especially in the 18th and 19th centuries, Bolama
offered an ideal defensive position but with easy access
to the interior. In 1753 Portugal claimed official ownership of the island, but their authority was weak and control fell back to local African leaders. The Africans sold
a portion of Bolama to the British trader Philip Beaver
and sold other portions for commercial purposes. By the
end of the 18th century these ventures failed and were
abandoned. In 1828 the Portuguese returned to fortify

the town and to restore their control.   The British pro-
tested and in 1837 sent the naval brig The Brisk to cut
down the Portuguese flag and hoist the Union Jack.   For
more than 30 years the conflict continued with various
acts of violence and ownership shifting back and forth
with the British occupying Bolama again in 1858 and claim-
ing ownership of the Bissagos Islands as well.   In 1860
the British declared that both territories were considered
incorporated with Sierra Leone.   At last, in 1868, the
tedious affair was presented to United States President
Grant, who ruled in favor of Portugal's claim.   The British withdrew in January 1869.   At this time Bolama became one of the four comunas of Guinea-Bissau and a
more intensive effort at colonization and "pacification"
was begun.
        In 1879 when Cape Verde ceased to govern the affairs
of Guinea-Bissau, Bolama was made the first capital of
the separate colony.   In 1941 the colonial capital was
moved from Bolama to Bissau and in 1946 the colonial
government issued a commemorative stamp noting Grant's
arbitration of Bolama.   Since the transfer of the location
of the capital Bolama has had only secondary importance.
The 1960 population was put at 5,000 while the 1967 population of the town fell to 3,000, no doubt related to the
nationalist war.

BOLANHAS.   Riverine marshes typical of coastal Guinea;
        areas suitable for rice cultivation given proper drainage
        and irrigation.

BRAMES.   These representatives of the Senegambian stock,
        Atlantic sub-family, are located in the area between Can-
        chungo and Bula on the right bank of the Mansoa River.
        Related to the Papel, Manjaco and Mancanha peoples,
        the Brames are hardly Islamized and mainly animist.
        Their economy is based on slash and burn agriculture
        with limited hierarchical political organization.   The 1950
        census showed 16,300 Brames while the 1960 estimate
        indicated the population to have risen to 35,000.

BRANCO AND RASO ISLETS (16° 40'N, 24° 40'W).   The two
        uninhabited islets of the Barlavento (northern, windward)
        portion of the Cape Verde archipelago.   Branco and Raso
        are located between Santa Luzia and São Nicolau.

BRAVA (14° 50'N, 24° 43'W).   The second smallest (24.7 mi.)
        of the ten major Cape Verdean islands, and the smallest

of the Sotavento group. Despite its size, Brava is rather
mountainous with a maximum altitude of 3,202 feet at
Fontainhas.   The main port is on the north coast at Porto
da Furna lying some 4 km. from the main town of Nova
Sintra situated in the interior hills.   With some permanent water sources Brava was very early to attract Europeans from Minho, Algarve, and Madeira and it is still
the most European of all of the islands.   New settlers
arrived from neighboring Fogo in 1680 following its eruption.   In 1798 the French attacked Brava in their unsuccessful effort to dislodge the Portuguese influence there
and on the coast.
      In the 1850's Brava began an early secondary school
which attracted students from throughout the archipelago
and from Guinea-Bissau.   The noted Cape Verdean poet,
Eugenio Tavares, was a native of Brava.   The small size
of the island and its limited agricultural land has resulted
in an historic pattern of emigration from Brava, perhaps
much more than other islands.   A very large portion of
the migration went to the northeastern United States.
Since independence the PAIGC has emphasized irrigation
and water conservation programs and efforts to develop
agriculture, animal husbandry and reforestation thus creating 410 new jobs.   The 1960 population of Brava was
8,646.

BULL, BENJAMIN PINTO.   Historian and secondary school
      teacher in Dakar who was President of the UNGP which
      sought independence from Portugal without revolution.
      He held talks in Lisbon in July 1963 to achieve this end.
      Benjamin's brother is Jaime Pinto Bull who was UNGP
      Vice President.   See also UNIAO DOS NATURAIS DA
      GUINE PORTUGUESA.

BULL, JAIME PINTO.   One of the few Africans from Guinea-
      Bissau who served as a deputy in the Portuguese National
      Legislative Assembly (NLA) in Lisbon in 1964.   J. P.
      Bull was also the Inspector of Administration and Sec-
      retary General of the colonial administration in Guinea-
      Bissau.   He served as the vice president of the UNGP
      and later as the president of FLING after 1966.   In 1969
      J. P. Bull was re-elected as the only African representa-
      tive of Guinea in the Portuguese NLA.   He was killed in
      a helicopter crash in July, 1970 while on a tour of the
      territory.   See also FLING; UNGP.

-C-

CABRAL, AMILCAR LOPES "ABEL DJASSI" (Sept. 12, 1924-
Jan. 20, 1973). Cabral was born in Bafata in Guinea-
Bissau of a Cape Verdean father, Juvenal Cabral, and a
Guinean mother. Since his father was educated, Amílcar
was sent to the Liceu Gil Eanes in São Vincente for his
secondary education. At the age of twenty-one he entered
the University of Lisbon Institute of Agronomy from which
he graduated with honors in 1950. In the early 1950's he
was associated with the Lisbon Casa dos Estudantes do
Império where he met and discussed with revolutionary
intellectuals from the other African colonies. While in
Lisbon he met and married his Portuguese wife, Anna
Maria who was herself a dedicated revolutionary. With
his training complete, Cabral entered the colonial agricultural service in 1950 where he applied soil science,
demography and hydraulics engineering. During the period 1952-4 Cabral traveled very extensively in Guinea,
conducting Guinea's first agricultural census and gaining
an intimate knowledge of the land and people that was to
be of great importance in organizing the PAIGC. Cabral's
first effort in forming a nationalist movement in Guinea
was in 1954 with the "Recreation Association" which was
parallel to the movement MING also founded by Cabral
in the same year. In the mid 1950's Cabral met with
his revolutionary friends from the CEI and they formed
the Movimento Anti-Colonialista (MAC). Finally, on September 19, 1956, Cabral, his brother Luis, Aristides
Pereira, Rafael Barbosa and two others met secretly in
Bissau to form the PAIGC. Cabral could not remain in
Bissau at the time as he had to return to Angola where
he was at work with a private sugar company. In December 1956 Cabral, Agostinho Neto and other Ango-
lans met secretly to form the Movimento Popular de Libertação da Angola (MPLA). The clandestine organizing
continued and sought to mobilize the workers of Bissau.
On August 3, 1959, a nationalist oriented dockworkers'
strike was met with savage colonial repression while Cabral was at work in Angola.
    Following this event Cabral returned to Bissau to dis-
cuss a change of tactics and the preparation for a protracted guerrilla war to achieve the independence of Guinea and the Cape Verde Islands. In 1960 Cabral secretly
left Bissau to continue building and to form the FRAIN in
Tunis, which was soon to be replaced by the CONCP in

April, 1961. After 1963 the PAIGC launched its war
which had control of two thirds of the countryside by the
end of the decade and in 1973 was able to declare itself
an independent republic. Cabral earned many international distinctions including the Nasser Award, the Joliot-
Curie Medal, and honorary doctorates at Lincoln University (U. S. A.) and from the Soviet Academy of Science.
On January 20, 1973, Cabral was assassinated in Conakry
in a Portuguese-backed conspiracy to overthrow the PAIGC.
Cabral is today considered a major African revolutionary
theoretician. He is survived by his brother Luis, his
three children (oldest born in 1958) and his wife, Anna
Maria, who now works in the Ministry of Health and Social Welfare. The 12th of September, Cabral's birthday,
is now celebrated as a national holiday. See also R.
BARBOSA; J. CABRAL; L. CABRAL; CONCP; FRAIN;
MAC; MING; PAIGC; A. PEREIRA; PIDJIGUITI.

CABRAL, JUVENAL (1889-?). Father of Amílcar Cabral and
author of Memórias e Reflexões (1947). J. Cabral studied at the Seminary of Viseu in Portugal and had a deep
understanding of the cultural aspects of Portuguese colonial rule which caused him great frustrations playing
an important role in the formation of the nationalist ideology of his famous son.

CABRAL, LUIS DE ALMEIDA (1931-). One of the six original founders of the PAIGC in 1956 in Bissau where he
was born. Cabral's training was as an accountant for
CUF. He left for Guinea-Conakry soon after the PAIGC
was formed since the Portuguese secret police were seeking his arrest. In 1961 Cabral became the founding Secretary General of the pro-PAIGC trade union group, the
UNTG. By 1963 Cabral was in charge of the strategic
Quitafine frontier zone which was militarily active at that
time. In 1965 he became a member of the PAIGC War
Council. Following PAIGC restructuring in 1970 he became a member of the Permanent Commission of the
CEL with the responsibility for national reconstruction
in the liberated zones. Since the independence of Guinea-
Bissau he became the President of the Conselho de Es-
tado and he is now the Deputy Secretary of the PAIGC.
Luis Cabral is the younger brother of Amílcar Cabral.
See also A. CABRAL; CEL; CUF; PAIGC; UNTG.

CABRAL, PEDRO ALVARES. Portuguese sea captain whose
fleet reached the Cape Verde Islands on March 22, 1500.

Rather than traveling along the West African coast he
went far to the southwest and accidentally discovered
Brazil in April 1500.

CABRAL, VASCO (1924?-). Cabral was born in Guinea-
Bissau but was one of the very rare few to study in Lisbon University in 1950. In 1954 he was arrested for his
political views and was held in prison for almost six years
including two years in solitary confinement. Upon his
release in 1959 he completed his degree in economics
and met with Amílcar Cabral who was also in Lisbon at
that time. V. Cabral fled from Portugal in July 1962
with A. Neto of the MPLA and soon joined the PAIGC to
serve on its central committee and on the War Council.
Cabral also served on the Executive Committee of the
Struggle with his specialty in party ideology. Currently
he is the Comissario de Estado (Minister) for Economic
Development and Planning. See CEL; CONCP; PAIGC.

CACHEN RIOS E COMMERCIO DA GUINE see CACHEU

CACHEU. Town in Guinea-Bissau (12° 10'N, 16° 10'W) located
on the south bank of the Cacheu River in an area populated by the Manjaco and Cobiana ethnic groups. The
Cacheu River was first reached by the Portuguese explorer Nuño Tristão in 1446. In the early 16th century,
slaving became the notable activity at Cacheu where there
was trade of salt and horses from Cape Verde for slaves
captured and sold by lançados along the coast and from
the interior kingdom of Mali. In 1588 Cacheu became an
official Portuguese captaincy in order to control the slave
trade and establish a post for regular trade and supplies.
With this prosperity beginning in the late 16th century a
special Crown agreement with Jewish merchants in 1601
gave permission to trade and settle in the Cacheu Rios
area and to establish a capitão e ouvidor which was subordinate only to the Portuguese governor of Cape Verde.
In the 17th century the slave trade was intensified and in
1624 the Dutch temporarily seized the Cacheu captaincy.
In 1630 Cacheu was fully returned to Portuguese control
as it began to be developed as the economic nucleus for
the province of Guinea. Security remained a problem and
Cacheu was fortified in 1641 against attacks by Luso-African lançados and various European powers.
    The 1660's brought the creation of the Cape Verdean-
based slaving company Cachen Rios e Commercio da Guiné
which had a slave trade monopoly from Senegal to Sierra

Leone including the rivers of Guinea. In 1676 this company was reorganized as the Companhia do Cacheu Rios e Cabo Verde, but its main slaving activities were still based at Cacheu which continued to dominate the slave trade in Senegambia. The Companhia do Cacheu Rios e Cabo Verde had relative prosperity but only until the close of the 17th century when it ceased its trade monopoly of the slave trade to Spanish America. With locust plagues and some reduction in local slaving, the importance of Cacheu declined into the early 18th century with Bissau's importance increasing, not to mention the expansion of slavery much further along the West African coast. In the 19th century European rivalries for African territory were intensified and the district officer at Cacheu in the 1830's, Honório Barreto, gained some prominence for his stalwart defense of Portuguese interests. In administrative reorganization in 1869, Cacheu had the status of one of the four territorial comunas, but when the government of Guinea-Bissau was separated from that of Cape Verde in 1879, the first capital became Bolama rather than Cacheu. Portuguese efforts at settlement and "pacification" of the Cacheu area were sharply resisted by the Papeis in 1891-4 and 1904. Today Cacheu is a small town of modest importance. See also BARRETO; LANÇADOS.

CADAMOSTA, ALVISE. Venetian navigator in Portuguese service who sailed in the Senegambian area between 1454 and 1456 in a 90-ton vessel. In 1455 Cadamosta and Usodimare, a Genoan, separately reached the estuary of the River Gambia. In 1456 the two navigators sailed on a joint 2-ship mission twenty miles up the Gambia River where the ships were strongly attacked by the local population and their ship crews mutinied. On the same voyate they reported active trade of merchandise and slaves at Arquim Island in Mauretania. Three or four armed caravels attacked coastal fishing villages in the Gulf of Arquim to capture slaves for the return voyage. Still in 1456 Cadamosta and Usodimare reached the Rio Grande (Geba) and the Bissagos Islands. See also HENRY.

CADERNETA. Labor passbook system started in 1920's in conjunction with contratado labor system. Similar to the South African system of passbooks for labor regulation.

CAETANO, DR. MARCELLO. Prime Minister of Portugal from September 1968, following the stroke of Prime Minister Salazar, until April 25, 1974, when he was over-

thrown by the Armed Forces Movement (MFA).   Caetano
was a professor of Public Law and the main author of
the 1933 Constitution.   He was the Minister of Colonies
from 1944 to 1949 and was instrumental in the 1951 revisions of the Portuguese constitution.

CANARY CURRENT.   South flowing ocean current off the Atlantic coast of Morocco enabling the Portuguese to pass
easily down the coast in the early days of exploration,
but making the return difficult with vessels which could
not sail close to the wind.

CANCHUNGO (12° 04'N, 16° 02'W).   Town in northwestern
Guinea-Bissau (also named Teixeira Pinto during the colonial era), named for the militarist who was responsible
for the "pacification" program.

CAO, DIOGO.   Born in the mid 15th century, he was a Portuguese navigator who, in 1482, was the first to explore
the West Coast of Central Africa just south of the equa-
tor.   He reached the Kongo Kingdom in 1483.   Pero Es-
colar and João de Santiago were on the voyage up the
Congo with Cão.   Christopher Columbus sailed along the
Guinea Coast between 1482 and 1484, possibly meeting
Cão.   Cão wanted to go around the Muslim world to India.   He reached 150 (50?) miles south of Lobito.   Cão
was the real forerunner and stimulus to Bartholomeu
Dias and Vasco da Gama.

CAPITAÇAO.   Head tax, especially as a source of revenue
during colonialism.

CAPITAO (Donatario).   Military commander representing the
Portuguese Crown, especially on Cape Verde.   Each capitão would rule a capitania or captaincy also known as
residêncas in Cape Verde.   See PRAZOS; DONATARIOS.

CASABLANCA GROUP.   African organization which sought to
unify the more progressive states such as Egypt, Guinea-
Conakry, Mali, Algeria, and Ghana in opposition to the
more moderate Brazzaville group formed in December
1960.   The Casablanca group was formed in January 1961
and was officially disbanded in 1963 with the formation
of the OAU.   As a result of the emergence of the Casablanca group the CONCP took place in April 1961 which
represented a major effort to unify the three leading nationalist movements fighting in the Portuguese colonies.
See also CONCP.

CASA DOS ESTUDANTES DO IMPERIO (CEI).   This semi-of-
   ficial African student center in Lisbon was a center for
   African assimilados and intellectuals including figures such
   as Marcelino dos Santos of Mozambique, Amílcar Cabral
   of Guinea and Mário de Andrade of Angola.   From the
   CEI, revolutionary thinkers formed the MAC in 1957.   In
   1965 the CEI was finally closed by the Salazar government which termed it subversive.   See also MAC.

CASAMANCE.   Region and river in southern Senegal forming
   a portion of the general area known as Senegambia.   The
   trade and administrative center of Casamance is at Ziquinchor which was a portion of Portuguese Guinea until
   the late 19th century.   French traders became quite numerous in the 1820's and 30's.   Following the Berlin
   Congress in 1886, Portugal gave up its claims to the
   Casamance Basin and Ziquinchor, meanwhile France withdrew its claims on Cacine in southern Guinea-Bissau.
   Other minor changes were made in the 1890's and early
   1900's to settle the frontiers of France and Portugal as
   the two colonial powers of the immediate area.   See also
   BERLIN CONGRESS; GABU.

CASSANGAS   see   BANYUNS

CENTRO DE INSTRUCAO POLITICO MILITAR (CIPM).   In
   order to develop ideological unity with the PAIGC cadres
   Amílcar Cabral founded the CIPM in the earliest period
   of the operation of an exile base in Conakry probably
   about 1961 when a number of the leading figures such as
   João Vieira, Francisco Mendes, Domingo Ramos, Constantino Teixeira, and others attended this seminal party
   school.   One of the functions was to link ideological and
   military training in the formation of "bi-grupos," the basic
   guerrilla army unit.   The CIPM also trained those returning from aboard and offered basic education.   In the early
   1970's, 200-300 students in groups of 25 would be trained
   through a series of formal, informal, and role-playing
   exercises during a program of several months.   The cur-
   riculum included national and world history, a PAIGC code
   of behavior, lessons on the party program and organization, military and political tactics, decolonization, foreign
   relations as well as developing a strong sense of national
   unity and purpose.   Stress was laid on the political, rather
   than military dimensions of the struggle.

CHAMPALIMAUD.   One of the major financial and industrial

conglomerates of Portugal with ties to the BNU and extensive colonial interests.   Champalimaud virtually con-
trols the Portuguese steel industry although it is, in turn,
dominated by West German finance capital.   Champalimaud
operated the cement and puzzolane company of Cape Verde
and a variety of firms in Guinea-Bissau.

CLASSES.   For small nations, the class structure of Guinea-
Bissau and Cape Verde is rather complex in its diversity
but simple insofar as both nations are overwhelmingly
geared to agricultural production.   Some scholars have
questioned the applicability of the European term "peasants," however, this term may be the best to describe
the dominance of agriculture and feudal-like social relations of production (especially in Cape Verde).   In Guinea-
Bissau much of the peasantry works at subsistence cultivation with income supplemented by cash crops such as
rice, peanuts, cashews, fruits and vegetables.   In Cape
Verde, sharecropping and systems of absentee landlords
are much more common.   Guinea has had little plantation
agriculture while Cape Verde has some modest plantations
of sugar cane and bananas, with coffee grown on some
islands.   The peasants of Guinea-Bissau may be divided
into the coastal, largely stateless, rice-farmers, and
the interior, more leader-oriented peanut-growers and
cattle-herders.   The acephalous peoples may be exem-
plified by the Balantas who have village level authority
and who are primarily animist in religious outlook.   The
most prominent centrally governed people are the Fulas
who have local and regional leaders who traditionally
command the respect of large numbers of their people,
especially with reference to their position in the colonial
structure and in the local Islamic religious hierarchy.
Such cephalous or semi-cephalous groups have chiefs,
local nobility and traditional religious leaders.
    The working class is very small in both nations and
is mainly concentrated in those concerns which prepare,
process or transport agricultural or livestock products.
In addition to basic industries such as lumbering, butch-
eries, dairies, traditional crafts and fish processing, one
of the largest concentrations of the wage-earning work
force is to be found among transport workers, particularly
in inter-island aircraft and ships in Cape Verde and river
and road transport in Guinea-Bissau.   To be included in
this general sector of transport workers would be the port
and docking personnel and airport workers.   Additional
members of the working class are repairmen, street ven-

dors and mechanics. Some traditional artisans or craftsmen such as weavers, blacksmiths and leatherworkers
may still be found as well as a subordinate wage-earning
service sector of servants, launderers, cooks and domestic help. Another group of wage-earners may be found
with those involved with public works such as road building. In earlier days these very poorly paid, unskilled
workers might have been slaves or later contract labor.
In the Cape Verde Islands, significant numbers of males
have temporarily emigrated from the islands to work in
various parts of the world and to send remittances to
families in the islands. With this demographic imbalance,
very large numbers of road building workers are women
and children.

Beyond the peasantry and the small working class there
is the "déclassé" lumpen proletariat which includes the
sector of prostitutes. These women were numbered in
the several thousands in and around Portuguese military
bases and in the larger towns during the war. Other
petty criminals and smugglers make up this small and
unreliable class stratum. Something of a minuscule petit
bourgeois class may be seen with some African officials,
those in the liberal professions, and some small scale
contract farmers. Members of a group of skilled professionals, such as engineers, doctors or lawyers are an
almost negligible portion of the total population and of
these, very few are Guinean, while larger numbers would
have a Cape Verdean heritage. Many Cape Verdeans
served in the colonial infrastructure in various Portuguese
colonies. Police and colonial military troops were drawn
from the local population to a certain extent, but were almost always officered by metropolitan Portuguese. Likewise, small scale merchants engaged in the sale of agricultural produce may be found in town markets. However, the commerce in textiles and light manufactured
items rested in the hands of Lebanese and Portuguese
in Guinea-Bissau and Cape Verdeans and Portuguese in
Cape Verde. In brief, the top political, commercial and
military positions were dominated by members of the ex-
patriot bourgeoisie and a very small sector of the local
petite bourgeoisie. At various points in the history of
Guinea-Bissau the Dyulas, a Mandingo-derived, itinerant
trading group controlled the trade to the interior with
Afro-Portuguese lançados working along the coast.

The class structure in Guinea-Bissau follows rather
sharp racial and rural-urban divisions. Aside from the
military, almost all Portuguese were found in the several

larger towns, but most were concentrated in Bissau. The
European plantation system was barely developed. Likewise, the top class positions were monopolized by Europeans including the high government officials and bureaucrats, many traders, representatives of foreign banks and
industries, business managers, and the "liberal" professions. At a somewhat lower level, assimilados and some
Cape Verdeans might be found in the government bureaucracy and as clerks and small merchants. In Cape Verde
the population is largely mestiço so the clear cut nature
of racial division is not so readily apparent although darker
Cape Verdeans tend to be clustered amongst the poorer
inhabitants.

Since the coming of national independence, the leadership of the two nations has attacked the traditional and
colonial class structure. The cephalous feudal-like authorities have lost considerable power and most of the
larger foreign monopolies and finance interests are either
nationalized or under strict regulation. The commercial
sectors are also under close state supervision. The new
leadership has formed a new state bureaucracy and large
scale private ownership has been abolished and placed in
the state sector. During Portuguese colonial rule the
process of class formation was very much repressed
and abbreviated by the colonial authorities. Because
only a small working class has come into existence,
the generation of surplus value was relatively underdeveloped. The post colonial period in many African
countries has been associated with a rapid class formation filling the vacuum left by the departing colonial
authorities, but the revolutionary nationalist movement
in Guinea-Bissau and Cape Verde incorporated a social
revolution with the acquisition of national independence.
With the rather sudden exit of the Portuguese the PAIGC
moved into positions of power and blocked the formation
of a local bourgeoisie based on private ownership of
the means of production.

COBIANAS   see   BANYUNS

COCOLIS (Kokolis).   This small Senegambian group is derived
    from the Bissagos peoples and occupies coastal stretches
    at the mouth of the Geba River near the Nalus peoples.
    See also BISSAGOS; NALUS.

COLA.   Fête, especially of holy saints, in Cape Verde.

COLI TENGUELLA see TENGUELLA; COLI

COLUMBUS, BARTHOLOMEW. Cartographer in Lisbon during the time of João II. He was the brother of Christopher Columbus.

COLUMBUS, CHRISTOPHER. Credited with being the first European navigator to reach the New World. Between 1482 and 1484 Columbus visited the Guinea coast which prompted a 1484 audience with King João II to gain financing for further voyages. João II turned down his offer, although Columbus visited him again in 1493 after his epic voyage. Some reports indicate that Columbus stopped in the Cape Verde archipelago before making his crossing.

COMISSAO PERMANENTE see PERMANENT SECRETARIAT

COMPANHIA DO CACHEN E CABO VERDE see CACHEU

COMPANHIA GERAL DO GRAO PARA E MARANHAO. This Brazilian slave trade company was formed in 1753(5) to supply the labor needs of the two northern, coastal Brazilian states of Pará and Maranhão. Initially there was a 25 (20?) year lease on the slave trade in Guinea-Bissau with indication that it continued well into the 19th century. This company revived a dying slave trade in Guinea and was important for rebuilding Bissau and stimulating Portuguese claims on Bolama. The Portuguese Marquis of Pombal was instrumental in arranging the charter of this company. See also BISSAU; BOLAMA; SLAVERY.

COMPANHIA LUSITANA DO ALUMINIO DA GUINE E ANGOLA. This Dutch firm was founded on August 16, 1957, to discover and process bauxites in Guinea-Bissau and Angola. The Portuguese government and Billiton Maatschappig N. V. of the Netherlands, with an initial investment of $172,000 (U.S.), agreed to prospecting in the Boe area for an estimated 200,000 tons of bauxite related to the same field of aluminum bearing ore in neighboring Guinea-Conakry. Regular productive exploitation is not yet achieved.

COMPANHIA UNIAO FABRIL (CUF). CUF is one of the very largest Portuguese conglomerates with large investments in Africa and with approximately 10 percent of Portugal's total corporate capital. CUF is a multi-national concern

involved in textiles, agriculture, petro-chemicals, steel
and shipbuilding. It has its own merchant ships and has
tens of thousands of employees.   CUF is primarily owned
by the powerful Mello family which, in turn, has links to
the BNU and the Champalimaud conglomerate which shares
CUF's dominance of the Portuguese, and formerly colonial, economies. CUF has important links to American
and French capital as well. In Guinea-Bissau the two
major CUF affiliates were Casa Gouveia, exporting palm
and peanut oil, and the Antonio Silva Corporation which
has very significant investments in shipping, insurance,
light industry and export-import concerns which dominated
Guinea's economy. See also BNU; CHAMPALIMAUD.

CONFERENCIA DE ORGANIZAÇOES NACIONALISTAS DAS
   COLONIAS PORTUGUESAS (CONCP). Founded in April
   1961 in Casablanca, Morocco, and held a permanent secretariat at Rabat under Marcelino dos Santos, who was
   to become a top leader of FRELIMO in Mozambique. The
   CONCP replaced the former umbrella organization FRAIN.
   The Second CONCP Conference was held in Dar es Sa-
   laam, Tanzania, in October 1965. In addition to other
   liberation movements and organizations, the PAIGC sent
   a five-man delegation consisting of A. Cabral, V. Cabral,
   V. Maria, A. Duarte, J. Araujo as well as representatives from the UNTG and UDEMU.

CONHAQUES. These small, isolated clusters of Senegambian
   people manifest considerable Mandingo acculturation as
   they were separated from the main coastal Senegambian
   groups during Mandingo expansion. They are now found
   in the hilly areas in the extreme southeast of Guinea-
   Bissau and some small pockets in the Madina Boe area.

CONSELHO DE GUERRA [War Council]   see   PERMANENT
   SECRETARIAT; CEL; CSL

CONSELHO EXECUTIVO DA LUTA (CEL). The CEL is
   elected during the annual meetings of the CSL and functions
   between CSL meetings. The CEL meets at least every
   four months or more often if needed. Its main function
   is to act as the Political Bureau of the PAIGC. There
   is, at present, only one female member of the CEL. After the 1964 Party Congress a 20-member (15 regular,
   5 alternate) Political Bureau was organized and functioned
   until it was replaced and enlarged by the CEL in 1970.
   The Conselho was central to the regulation of political

and military affairs during the period of the nationalist war.   This regulation was achieved insofar as the CEL contained the 7-member Conselho de Guerra (War Council) and the powerful PAIGC 3-member Permanent Secretariat (Commission).   Members of the CEL constitute about a third of the CSL.   See also CSL; PAIGC.

CONSELHO SUPERIOR DA LUTA (CSL) [High Council of the Struggle].   The CSL functions within the PAIGC as an organ roughly equivalent to a Central Committee, that is, it is the highest body except for the irregular meetings of the Peoples National Assembly (ANP).   Within the CSL are the CEL, the War Council, and the Permanent Commission.   The CSL meets, annually since its first session in August 1971 when it replaced the PAIGC Central Committee (65 members) that emerged from the Second Party Congress.   In 1964 the Central Committee had seven departments but these were reduced to five by 1967.   In 1970 the Central Committee was initially enlarged to 70 members and was newly named the CSL with about one third of its members also being on the CEL.   At the time of the 1973 Second Party Congress the CSL increased its membership from 81 to 85.   The membership was raised to 90 at the 1977 meeting of the Peoples National Assembly.   During the CSL meetings members of the CEL are elected to serve between the yearly CSL meetings.   See also CEL; PAIGC.

CONTRATADO.   A contract laborer who agrees to sell his labor power for a proscribed period of time to a specific employer, used extensively in Cape Verde to reduce the population on the poor desiccated islands and to generate funds which can be sent home.   Often used for large public works and in the agricultural sector.

CORUBAL, RIO [Corubal River].   This major river of Guinea-Bissau has its headwaters in the vicinity of Labé in the Futa Jallon plateau of Guinea-Conakry.   Before it reaches Guinea-Bissau it is known as the Koliba River until it enters the eastern frontier of Guinea-Bissau south of Buruntuma curving back south through the Gabu and Boe areas before swinging northward again to empty into the upper portion of the Geba estuary.   The Corubal is about 280 miles in length and provided a convenient route for the export of slaves to the coast.   See also GEBA, RIO DE.

CRIOULO.   Cape Verdean dialect of Portuguese, based essen-

tially on a Portuguese morphology and African phonetic
system with loan words from both stocks. Sometimes
used to infer mixed Cape Verdean cultural heritage. Spoken
in Guinea-Bissau with somewhat greater portion of African loan words.

-D-

DA GAMA, VASCO. Da Gama was the first Portuguese sol-
    dier-navigator to round the Cape of Good Hope and travel
    up the east coast of Africa to India. He initiated the
    Portuguese trade monopoly of the region. With advanced
    navigational equipment, da Gama sailed directly from the
    bulge in West Africa to the South African cape on his trip
    to the region during the years 1502-1504. On his first
    trip, 1497-99, da Gama rounded the Cape with three ships.
    In 1498 he encountered Muslims at Quilemane on the east
    coast, then sailed to Malindi and on to Calicut and Mala-
    bar, India. On the 1502 trip he subdued Kilwa at gun-
    point, opening the age of early 16th-century rivalry be-
    tween the Portuguese and Moslems for east coast trade.

DEGREDADOS. Exiled Portuguese criminals, often charged
    with political crimes, who settled in Cape Verde Islands
    or were confined there for a punishment period. Some
    degredâdos became a permanent settler population in
    Guinea-Bissau known as lançados.

DEMOCRATIC ACTION GROUP OF CAPE VERDE AND GUINEA
    (GADCVG). The GADCVG emerged in the period after
    the fall of the Caetano government in Lisbon and essen-
    tially represented the position of the PAIGC regarding
    unity with Guinea and Cape Verde. The GADCVG rapidly
    became a mass organization which blocked the organizing
    efforts of the UDCV and the UPICV particularly in mid-
    November 1974 when it organized a 24-hour general strike
    to back the PAIGC demand that it alone would be in the
    negotiations with Portugal regarding independence in 1975.

DEMOGRAPHY see POPULATIONS

DE NOLI, ANTONIO see NOLI, ANTONIO DE

DGS see PIDE

DIALONKES (Djalonkes, Jaloncas, Jallonkes). This small

group appears to be of the Senegambian stock but with
very pronounced Mandingo acculturation so that it is sometimes placed in the latter category.   They are partly Islamized as a result of the 18th-century Fulani migrations
from Futa Jallon and are now located east of Duas Fontes
(Bangacia).   The Dialonkes are the neighbors of the Quis-
sincas, a Manding group.

DIAS, BARTHOLOMEU.   Portuguese navigator who rounded
the Cape of Good Hope, South Africa, in 1488 and returned
to Portugal in December of that year.

DIAS, DINIZ.   Portuguese navigator who "discovered" the
mouth of the Senegal River and Cap Vert of Senegal in
1444-5.

DIOLAS (Djolás).   This group of the Senegambian stock is related to the Senegalese Serer and is thought to have split
from them in about the 14th century with the creation of
the Sine and Salum kingdoms.   These animistic rice cultivators are found between the Casamance and Cacheu rivers in the northwest and coastal portions of Guinea-Bissau
and they have absorbed some of the Banyun population
living to the east.   The term Diolás must be distinguished
from the Manding derived Dyulas.   The Diolás were frequent targets of Manding slave raiders who sold their
captives to the lançados and other Portuguese.

DONATARIOS (Capitães).   System of local rule in Cape Verde
and other Portuguese islands.   Local nobility was appointed by the Crown and subject to inspection and appeal
by Lisbon.   The regulation of a donatario was sometimes
in the hands of a capitão.   The recipients of these royal
land grants usually farmed their holdings with slaves.
See CAPITAO.

DROUGHT.   The Sahelian drought in Africa is a continuation
of centuries of desiccation of the Sahara and the Cape
Verde archipelago.   The drought in Cape Verde is accompanied by a major demographic transformation of the
population of the islands.   On the one hand, resultant
famines have commonly cut the population by a third or
more.   Statistics have been kept from 1747 to 1970 which
show 58 years of famine and over 250,000 related deaths.
On the other hand, the unpredictable role for agriculture
has forced emigration from the islands to seek employment elsewhere.   Thousands of Cape Verdean male con-

tract laborers have left a population composed dispropor-
tionately of elderly, children and women. A large factor
in the drought is a serious lack of proper land manage-
ment and water conservation. Colonial rule actually benefited from cheap Cape Verdean labor and had little in-
clination to invest the necessary funds for meaningful
economic or resource development of the islands. Currently another drought is underway, but it appears to be
drawing to a close. The PAIGC leadership is projecting
plans for reforestation, deep well drilling, desalinization of
plants, erosion control and catchment dams to reduce the
disastrous effects of the natural and political problem.

DUARTE, ABILIO MONTEIRO. Minister of Foreign Affairs
for the Republic of Cape Verde, Duarte studied beaux
arts at the Sorbonne in Paris. As a PAIGC militant he
was made a member of CEL in charge of reconstruction.
Subsequently he was a member of the PAIGC General Secretariat. After the independence of Cape Verde Duarte
has served as the President of the Cape Verdean National
Assembly, Chairman of the Unity Commission and as Cape
Verdean Ambassador to the United Nations.

DYULAS (Diulas, Joolas). This economically important ethnic
group of Manding derivation must be distinguished from
the Senegambian Diolas. The Dyulas are mainly from
the Soninke branch with some Fula admixture. Function-
ing as a specialized class of itinerant traders, the Dyulas
integrated the Portuguese economic concerns along the
coast with those of the people in the interior, especially
in the early 16th century until the arrival of the colonial
era. During the decline of Mali, the influence of the
Dyulas appeared in a series of petty chiefdoms on the
shores of the Gambia and Cacheu Rivers and at the Dyula
commercial center at Kankan. The Dyula stimulated local production of gold, kola nuts and the exchange of
slaves for imported products such as salt, textiles and
firearms during the pre-colonial era. These items were
traded throughout Guinea-Bissau and in much of the Upper Niger River. The Dyulas often worked in close association with Mali and the Mandingo kingdoms. Most
Dyulas were Moslems, but they did not carry out con-
versions or jihads. The penetration of the interior by
the Portuguese broke into the Dyula commerce which
helped to cause the Dyula "revolutions" from 1835 to the
1880's in the Upper Niger and in Guinea-Conakry during
which they tried to re-establish their commercial authority. See also GABU; MANDE; SONINKE.

-E-

EANNES, CONSALO. As a representative of the Portuguese
    Crown, Eannes was sent to visit the Prince of Tekrur
    and the Lord of Timbuktu in the last quarter of the 15th
    century. See MALI.

EANNES, GIL. Sailing for Prince Henry in 1434 and 1435,
    Eannes made two trips in a cumbersome 50-ton square
    sailed barca. More efficient caravels were operational
    after 1441. After returning to Lisbon in 1435 he later
    set sail with Afonso Gonçalves Baldaio and went south of
    the tropic of Cancer ($23\frac{1}{2}°$). These voyages were the
    first recorded in that region since the time of the Phoe-
    necians in 813 B. C. In subsequent expeditions, Eannes
    made three consecutive trips in 1444, 1445 and 1446 us-
    ing the more advanced caravel type of ship.

ECONOMICS (Trade).
        Guinea-Bissau: Under colonialism approximately 90
    percent of the exports of Guinea-Bissau went to Portugal
    and the other Portuguese African colonies. West Ger-
    many was the next largest importer of products from
    Guinea-Bissau but this was only a very small portion of
    the total colonial monopoly. The largest portion of im-
    ports were also from Portugal which represented 50-55
    percent in the early 1970's with the rest shared with other
    European powers, Japan and the United States. The cur-
    rent trade policy has been to diversify trading partners
    with some trade now going to socialist nations in eastern
    Europe, the Soviet Union and Cuba. During the heyday
    of Portuguese colonial rule Guinea was a relatively strong
    exporter of rice and peanuts but the war (1963-1974) con-
    tinuously eroded this position so that from the mid 1960's
    food was a chief import, in fact by 1975, 75 percent of
    the nation's food was imported. However, by 1976, only
    one full year after national independence, agricultural pro-
    duction had been partially restored and food imports fell
    to only 20 percent of the total. It is realistically expected
    that food will soon return to being an important export of
    Guinea-Bissau in the coming years.
        The following table provides the basic patterns of for-
    eign trade showing a steady increase in imports. Exports
    fluctuated noticeably but never regained the 1960 high.
    After the war began in 1963, rice production fell off mark-
    edly and thus reduced the role of this major export. As
    a consequence, the deficit steadily increased, reaching

822,000 contos in 1971 (1 conto = ca. $35 U.S.).   The
1973 data are atypical and only represent the economic
upheaval caused by the final phases of guerrilla war.   The
1975 data show a very substantial rise in exports and the
beginning of a decline in the deficit now that the nation
is under nationalist control.   The chief exports of Guinea-
Bissau continue to be rice, peanuts and other agricultural
commodities.   Under colonialism, textiles represented 20
to 25 percent of the total value of imports

Guinea-Bissau: Balance of Trade*
(in 1,000 contos)

Date	Exports	Imports	Deficits
1951	168.3 ·	188.1	-19.8
1953	211.2	188.1	+23.1
1955	178.2	221.1	-42.9
1957	221.1	267.3	-46.2
1959	224.4	283.8	-59.4
1961	211.2	292.1	-80.9
1963	166.5	407.2	-240.7
1965	105.8	419.3	-313.5
1967	91.2	471.9	-380.7
1969	105.0	672.3	-567.3
1971	57.0	879.0	-822.0
1973	47.1	140.2	-93.1
1975	282.3	894.1	-611.8

*Sources sometimes give conflicting figures.
(Exports 1951-75 increased 1.6 times; imports 1951-75 increased 4.7 times.)

while the colonial monopoly only permitted 6-8 percent
of imports in the sector of machines and tools thereby
locking Guinea-Bissau into agricultural production.   During the colonial period in the 1950's to 1974, manufactur-
ing industries in Guinea-Bissau contributed only between
1-2 percent of the Gross Domestic Product.
     Cape Verde: The trade of Cape Verde has been vir-
tually strangled by Portuguese colonial monopolies.   Decades have gone by with a major deficit in the balance of
trade.   Between 1951 and 1973 imports have increased
almost 11 times in value while exports have not even increased three-fold.   In other words, the deficit between
exports and imports between 1951 and 1973 increased 370
percent (while for Guinea-Bissau in the same period it
increased 290 percent).   A contributing source of the fundamental economic imbalance has been the prolonged
drought which necessitated, in the 1970's, the major

importation of food (about 2/3 of the total import value).
Approximately 75 percent of all imports were from Portugal and its African colonies.   Other important imports
included cement and textiles.   Like imports, the major
recipient of Cape Verdean exports was Portugal and the
Portuguese African colonies which received about 2/3 of
the meager volume of total exports.   The other major
recipient of Cape Verdean exports was the United States
which purchased 15-25 percent of the total exports (especially fish).   By value, exports in recent years have cov-
ered only 5-6 percent of all imports thus requiring heavy
government subsidies, emigration, burdensome poverty
and remittances from Cape Verdeans overseas.   The estimated per capita income in 1974 was $250 per year.

Year	Imports from Guinea and Cape Verde to Portugal (% of colonial imports)	Exports from Portugal to Guinea and Cape Verde (% of colonial exports)
1959	16. 3%	12. 1%
1963	11. 5%	10. 7%
1964	9. 8%	10. 2%

Cape Verde: Balance of Trade*
(in contos)

Date	Exports	Imports	Deficits
1951	16,342	77,112	-60,770
1953	21,715	76,836	-55,121
1955	22,536	103,91?	-81,383
1957	23,708	151,30?	-127,595
1959	42,282	132,231	-89,949
1961	27,809	185,517	-157,708
1963	24,116	170,242	-146,126
1965	30,913	228,283	-200,322
1967	40,772	258,800	-227,887
1969	47,731	418,801	-374,245
1971	45,600	573,500	-527,900
1973	47,700	833,600	-785,900
1975	?	911,400	?

*Statistics may vary by source.

EDUCATION.   Metropolitan Portugal is notable in Europe for
a particularly low level of public education.   For example,
in 1960 in Portugal 9. 8 percent of the population was enrolled in primary school while the comparable statistic
for Holland was 13. 0 percent, the U. S. S. R. 14. 2 percent,
the U. S. A. 18. 4 percent.   In Portugal's overseas territories the situation was expectedly even worse.   The per-

centages for enrollment in primary school were 4.7 percent for Cape Verde and 3.8 percent for Guinea-Bissau.
These low rates were typical for the European colonies
in Africa, but after independence the percentage in primary school tends to increase rapidly as the function of
education has changed from producing an effective colonial
administration to one of nation-building and social reconstruction.

The main function of Guinea-Bissau was for primary
production and labor recruitment. In Cape Verde, contract labor was an essential element of the colonial economy but also Cape Verdeans were important in the entire
African colonial infrastructure. In 1860 a secondary
school (Lyceu) was constructed in Praia, Cape Verde,
and by 1945 there were 45 primary schools operating in
Guinea and 100 in Cape Verde, yet it is clear that these
few schools were grossly inadequate in meeting the social
needs since the rate of illiteracy in Guinea-Bissau in 1950
was placed at about 98 percent and 72.8 percent for Cape
Verde. Mission education played an important role in
Cape Verde, but there was no serious mission education
in Guinea-Bissau until 1950 when no more than 2 percent
of the African population was mission-educated. The
Portuguese budget for education in 1972 was only 6.2
million escudos (1.6 percent of the total budget) or $217,000
(U.S.). This low level of spending represented $.41 per
student per year although Cape Verdean students were
budgeted almost $2.00 per year. This inequality in the
educational budget helped to foster antagonisms between
Guineans and Cape Verdeans. Students in neighboring
Guinea-Conakry and Gambia were receiving about $3.00
per capita annually at this same time.

Educational statistics are conflicting and contradictory
as it is not always clear whether students simply enrolled,
actively attended, or actually completed a given level of
education. The 1973 Provincial Report on Educational
services of Guinea-Bissau offers the following data just
before independence, these data should be considered as
maxima for the various categories:

Education In Guinea-Bissau*

	Primary		Secondary	
	Students	Teachers	Students	Teachers
1962-3	11,827	162	987	46
63-4	11,877	164	874	44
64-5	12,210	163	1,095	45
65-6	22,489	192	1,293	42

66-7	24,099	204	1,039	43
67-8	24,603	244	1,152	40
68-9	25,213	315	1,773	111
69-70	25,854	363	1,919	147
70-71	32,051	601	2,765	110
71-72	40,843	803	3,188	158
72-73	47,626	974	4,033	171

*Source: February 12, 1973, Repartição Provincial do Serviços de Educão, Provincia da Guiné.

While education in Cape Verde is uniformly higher than in Guinea-Bissau it should be stressed that of the 25-28 percent literate, about 90 percent are only literate at the primary level. Most of the primary school teachers have themselves had only four years of primary education with only 8 percent fully qualified teachers. There is only one teacher training school. The two licensed secondary schools are in Praia and Mindelo. Higher education really does not exist in either Guinea or Cape Verde. Except for some specialized vocational training anyone with higher education had received it from abroad. The following data show the sharp differences in enrollment between primary and secondary levels and although the numbers in the various categories tend to increase, the increase in population at this time has not resulted in a significant reduction of illiteracy.

Education In Cape Verde*

	Primary		Secondary	
	Students	Teachers	Students	Teachers
1953	6,167			
1964	18,150			
1968	23,986	456	2,420	
1969	40,685	795	2,400	203
1970	45,103	731	2,895	
1971	53,862	837	3,230	
1972	53,195	872	4,134	
1973				
1974	70,000	1,220	7,000	247

*Compiled from Portuguese Government Sources.

The educational system described above was designed to meet colonial needs of ideology, labor, and services. As the data painfully illustrate, it was not in the interests of colonial Portugal to have a large, well-educated populace, for example, there were only 14 university graduates in Guinea-Bissau in 1960, while between 1964 and

1973, the PAIGC sent 422 students overseas for advanced
education.   In 1973 there were 35 PAIGC-backed university graduates.   In addition, the PAIGC constructed its
own rival educational system in the liberated areas. While
the PAIGC educational effort did not overtake the Portuguese it was a very remarkable experience given the im-
mensely adverse conditions of air attacks and security for
the students.   The fluctuations in the statistics may be
attributed to periods of intensification of counter-insurgency by the Portuguese thereby upsetting enrollment and
pedagogical programs.   As with the health system, schools
in the liberated areas were very simply constructed and
were moved periodically and new trenches dug as protection against air raids.   The leading PAIGC facility was
the Pilot School in Conakry which usually had about 120
students (about 80 boys and 40 girls).   This secondary
school was very disciplined and often led to direct recruitment into the PAIGC through the operation of the Pioneers of the Party youth organization.   A kindergarten
for absent PAIGC parents and war orphans was also located in Conakry.   Each of the three regions inside liberated Guinea-Bissau also had a boarding school as well
as the more than 200 primary day schools under the forest canopy.   The data on PAIGC schools during the war
for primary students (ages 7-15) are as follows:

Liberated Areas of Guinea-Bissau*
(PAIGC Primary Education)

Year	Students	Teachers	Schools
1965	13,361	191	127
1966	14,380	220	159
1967	9,384	284	158
1968	8,130	243	134
1969	8,559	248	149
1970	8,574	251	157
1971	14,531	258	164
1972	20,000	251	200
1975	60,000		400

*Source: PAIGC Document.

Since independence the PAIGC now claims a precipitous decline in illiteracy from about 98 percent of the
population to 75 percent now that the educational facilities
can operate openly under peaceful conditions.   Not less
remarkable are the 60,000 students now receiving primary education in 400 schools; the 2,000 students in secondary schools and 5,000 students in other educational

training including some 495 receiving secondary, university or specialized training (such as medical, vocational, construction, or organizational) in a variety
of foreign countries.   Aside from formal education,
there are mass circulation newspapers, radio programs
and community organizations which play a direct role
in mobilizing the people for the task of national reconstruction.

ESSO EXPLORATION OF GUINEA, INC.   Esso (Exxon) is the
second largest American oil corporation after Gulf Oil.
In March 1958 Esso was established in Guinea-Bissau and
was given exclusive oil prospecting rights at the cost of
a quarter of a million dollars (U. S.) each year.   An additional $14 to $60 were paid for each square kilometer
where prospecting actually took place.   Beyond this there
was a 12. 5 percent tax on production and a 50 percent
tax on profits.   In 1966 and 1973 the contract between
the Portuguese colonial government and Esso Exploration
was renewed and expanded to include other minerals.   The
on-shore and off-shore results of the prospecting were
not conclusive but there are appropriate conditions for
potentially oil-yielding strata.   The revenue generated
by the terms of this contract gave the Portuguese badly
needed financial support during the period of nationalist
insurgency.   Since independence the contract with Esso
has been suspended and a new contract has been written
with the Italian petroleum company, AGIP.

-F-

FARIM-CACHEU, RIOS [Farim-Cacheu Rivers].   With headwaters to the north of Contuboel on the Geba River, the
Farim River flows almost directly west until it reaches
the town of Farim.   At this point it begins to widen and
proceed westward until it becomes known as the Cacheu
River since it is in the vicinity of the town of that name.
As with the other rivers penetrating the coastal swamps
the Farim-Cacheu was an important corridor for the export of slaves and for commerce through lançados and
Dyula traders with the interior.   The combined length of
these rivers is about 160 miles, although ships of 2, 000
tons are only able to navigate 62 miles to the interior.
See CACHEU.

FELUPE.   A minor Senegambian group most closely related

to the Balantas and Baiotes.   They have a limited hierarchical structure, but there are some reports of a secondary kingdom of the Mali among the Felupes in the 15th
century, however, this may simply be an imposition of
rule from Mali.   The Felupes are famed rice cultivators
using the flood irrigation technique.   They are mainly located in the northwest corner of Guinea-Bissau especially
south of the Casamance north of the Cacheu River and
reaching to the ocean coast in that region.   During the
period of aggressive Portuguese colonization, military reports show acts of resistance by the Felupes in 1878-90,
1901, 1903 and finally in 1915 when they were repressed
in the campaigns of Teixeira Pinto.   See also BAIOTES;
DIOLAS.

FERNANDES, GIL VINCENTE VAZ (May 10, 1937-   ).   Born
in Bolama Guinea-Bissau, Fernandes attended high school
in Bissau.   Because of his affiliation with the PAIGC he
fled to Senegal in September 1960.   With plans to study
in Poland he was recruited to attend the University of
New Hampshire from which he earned a B.A. in Political Science in 1965.   Later he received a M.A. from
American University in Washington, D.C.   Fernandes is
a pioneer of the PAIGC on the international scene.   From
1970-72 he was the party representative in Cairo; 1973-
74 in Scandinavia.   At the time of independence he was
a roving Ambassador of the Foreign Affairs Commission.
He has played a significant role in representing the party
at the United Nations.   He is currently a member of the
CSL and the first Guinea-Bissau Ambassador to the United
States.   See UNITED NATIONS; CSL.

FISHING see AGRICULTURE

FOGO (14° 55'N, 24° 25'W).   Fourth largest island (183. 7 sq.
mi.) in the Cape Verde archipelago.   Fogo also has the
highest point (9, 281 feet) among all of the islands.   The
round, rocky cone-shaped island continues to have periodic volcanic eruptions.   Some of the more notable activity was in 1680, and in 1951.   The most recent activity was in March 1962.   Fogo is just east of Brava, but
may be seen from São Tiago on a clear day.   It is one
of the four members of the Sotavento (southern, leeward)
islands.   Fogo was the second island to be settled and
was known as São Filipe for which its leading town
and port is now named.   The island has about 12. 5 percent of the population of the archipelago and São Filipe

(pop. 3,500) is the third largest in all the islands.   The
two other main villages are Igreja and Cova Figueira.
The earliest settlement was based on slaves from the
mainland as early as the late 1460's.   The land was initially a Crown grant (donatario) to settlers related to
Prince Fernando.   The settlers grew some agricultural
trade items and dealt extensively in slaves.   Most of the
first settlers left by the end of the 15th century and only
after 1510 was the island settled more widely.   By 1582
the slave population of the island had reached 2,000 and
the relative autonomy in trade on the coast gave some
atmosphere of prosperity.   An eruption of the volcano in
1680 drove some of the population to neighboring Brava.
This island attracted a number of Europeans, particularly
from Madeira.
    Since independence the PAIGC has organized construc-
tion of some 330 water conservation dikes (73 km.) and
42 km. of terracing.   In addition, the new government
has restored and maintained considerable numbers of former dikes and terraces.   A reforestation project has fo-
cused on São Filipe and Monte Verde while major efforts
at road construction and coffee production have created
3,200 jobs.   There are also plans to build a tourist hotel on Fogo island.

FONIO.   This important cereal grain is native to West Africa
    as a member of the Sudanic food complex.   The scientific
    name is Digitaria exilis.   In Portuguese fonio is known
    as fundo.   It is a hardy plant needing little rain or cul-
    tivation and was a basic food stuff in the Empire of Mali
    and surrounding secondary kingdoms.

FORÇAS ARMADAS REVOLUCIONARIAS DO POVO (FARP).
    This is the regular armed forces of the PAIGC.   FARP
    was formed in 1964 in order to wage a more aggressive
    war against the Portuguese.   The original function of ci-
    vilian defense was then handled by PAIGC local militia
    units (FAL).

FRENTE DE LIBERTAÇAO DA GUINE (FLG).   In 1961 the
    FLG emerged with unity between Mendy's MLG and the
    RDAG.   By 1962 the FLG had combined its forces with
    the moderate FLING.   See FLING.

FRENTE DE LIBERTAÇAO DA GUINE PORTUGUESA E CABO
    VERDE (FLGC).   The FLGC emerged in 1960 under the
    leadership of Henri Labéry the founder of the UPG in

1957.   Essentially the FLGC replaced the MLGCV of Dakar and its three constituent organizations.   The FLGC
also included the MLGP and the MLICV so as to broaden
the base of support to provide an effective rival to the
PAIGC which was founded four years earlier.   While the
FLGC united new groups it lasted only one year until it
was replaced by FUL following factional divisions within
the FLGC, FUL and the former FLGC members led to
the formation of FLING in 1962.   See FLING.

FRENTE DE LUTA PELA INDEPENDENCIA NACIONAL DA
    GUINE-BISSAU (FLING).   FLING was the only serious
    rival of the PAIGC.   The principal differences lay in the
    moderate program, ethnic allegiances, and exclusion of
    Cape Verde for FLING versus the social reforms, anti-
    tribal program, and Guinea and Cape Verde unity for the
    PAIGC.   FLING emerged in a July-August 1962 meeting
    in Dakar, Senegal which formed a coalition of seven eth-
    nically-based groups such as the MLG, UPG and RDAG
    under the leadership of Henri Labéry.   In 1966, Jaime
    Pinto Bull became the president and the main operation
    continued from a Dakar office.   As the successes of the
    PAIGC mounted, FLING undertook direct actions against
    the PAIGC and was implicated in the assassination of
    Amílcar Cabral.   FLING undertook some military activ-
    ities shortly after being founded but not after 1963.   Some
    members of FLING were openly hostile to Cape Verdeans
    given the role of Cape Verdean merchants during slavery
    and some Cape Verdean administrators during colonialism.
    Between 1963-1967 the OAU sought to merge FLING and
    the PAIGC with active encouragement by Senegal's mod-
    erate President Senghor.   After 1967 Senghor reluctantly
    accepted the supremacy of the PAIGC although Senegal's
    support for FLING continued quietly from 1967 to 1970.
    It was long assumed that the Portuguese PIDE and the
    American CIA favored FLING to divide the supporters of
    the PAIGC.   The most militant elements of FLING were
    the former MLG members, while most of the other mem-
    ber groups held rather moderate, reformist views.   In
    1970 FLING was reorganized with Domingos Joseph Da
    Silva as the new Secretary General of FLING-UNIFIE.
    In 1973 the leadership passed again to Mario Jones Fer-
    nandes.   FLING was charged with creating disturbances
    in Bissau, Bolama and Bafata in May 1974 and FLING
    members were arrested by the Guinea-Bissau government
    in April 1976.

FRENTE REVOLUCIONARIA AFRICANA PARA A INDEPEN-

DENCIA NACIONAL DAS COLONIAS PORTUGUESAS
(FRAIN). This umbrella organization was formed in
Tunis, Tunisia in 1960 to link the PAIGC and the MPLA
of Angola in their common programs. The first leader
of FRAIN was Mario de Andrade of the MPLA. Just as
FRAIN replaced MAC, (Movimento Anti-Colonialista) it
was replaced in 1961 by the CONCP, which continued the
same function. See CONCP.

FRONT UNI DE LIBERATION [de Guinée et du Cap Vert]
(FUL). In July 1961 Amílcar Cabral again sought to
unite the PAIGC with Henri Labéry's FLGC and some
other leaders. This attempt to make a united front failed
because of the hesitating support of the FLGC and the re-
fusal of the MLG to participate. Once FUL became moribund Cabral returned to organize the PAIGC in Conakry
in 1962. The other leaders agreed to form FLING which
proved to be the only serious rival to the PAIGC. See
FLING; PAIGC.

FULA (also known as Fulbe, Fulani, Peul, Fellani, Ful,
Foulah, or Fellata, depending upon local usage). The
Fula peoples are members of the West Atlantic sub-branch
of the Niger-Congo language stock but their history differs
from the other more typical members of the Senegambians.
The Fulani language is much closer to that of the Serer
of Senegal from which they originated, although some
scholars have attributed the Fula origins to the Nile valley
in prehistoric times with westward migration along the
southern fringes of the Sahara desert. Fula-like people
are shown in Saharan rock paintings drawn during periods
of much greater Saharan moisture, but such cultural reconstruction is still speculative. At large, the Fula may
be distinguished by two main categories, i.e., the sedentary, more fully Islamized Fula and the migratory pastoral Fula who have syncretic forms of Islam and anim-
ism. The sedentary Fula are rather strongly hierarchical
in socio-political organization and were influential in the
spread of Islam through much of the sub-Saharan region.
In the southward migration to and through Guinea-Bissau
some Fula adopted some Mandingo cultural patterns and
became known as the Fulas pretos or Fulacundas who are
much less cephalous than the Fulas of Futa Toro or Futa
Jallon. Where the Fulas did not establish their own local rule they often served as herdsmen for the various
kingdoms in the western Sudan. The origins of the Fula
are now clearly traced to Tekrur and Futa Toro in the

Senegal River valley.   The Fula are related to the Berber,
Tukulor, Wolof and Serer peoples.   The 1950 census of
Guinea-Bissau put the Fula population at 108,400 or 21.5
percent of the total population.   In 1960 the Fula population was estimated at 100,000.   As one of the major ethnic groups of Guinea-Bissau the Fulas are sometimes divided into three sub-groups, but there are numerous over-
lapping regional terminologies.

First there are the most numerous Fulas pretos,
"Black Fulas," concentrated in a wide area between Gabu
and Bafata and in scattered groups in the southeast of
Guinea-Bissau.   The Fulas pretos also include the Fulas
forros (Free Fulas) or Fulacundas (Futacundas, Foula-
coundas) found in the northeast and with sizable groups
in the vicinity of Aldea Formosa and in the south central
areas.   The large numbers and wide distribution of this
major Fula grouping attest to the centuries of admixture
with local Malinke people long before the conquest of Kansala by the Futa-jalonkas.   The second Fula grouping is
known as the Futa-jalonkas (Foutajalonkes) including the
Futa-fulas of the north-central Gabu-Pitche area.   Sometimes the Futa-fulas are known as the Quebuncas since
it was these Fulas from Futa Jallon (Labé province) who
brought the end of the Mandingo kingdom of Quebu (Gabu).
The Futa-jalonkas also incorporate the Boencas, just to
the north of Gabu and the Futa-fulas pretos in the extreme
southeast near Madina Boe and adjacent to the former
Labé province from which they originated.   The third
group of Fulas is considered to have its origins in Futa
Toro in Senegal.   They are known by several names,
such as Torancas, Futancas, Tocurures, Fula-forros or
Vassolancas depending upon local usage.   Members of this
group are found in the northeast and especially in scattered groups in the southeastern regions which they share
with the Futa-fulas pretos.

Some non-Islamic pastoral Fula may have spread into
remote eastern parts of Guinea-Bissau as early as the
12th or 13th centuries.   More significant numbers of cattle herding Fula arrived in Guinea-Bissau in the 15th century from Futa Toro.   From the 15th to 18th centuries
the Fulacunda (Fulas pretos) population was in formation
although there was continued peaceful settlement of other
Fula peoples who arrived and mixed with the Mandingos.
Another wave of Fula migrants came from Massina after
Fula and Mande peoples allied in their joint effort to destroy Songhai in 1591.   These migrants paved the way for
the open Fula conquest of Futa Jallon during the later

period of revivalistic theocratic states based on Islamic
brotherhoods; this was especially important for the sedentary town Fula.   This epoch was filled with religious and
military campaigns against the Wolof and Serer of Senegal, the local peoples of Futa Jallon and against the various secondary states of Mali including Gabu of Guinea-
Bissau.   Still another wave of migration took place when
the Fulacundas left Futa Toro between 1650 and 1700 with
Dialonkes to settle in Futa Jallon and eastern Guinea-Bissau.   In general the Fulas were pastoralists while the
Mandingos were agriculturalists.   The policy of Fula settlement in Guinea-Bissau was endorsed by the 15th-16th
century Fula leader, Coli Tenguella.   Fula migration was
stepped up in the 18th century although the Fula of Guinea-
Bissau were still subordinate to the Mandingo state of
Gabu.   Up until this time the Fula were essentially stateless pastoralists, although the most important and numerous of such groups in West Africa.   By the 19th century
Fulas (Fulani) were expanding everywhere in Sahelian
West Africa such as the jihads in northern Nigeria in
1804-1820 and the arrival of the Fulani in the Cameroons
in about 1900.
   From the mid 18th century until 1867 the Fulas from
Futa Jallon and especially from Labé frequently attacked
Gabu until it finally collapsed.   Following its fall in 1867,
the entire eastern portion of Guinea-Bissau was admin-
istered from Labé province.   This would exclude the remaining fragment of Mandingo rule at Braço, but Fula
influence reached as close to the coast as areas south
of Buba.   In 1880-2 and 1900 the Portuguese colonial authorities carried out military expeditions against the Fula
and brought them under control by means of the Fula's
hierarchical political system which had been developed
for the administration of their conquered territory.   Later, the centralized Fula society proved to be well suited
to a form of indirect colonial rule which reinforced the
traditional chief structure by paying them and giving them
special privileges within colonial society.   See also ALFA
MOLO; ALFA MUSA; COLI TENGUELLA; DIALONKES;
FUTA JALLON; FUTA TORO; GABU; TEKRUR.

FUTA JALLON (Fouta Djallon, Djalonke, Jalonke, Dialonke,
   Jaalo).   A plateau area of the interior of Guinea Conakry
   which has served as the homeland for a portion of the
   Fula people of Guinea-Bissau and a major source for the
   regional spread of Islam.   Fula peoples arrived in Guinea-
   Bissau at least by the 15th century particularly as an ef-

fect of the movements of Coli Tenguella (I) but the greatest period of Fula migration took place between 1654 to
about 1700.   The Fula were disorganized and nomadic and
at first lived peacefully with Mande and Dialonke peoples
but paid tribute to the Mandingo state of Gabu.   In 1725
the first Fula jihad against the Dialonke of Futa Jallon
took place but it was indecisive.   By the mid 18th century Gabu was increasingly under attack by the Labé
branch of the Fulas from Futa Jallon.   This period of
intense and complex conflicts was related to the heavy
demand for slaves and the widespread use of firearms.
Which ever group was the victor in any given battle there
was a ready market for slaves at such places as Cacheu,
Bissau, or on the Casamance or Gambia rivers.   Late
in the 18th century the Fula peoples had conquered the
Dialonke branch of Mali in Futa Jallon.   A constitution
of this theocratic military state was drawn up by nine
Fula leaders.   The influence of Futa Jallon went out in
many directions including the formation of Labé province
adjacent to Guinea-Bissau.   By 1788 the Fula ruling ar-
istocracy had been stabilized and such former residents
like the Susu had been pushed toward the coast in Guinea-
Conakry and into southern Guinea-Bissau where they assimilated coastal cultural patterns.   Islamization of many
neighboring peoples grew considerably in extent.   At the
close of the 18th century a holy war had been declared
against the non-believers in Gabu and while the Mandingo
state lasted another seventy years it underwent rather
steady weakening.   In one case in 1836-7 the Mandingo
state of Braço in Guinea-Bissau attempted resistance and
defeated Almami Bubakar of Labé, but this represented
only a short-lived halt in the deterioration of Gabu.
      Throughout the first quarter of the 19th century the
Fula jihads intensified and the power of Gabu continued
to decline.   No less than a dozen military missions were
thrown against Gabu from Labé.   The holy war was justified by the fact that the Mandingo were mainly animists
even though some had converted to Islam as early as the
time of Coli Tenguella.   Ironically, even the Fula founder
of Labé, Kalidou, was not a Moslem himself although he
was not opposed to Islam.   One of the most prominent
19th century jihad leaders was Al-Haj Al-Mami Umaru,
a Tukulor from Futa Toro who had joined a Tijaniya religious brotherhood during his pilgrimage to Mecca.   Upon
his return he revitalized the holy war movement in
Futa Jallon; prepared his disciples and entered into
a full scale slave trade to acquire firearms on the Atlan-

tic coast.   In 1848 Al-Haj Umaru declared his hegira or
holy emigration from Futa Jallon to Dinguiray, a small
kingdom near Futa Toro.   On the way north he passed
through Guinea-Bissau and killed the king of Gabu, Yangi
Sayon, in 1849.   Gabu was also suffering internal weak-
nesses from various revolts of indigenous Fula peoples
such as the 1850 upheaval which led to the creation of
the small Fula state of Forea on the Corubal River.   In
1862 Al-Haj Umaru initiated his major jihad, first against
Futa Toro where he met defeat, however his army still
grew in size and later went on to capture Segu and Mas-
ina.

In 1865 Al-Haj Umaru made preparations for the final
conquest of Kansala, the capital town of Gabu.   In direct
association with Alfa Mo Labé (Yaya Maudo) and Musa
Mo Labé a siege by Al-Haj Umaru was laid against Kansala from 1866 to 1867 when the Mansa (governor) Dianke
Walli finally capitulated thus bringing the collapse of Gabu.
This shift in power brought about relocation of many of
the peoples of Guinea-Bissau.   On the one hand it represented the start of another wave of assimilation by Fula
migrants from Futa Jallon.   On the other hand, the fall
of Kansala also stimulated Malinke migrations of the Gambia area where their town of Braço remained unconquered
although some Fulacunda in Braço drove Malinke people
out of the lower Casamance and lower Gambia regions.
In addition Beafadas and Nalus who had been living under
the control of Gabu were driven west to the coastal river
lowlands where they resettled, with Portuguese aid, at
the forts at Geba and Buba.   With the end of the military
campaign, Gabu was placed under the authority of Alfa
Mo Labé, the Fula head of Labé Province.   As Haj Umaru
went back to Futa Toro where he was engaged in battle
with the French general Louis Faidherbe who blocked his
advance into the middle of the Senegal River valley.   In
1878 Faidherbe completed his task and gave Al-Haj Umaru
his final defeat.   At the height of his conquests (1862-1878)
Al-Haj Umaru briefly controlled an area about as large as
the former Empire of Mali.   See FUTA TORO; FULAS;
COLI TENGUELLA; TEKRUR; GABU; NALUS; BEAFADAS;
MANDE.

FUTA TORO.   Geographically adjacent to the Senegal River
valley is the plateau region of Senegal known as Futa Toro
which is the name usually given to the Fula state built
upon Tekrur known from ancient times.   In any case, by
the 11th century the Islamic state of Tekrur at Futa Toro

was ruled by peoples from the mergers of Berber, Tukulor and Soninke ethnic stocks who controlled local Wolof
and Serer populations.   In the 11th century some Serer
left Futa Toro to resist the Islamization from Tekrur and
then went to the Sine and Salum areas of Senegal where
they set up their own small, but powerful states.   Between the 13th and 15th centuries Sine and Salum assimilated local Malinke and Serer culture and society which
was highly stratified with Malinke warriors in the dominant
positions.   The Malinke penetration of the upper Gambia
was limited to that area because it was at the frontiers
of control from Futa Toro.   Some Wolof also left Futa
Toro in the mid-14th century in opposition to the Tekrur
rulers thus starting some small Wolof states in Senegal.
     From Futa Toro the Fula peoples spread widely in the
12th and 13th centuries as the most important pastoralists
of West Africa.   As Mali grew in power and influence in
the 13th and 14th centuries under Sundiata and his followers the Fula ruling class of Futa Toro was composed
mainly of Fula refugees from the kingdom of Kaniaga
which had fallen to the Malian Keita dynasty.   Under the
rule of Mansa Kankan Musa (1312-1337?) of Mali the
Wolof and Tekrur areas were maintained as tributary
states thus extending the rule of Mali virtually to the
Atlantic coast.   When Mali declined in the 15th century
both Tekrur and Wolof states re-emerged.   The best
known Fula leader of this period was Coli Tenguella who
established the new Denianke dynasty in Futa Toro in
about 1490 when he attacked the western flanks of Mali.
The Denianke dynasty of Futa Toro lasted until the 1770's.
During the period of the Denianke dynasty the Portuguese
made some of their first contacts with the interior.   King
João II sent missions to Mali in 1494 and under the reign
of João III another mission was undertaken in 1534.   Portuguese trade to the African interior between the 15th and
16th centuries was largely conducted on the Senegal River
for slaves, gold, and ivory from Mali and Futa Toro and
on the river systems on the Gambia and the Geba which
gave some access to the Futa Jallon plateau region to
which some Fula from Futa Toro had already migrated.
     Throughout the 15th century Fula from Futa Toro
drifted eastward and southward to Guinea-Bissau where
they settled peacefully with the existing Mande-speakers
and other Senegambians.   Between 1654 and 1694 (?) the
greatest wave of Fula and Dialonke migration left Futa
Toro.   In 1750 the theocratic state in Futa Toro launched
a jihad against the animist Dialonke located, in small part,

in Guinea-Bissau and against various Senegambians inhab-
iting Futa Jallon.   This jihad resulted in a cultural admixture known as the Futa-jalonke.   A second major period of Fula migration and jihad or holy war left from
Futa Toro in 1770.   Then between 1770 and 1818 two additional jihads were initiated in Futa Toro.   With this
pattern clearly established it was Al-Haj Umaru, originally from Futa Toro, who began his own series of jihads
against Futa Toro which brought an end to the Denianke
dynasty.   Despite his final defeat by the French General
Faidherbe, Al-Haj Umaru and his army briefly held an
area about the equivalent for former Mali reaching as
far east as Jenne.   During these migrations and jihads
the Fula people crossed over eastern Guinea-Bissau and
added to the already existing Fula population centers.
See FUTA JALLON; COLI TENGUELLA; MALI; FULAS;
TEKRUR.

                            -G-

GABU (Kaabu, Quebu).   Tiramakhan Traore, a general of
   Malian King Sundiata, brought his soldiers to regions
   around northeastern Guinea-Bissau and the Casamance in
   the mid 13th century to lay the foundation for the secondary Manding kingdom of Gabu.   Subsequently local Mandingos were appointed to serve as regular administrators.
   The first king (Mansa) of Gabu, Sama Coli (Kelemankoto
   Baa Saane) was said to have been the son or grandson of
   Traore.   Some historical accounts consider that Gabu
   formally began with Sama Coli rather than his ancestor.
   Early in the history of Gabu there were three royal Provinces: Pachana (Pathiana) on the headwaters of the Geba,
   Jimara (Djimara) in Senegal south of the Gambia's headwaters, and Sama on the Casamance.   The capital town
   of all of Gabu was at Kansala in northwestern Guinea-
   Bissau just south of today's border with Senegal.   Mali
   used the well-situated Gabu to secure the trade in salt,
   gold, and slaves on the coastal river estuaries.   The
   Mande-derived Dyulas were important links in this early
   trade with the Portuguese.   Gabu's influence extended
   from the Gambia to the Corubal Rivers, that is, most of
   the upper Casamance and virtually all of eastern Guinea-
   Bissau.
       During the period of subordinance to Mali each pro-
   vincial Farim (Faren) or governor had considerable local
   authority and was accorded his own administrative council,

symbolic war drums, and personal army. On the other
hand, the rule of the Mansa was considered sacred and
even followed a matrilineal line of succession rather than
the patrilineal descent for the Farims and ordinary people.
The Mansa of Gabu was selected from the eldest of the
leaders of the royal Provinces.   Each provincial capital
town was fortified and had a regular guard.   Some of
these armed forces would be supplied to the Mansa during time of war.   The degree of centralized control of
the Empire of Mali slipped away into the 16th century as
it increasingly fell to the attacks from Songhai after 1546.
At this time Gabu gained full autonomy and was able to
expand and maintain its own kingdom until 1867.   Between
the mid 16th century until the 18th century, Gabu was
still ruled from Kansala but it also included some 20-30
royal trading towns and several additional royal Provinces,
e. g. , Manna, Payinko, Paquessi, Kusara, Badora, Tumanna, and Koliba.   Gabu became the most important and
strongest and under its direct stimulation it launched the
growth of the small, but strong Serer states of Sine and
Salum when they came under the authority of Gabu's Guelowar (Gelwar) dynasty.   Salum was just north of the
River Gambia and Sine was to the northwest of Salum in
Senegal.   However Mandingo rule from Gabu did not last
out the 16th century and the Guelowar dynasty was assimilated by the Serer who restored independence to Sine and
Salum as small, centralized, Senegalese states.

     Also coming under the control of Gabu were the two
Provinces of Oio and Braço, but these two maintained a
greater degree of local autonomy rather than the other
Provinces.   Oio was south of the headwaters of the Cacheu River and Braço to the north of the headwaters.
Just beyond Braço's control further north lived the Cassangas with their capital at Birkama.   The Cassangas
are related to the Banhun of Guinea-Bissau, and formed
their own secondary Mandingo kingdom on the south bank
of the Casamance River.   The Cassanga king was called
Cassa Mansa from which Casamance is derived.   These
various Mandingo kingdoms had all been under Malian authority at Niani until 1546.

     In the 17th and 18th centuries various military opera-
tions gave Gabu great strength and produced many slave
captives.   Perhaps as many as half of all African slaves
in the late 16th and early 17th centuries were generated
from Gabu's wars, although the state of Gabu later became quite stable.   As Gabu gained in power the Fula
pastoralists and farmers, with whom the Mandingo lived,

became a subordinate population. At times there was
comparative harmony between the ruling Mandingos and
the Fulas, however other periods were marked by struggle, conflict, insult, and oppression by the ruling class
of Gabu. These precarious social relations led to a long
pattern of Fula revolts. At the end of the 18th century
Gabu was increasingly the victim of Fula attacks from
Futa Jallon sometimes in local alliances with the Fula of
Guinea-Bissau. Into the 19th century the Fula pressed
their attacks and at least one Farim of the royal Province of Paquessi was converted to Islam, while the Fula
jihad leader, Al-Haj Umaru killed Farim Yangi Sayon in
1849. The following year local Fulas in Guinea-Bissau
broke away to form their own small states. In the mid
19th century King Siibo ruled Gabu but he died with no
clear successor. The throne was contested by Saama,
Tumanna, and Waali groups, but with Mansa Janke (Djanke)
Waali finally prevailing. In 1867 Mansa Waali of Kansala
capitulated to the Fulas under a purported force of 12,000
soldiers under Alfa Molo and led by the Fula marabout of
Timbo, Abdul Khudus. After three days of siege Janke
Waali saw the end and blew up his powder magazine with
many family members inside.

The centuries of Gabu were at an end, although some
small Mandingo states lingered on in the 19th century.
Taking advantage of this state of internal disorganization
the Portuguese initiated a series of protracted military
campaigns between 1891 and 1910 and concentrated attacks
on the Oincas (Oio Mandingos) in 1897, 1902, and in 1912-
15. With attacks, first from the Fula, and second by the
Portuguese, the Mandingos were stripped of their former
glory and power. The eastern city of Guinea-Bissau once
known as Gabu, was renamed Nova Lamego to commem-
orate the Portuguese military conquest. See MANDINGO;
MALI; FUTA JALLON; SERER; PINTO; COLI TENGUELLA;
ALFA MOLO; TIRAMAKHAN; SAMA COLI.

GEBA, RIO DE [Geba River]. The Geba River has its headwaters in northernmost Guinea-Conakry but then curves
through regions of the upper Casamance area of Senegal
before turning back toward the southwest and into Guinea-
Bissau through the northeast. At the town of Bafata the
Geba is joined by the Colufe River flowing from Gabu
town. The river remains relatively narrow flowing by
Geba town and Bambadinca but at Xime it broadens very
widely, joined by the Corubal to become, ultimately, an
estuary with a mouth of about 10 miles near Bissau. The

Geba was an important route for commerce and slavery
in the interior and gave an axis around which the Gabu
states formed. The Geba is about 340 miles in total
length, but only navigable for ships up to 2,000 tons for
93 miles. See CORUBAL, RIO.

GOMES, DIOGO. Portuguese navigator and pilot. In 1455,
   along with the Venetian Cadamosta, Gomes established
   commercial relations with the Wolof people at the mouth
   of the Senegal River and with the Malinke states on the
   Gambia thereby strengthening these early Portuguese relations with Mali itself. In 1457 Gomes reportedly arrived at Arguin with four horses, where one horse usually brought 10-15 slaves. Gomes found Gonçalo Ferreira and the Genoese Antonio da Noli already trading at
   Arguin at that time. By exercising the royal Portuguese
   trade monopoly Gomes gave da Noli and Ferreira seven
   slaves per horse, but received 14-15 slaves per horse
   from the African traders. Gomes is credited with being
   one of the discoverers of the Cape Verde Islands. This
   occurred when he was blown off course returning from
   coastal exploration in 1460. He landed at what is now
   São Tiago and also visited Fogo. Later he reported on
   Boa Vista, Maio and Sal Islands as he sailed northward.
   In 1461 Gomes sailed to coastal Liberia and Sierra Leone.
   See NOLI.

GOMES, FERNAO. Gomes was a Lisbon merchant. In 1468
   Gomes received a lease for Guinea trade for five years
   from King Afonso V (1438-1481) for the price of 200 mil-
   reis a year on the condition that he explore 100 leagues
   of West African coastline to the east of Sierra Leone.
   This lease excluded land opposite the Cape Verde Islands.
   Gomes was also required to sell ivory to King Afonso V
   at a fixed price. Between 1469 and 1475 Gomes carried
   out his explorations and he is credited with the discovery
   of the Gold Coast during this period. In 1477 Gomes
   reached the Bight of Biafra. In 1482 a Portuguese fort
   was constructed at El Mina as a result of Gomes' travels
   and reports. The Crown granted Gomes a trading monopoly along the Guinea Coast, but the operation was based
   in the Cape Verde Islands, which had been settled only a
   few years earlier.

GONÇALVES, ANTAO. With Nuño Tristão, Gonçalves was
   the first to capture Moorish slaves at Cape Blanc and
   thus begin the age of slavery in 1441. The Africans were

seized for information and ransom. With this cargo of slaves and gold dust Gonçalves returned to Portugal to stimulate further exploration. Gonçalves made at least five voyages in 1441, 1443, 1444, 1445 and in 1447 to the upper West coast of Africa. See HENRY.

GRIOT. Greatly respected poet, oral historian, itinerant musician, arbitrator and keeper of lineages, especially in Senegambia.

GROUNDNUTS see AGRICULTURE; PEANUTS

GRUMETTAS. African ship crews, occupying the lowest rank in the navy, considered to be para-military; or christian- ized slaves, especially as private slave armies of the lançados; African auxiliaries, associates of the lançados.

-H-

HAWKINS, SIR JOHN (1532-1595). Like his father, William Hawkins, John was a merchant adventurer from England, but the main items of commerce for John Hawkins were African slave captives. In 1559 John moved from London to the port town of Plymouth where he married the daugh- ter of Benjamin Gonson, Treasurer of the Navy, an office that John Hawkins was later to hold. Backed by English merchants Hawkins left for Africa in 1562 in three small ships named Salomon, Swallow and Jonas. This first ad- venture in English slaving was sufficiently profitable that it attracted the secret financial backing by Queen Eliza- beth and several of her Privy Councillors as secret stock holders. The second voyage took place in 1564 and met armed resistance by the Portuguese which was forcefully broken by Hawkins, who seized several Portuguese ships. For these successes Hawkins was knighted by the Queen and given a Royal emblem showing an African slave in chains. The rapid gain in popularity of sugar as a sweet- ener encouraged a third voyage in 1566 under a different captain and in 1567 with Hawkins in charge again. On his last trip Hawkins was attacked and beaten by Spanish ships, thus ending this first period of English slaving.

HEALTH.
    Guinea Bissau. In 1972 the Portuguese health budget for Guinea-Bissau was 10 million escudos (2.7 percent of the total budget). The processing industries took 56 per-

cent of the budget while transport used 26 percent of these
revenues.   These percentages indicate the limited concern
for African health by the colonial government and they
demonstrate the financial base for the extremely low level
of health delivery systems.   In all the Portuguese spent
about $350,000 (U.S.) or $.66 per person for health in
one of their last years as the colonial power.   In Guinea-
Bissau there are numerous debilitating tropical diseases
such as malaria, bilharzia, filariasis and various intes-
tinal disorders.   Tuberculosis and nutritional deficiencies
are also common problems.   To meet these needs in 1959
the Portuguese budgeted 16.6 million escudos or about
$1.10 (U.S.) per person.   There was one doctor for
every 20,000 inhabitants which was, at that time, worse
than Cape Verde which averaged one doctor for 14,000
people.   This ratio was about the same for the former
French colony of Senegal but far better than that of Mali
having only one doctor for 39,000 people in 1962.   Although thousands of people never saw a doctor there were
gains in the health services in the 1960's as the following
data indicate:

	1960	1961	1963	1966	1971
doctors	25	26	34	48	46
nurses	100	150	202		285
hospitals	10		31	34	
beds	300		839	850	1,027

By 1964 the doctor-to-inhabitant ratio had improved to
one for every 15,400 people and the per capita expendi-
ture had risen to $1.45 (U.S.) per person annually.   Ob-
viously the improvements were still hopelessly inadequate
and many of the increased services were simply involved
with the treatment of war-related injuries as the war intensified.
     During the course of the nationalist struggle the PAIGC
began to develop its own health and military facilities to
treat war casualties and to serve the increasing numbers
of people in the liberated zones.   In the midst of guerrilla
warfare the services were crude and decentralized but
rather effective.   Each village committee had specific
health assignments and the close personal contacts resulted in the fact that the number of sanitary posts (dress-
ing stations) of the PAIGC exceeded those of the Portuguese by 1970.   Throughout the war the PAIGC sent people
overseas for nursing and medical training while some
numbers of foreign doctors, especially from eastern Eur-

opean nations and Cuba, came to serve as doctors in the
liberated regions.   In addition to the village health com-
mittees the PAIGC organized traveling health brigades.
By 1972 there were five PAIGC hospitals in the south,
two in the north, and two in the east.   These primitive
facilities were concealed under the trees and were sometimes moved several times a year for security reasons.
Operations such as Caesarean sections, amputations, and
appendectomies were performed using blood plasma, local
anesthetics, and antibiotics to which there was an unus-
ually good response.   The main goal in these field hospitals was to get patients ambulatory to go to the 123-
bed PAIGC hospital at Boke, Guinea-Conakry or to the
50-bed facilities at Koundara or Ziguinchor, Senegal.   In
1972 Boke processed 5,000 outpatients.   By the same
year the total number of doctors working with the PAIGC
was 41, thereby approximating the number used by the
Portuguese at that time.

Since coming to state power the PAIGC has inherited
the colonial facilities and thus has shown even further
expansion in the health services.   In absolute terms these
services are still very underdeveloped and much further
growth is still required.

Cape Verde: Unlike Guinea-Bissau the PAIGC did not
organize any health service infrastructure in the islands
as there were no liberated zones in the sense that there
had been on the mainland.   At the time of independence
Cape Verde had only 12 doctors, or one per 25,000 inhabitants.   Several islands had no doctors and Santo Antão, the second largest, had only one.   The archipelago
had only two hospitals: one 200-bed facility in Praia and
a 120-bed hospital in Mindelo or 2.2 beds/1,000 inhabitants.   Not only are the facilities very inadequate, the
basic diet does not even yield the minimum daily caloric
intake thus making disease and a short life expectancy endemic.   Aside from the two main hospitals there
were 21 health posts and 54 nurses in the islands at independence in 1975.   Even with various additional technical and medical assistants the health delivery system
was notably deficient.   In the mid 1960's there were at
least double the number of doctors, but many left just
before independence.   Since 1975 a dozen or more Cuban
doctors have arrived to make up for this void.

HENRY, PRINCE ["The Navigator"] (1394-1460).   Prince
Henry was the son of João I (1358-1433) and Philippa,
daughter of the Englishman, John the Gaunt.   Henry was

responsible for organizing about one third of the early
Portuguese exploration of the West African coast during
the great age of Portuguese maritime innovation during
the first half of the 15th century. Henry led the military
expedition against Ceuta, Morocco in 1415 for the Royal
Portuguese House of Avis. Stimulated by reports of the
mysterious Christian, Prester John, and lured by the
knowledge of gold mines feeding trans-Saharan trade Henry
sent ships along the coast of Morocco looking for an eas-
ier sea route to the interior of Africa. When the Moors
left the Iberian peninsula they had blocked Christian entry
into Africa's trade and territory. In 1434 ships of Prince
Henry reached Cape Bojador (S. A. D. R.), the furthest
point reached by Portugal until that time, due to the limitation of prevailing winds and navigational skills. In
1436 Prince Henry led an unsuccessful military effort
against Tangiers. In 1441 a ship captained by Antão
Gonçalves, sailing for Prince Henry, returned to Portugal with the first documented African slaves (Moors from
an area probably along southern coastal Morocco). Prince
Henry received 20 percent of slave cargos.
    In 1453, Gomes Eanes de Azurara, a well-known chron-
icler for Prince Henry, wrote "Cronica de Guine" which
described some of the aspects of this early exploration
and slave trading. In 1456 the Genoan captain Usodimore
and the Venetian captain Cadamosta both sailed under
Prince Henry's flag when they reached the Geba River
in today's Guinea-Bissau. During the period 1419-1460
there were at least 35 voyages under the Portuguese flag.
Of these, eight were initiated directly by Prince Henry
and two were co-sponsored by him, although at his death
he had never actually participated on an exploration mission as it was not considered appropriate for a man of
his status. See A. GONÇALVES; CADAMOSTA; AZURARA.

HODGES, SAMUEL (January 27, 1792-October 26, 1827).
    Born in Taunton, Massachusetts (U. S. A.), he was ap-
    pointed as the first U. S. Consul to Cape Verde in 1812
    to regulate commerce and shipping of American ships in
    the islands. Hodges was not officially recognized by the
    Portuguese until 1823. Tension was high because Amer-
    ican privateers raided the islands for salt, booty and
    slaves. Hodges formed an alliance with a wealthy Cape
    Verdean merchant and was deeply involved in a wide va-
    riety of commercial ventures including smuggling. He
    died in Praia of malaria and was succeeded by William
    G. Merrill on December 19, 1828. Hodges wrote an
    early Crioulo-English dictionary.

-I-

ILHAS DE BARLAVENTO. Northern, windward islands of
Cape Verde including Santo Antão, São Vicente, (includ-
ing Santa Luzia), Santa Luzia, São Nicolau. (Easterly--
Sal, Boa Vista.)

ILHAS DE SOTAVENTO. Southern, leeward islands of Cape
Verde including Maio, São Tiago, Fogo, Brava.

-J-K-

JACANCAS. A very small ethnic stock related to the Manding and located to the northeast of Bafata.

JOAO II (ruled 1477, 1481-1495). The son of King Afonso V.
During his reign, settlers began arriving in the Cape
Verde Islands. Under João II, chartmaking began in
Lisbon, including the work of Bartholomew Columbus,
brother of Christopher. In 1484 João II turned down a
request by Christopher Columbus to finance further voyages after he had visited the Guinea Coast between 1482-
1484. Columbus visited João II again in 1493 after his
historic voyage.

JUVENTUDE AFRICANA AMILCAR CABRAL (JAAC) see
PIONEERS OF THE PARTY

KANSALA (CANSALA) see GABU; FULA

-L-

LABERY, HENRI. Founder of the UPG in 1957 which led to
his direct involvement of the founding of the FLGC in
1960. Some elements of the FLGC appeared in 1961 as
FUL. In 1962 Labéry emerged as the head of FLING.
Labéry is of Cape Verdean extraction and was an early
associate of Amílcar Cabral. He went to schools in
Lisbon, but lived mainly in Guinea-Bissau. Labéry's
program was less clear on ideological matters, and was
essentially concerned with the independence of Guinea.
See FLING.

LADINOS. Baptized African slaves who were fluent in Crioulo and Portuguese and who were sometimes interpreters

and middlemen; from Portuguese meaning "crafty" or
"adroit" or because they were "Latinized."

LANÇADOS. Portuguese settlers; including fugitives, known
for having courage and initiative, also, half-caste traders
living in or near African coastal communities, who maintained semi-autonomous control of local coastal communities. They often had African wives of the local group;
they were intermediaries or middlemen for the Portuguese or Cape Verdeans; literally, out-caste.

LANDUMAS. This is a very small Senegambian grouplet in-
habiting the area immediately around the southern town
of Catio.

LEGISLATIVE ASSEMBLIES (PORTUGUESE). The 130-mem-
ber Legislative Assembly of Portugal provided for two
representatives from Cape Verde and one from Guinea-
Bissau. In the two colonies there were separate Legislative Assemblies replacing the former Legislative Coun-
cils. In Guinea-Bissau the Assembly consisted of 17
members: 5 elected, 3 traditional chiefs, 3 administrative representatives, 2 commercial representatives, 2
from workers organizations, and 2 representing "cultural
and moral" concerns. In Cape Verde there were 21
members of the Assembly expanded from the 18-member
Council. The composition included: 11 elected by vote,
4 administrative appointments, 2 commercial representatives, 2 workers representatives, and 2 representing
"moral and cultural" concerns. Both Guinea and Cape
Verde were "Overseas Provinces" of Portugal after 1971
with subdivisions of concelhos (municipalities) and civil
parishes (administrative posts). In Guinea-Bissau a pro-
vision was made to have traditional ethnic group leaders
meet in an annual Peoples' Congress, which had no real
power.

LIGA DA GUINE. This was the first modern African volun-
tary association in Guinea-Bissau. This proto-nationalist
formation emerged in 1911 under the leadership of Oliveira
Dugu. The Portuguese government forced it to disband in
1915.

LIVESTOCK. In both Guinea-Bissau and Cape Verde the Portuguese paid only marginal attention to systematic livestock
raising. Although both nations are overwhelmingly agricultural, the Third Development Plan of the Portuguese

for 1968-1973 for Guinea-Bissau only budgeted between
3 and 4 percent for agriculture and livestock production
and development.   Virtually all meat and milk produced
was for local consumption although in 1969, for example,
there was an export of 1,059 tons of animal hides from
Guinea-Bissau; 100 percent of this export went to Portugal.   The areas in the north and east are the chief regions for cattle raising by the Fula peoples although cattle
are found elsewhere.   Between 1967 and 1974 the cattle
population has shown variation between 245,000 to 253,000
head reflecting the marginal role for a market economy.
Pigs are raised by the non-Islamic populations and apparently the number of pigs has increased from 107,000 in
1967 to 165,000 in 1974.   In the same year there were
178,000 goats and 68,000 sheep reported in Guinea-Bissau.

   Livestock statistics in Cape Verde show radical fluctuations depending upon the presence or absence of drought
conditions.   At times in the 16th century Cape Verdean
horses were much prized for use in the slave trade; at
other times the livestock population on some islands is
virtually brought to zero.   The following statistics describe the current period of precipitous decline in livestock population:

	1968	1973	1974
horses	21,292	------	9,085
cattle	27,689	18,000	7,933
goats	79,352	------	41,603
sheep	3,394	3,000	803
pigs	------	17,000	------

Not only do these data point to the drastic nature of the
effects of the drought, but the two most numerous animals
today are pigs and goats which often survive by foraging
and are, consequently, not particularly healthy.   In 1971,
728 tons of meat were slaughtered.   This minuscule
quantity represents 2 kg. of meat per person annually
and shows the basis of the gross protein deficiencies
endemic to the islands.   The small number of animals
butchered makes a very little contribution to the export
economy of hides.   See AGRICULTURE; ECONOMICS
(TRADE).

                              -M-

MAC   see   MOVIMENTO ANTI-COLONIALISTA

MAIO (15° 10'N, 23° 10'W). Sixth largest island (103. 8 sq.
mi.) in the Sotavento (leeward, southern) group of the
Cape Verde archipelago. This low (maximum altitude,
1,430 feet), sandy island lies just to the east of São
Tiago. Maio has the two main towns of Vila do Maio
and Santo Antonio, but the population is small. The island was not effectively settled until the early 16th century and its economy was based on livestock and slave
trading. The periodic droughts in Cape Verdean history
have always had the most disastrous effects on Maio and
frequently the lack of water and grazing land has decimated the livestock. As early as 1643, slave ships from
New England (U. S. A.) traded at Maio. American ships
did not always come in peace and coupled with weak Portuguese control a pirate ship from Baltimore sacked the
port of Maio in December 1818. Trade in salt was also
an important feature of the Maio economy until about 1850.
Salt was traded on the coast for slaves and to passing
ships for manufactured goods. Since the working population was small, and Portuguese administration slight,
some ships stopped at Maio and gathered their own salt
supplies. With a 1,400 meter airport there was a colonial plan under consideration to develop tourism through
the TURMAIO agency, but little progress had been made
at the time of independence in 1975.

MALFANTE, ANTONIO. Genoese merchant who visited Timbuktu in 1447. See CADAMOSTA; MALI.

MALI. Following the collapse of the Empire of Ghana, the
Empire of Mali entered its formative phase in the late
11th century. Mali's early capital was at Kangaba on
the Upper Niger River. Mali's economy was based on
trade, especially of slave, and subsistence agriculture
of the Sudanic crops. The gold traded in Mali was mainly
from the Bambuk goldfields south of Niani and out of
Mali's military control and Islamic influence. Likewise
the source of ivory was mainly south of the Sahel, but
trade in ivory, gold, and slaves was what built the Sudanic states. The most important group of Mande traders upon whom Mali was built were the Soninke-derived
Dyulas (sometimes known as Wangarawa) who were instrumental in the Islamization of Mali. Islamic conversion
of the Malian ruling class and large numbers of the farming people took place between the 11th and 13th centuries.
Perhaps the first member of the Malian ruling class to
be converted was Barmandana Keita in 1050. Mali was

very hierarchical in socio-political structure including nobility, soldiers, traders, artisan castes, and slaves.

Mali's formal beginning occurred in 1230 when Sundiata (Sundjata) and his general Maridiata defeated the Susu leader Sumaguru at the battle of Kirina, thus ending the Susu resurgence. Sundiata was the son of Nare Famaghan, of the Keita dynasty of Mali (at Kangaba). Earlier Famaghan had been defeated by Sumagura in the effort to reestablish the Empire of Ghana. Sundiata ruled Mali from 1230 to 1255 and made Islam the state religion. Sundiata's son, Mansa Uli (1255-1270) extended the rule of Mali to the trade center at Gao. Under Mansa Sakura (d. 1300) Tekrur was conquered in 1285. According to the Arab historian Umari, Mansa Musa related to the Governor of Cairo that sea-faring Malians had actually ventured to the New World before 1312. Under the rule of Mansa Muhammad (son of Qu) 200 ships of men and 200 of gold, water and supplies were sent. One of the ships returned to be followed by another 1,000 of men and 1,000 of supplies. These interesting reports have not been fully substantiated.

It was during the reign of Mansa Kankan Musa (1312-1337) that Mali reached its greatest influence. In 1324-5 for example, Mansa Musa is reported to have made a flamboyant pilgrimage to Mecca with an entourage of thousands of followers carrying gold gifts of astonishing abundance. In the year of his return his soldiers occupied Dar Tichitt, Walata, and other key trading centers. The following year Gao (of Songhai) and Timbuktu also came under the armies of Mansa Musa. By 1375 Mali was noted on European maps even though Europeans had still not traveled along the West African coast. At its peak Mali included the Mandingo kingdom of Gabu in an area between the upper Corubal, upper Cacheu, to the Gambia River, then all the way to the Atlantic coast through Wolof, Serer and Tukulor areas northward up the coast until just north of the mouth of the Senegal River. At this time Mali also controlled Futa Jallon through the Dialonke tributary chiefs and a lesser degree of control existed in subduing rebellions in Tekrur. Through the late 14th and early 15th centuries Mali thrived as Mali supplied as much as 1/16 of the entire world supply of gold. The Arab traveler and historian Ibn Batuta visited Mali in 1352-3 and brought reports of its glories to northern Africa and southern Europe. In the 15th century Mali's fortunes began a long decline. Tekrur and the Wolof provinces rebelled and regained their independence

in the early 15th century and by 1433 Timbuktu was
lost.

The Portuguese were on the scene in the late 15th
century and noted the state of hostility between Mali and
its neighbors, but the Portuguese, who only wanted African products and slaves could not be concerned with the
outcome and gave no aid to Mali.   In 1473 Jenne was also
lost.   Mansa Mahmoud I of Mali sent a message to King
João II of Portugal requesting military aid against his
Fula and Songhai enemies, however the Portuguese still
did nothing and in the 16th century Mali's power eroded
even further, although it was still producing more gold
than the New World gold mines of the time.   In 1534
another request for aid was directed to Portugal's King
João III and ambassadors from Mali actually traveled to
Portugal.   Needing slaves and war captives and not want-
ing to back a loser Portugal again declined aid.   This
trend was climaxed in 1546 when Songhai invaders sacked
Niani, the Malian capital, bringing an end to a major
West African epoch.   See BAMBARA; GABU; FUTA JAL-
LON; FUTA TORO; SONGHAI; SUSUS; TEKRUR.

MANCARRA see PEANUTS

MANDING (Mandingo, Mandinga, Malinke, Mali).   The Man-
    dingo and related peoples of Guinea-Bissau are repre-
    sentatives of the Nuclear Mande or Manding language fam-
    ily of the Niger-Congo linguistic stock.   Manding is a
    principal language of Africa and is spoken in one form
    or another in 9 West African countries with as many as
    10 million speakers.   As with many West African lan-
    guages it is tonal with no uniformly accepted written form.
    The Mandingo began to arrive in the mid 13th century
    with the expansion of the Empire of Mali to which they
    are related.   After the fall of Mali in 1546 the local Man-
    dingo state of Gabu continued until 1867.   Before the con-
    solidation and expansion of Gabu, many Senegambians such
    as the Papeis, Manjacos and Brames were found in east-
    ern Guinea-Bissau.   These three groups assimilated a
    moderately hierarchical system of political administration
    from the intrusive Malians.   Other Senegambians such as
    the Balantes, Banhuns and Beafadas were either driven
    far closer to the coast or were simply stranded as pock-
    ets within expanding Gabu.   Various Fula peoples became
    interspersed in Gabu as cattle herders until, of course,
    when they took over completely after 1867.

    When the Portuguese arrived they called the language

of the Mande peoples, Mandunca, from which the term
Mandingo is derived.   Throughout the centuries of slaving
the Mandingos of Gabu had important trade centers at
Farim on the Cacheu River headwaters, at Cacheu at the
River's mouth, at Ziquinchor on the Casamance, and at
Geba on the Geba River.   These posts permitted contact
with Europeans (e.g. Portuguese, French, and English)
and access to firearms in exchange for war captive-slaves.
The local Fula herdsmen provided livestock while the
Mandingo farmers grew the basic staples of the Sudanic
food complex.   In the mid 19th century the Fula of Futa
Jallon expanded and brought an end to Mandingo dominance.
By the end of the century, after the Berlin Congress,
Portuguese incursions to the interior were laying the
ground work for the colonial wars against the Mandingo
of the early 20th century.   In 1900 the Mandingo formally
submitted to Portuguese rule but the Oio branch showed
continued resistance to Portuguese "pacification" in the
campaigns of 1897, 1902, and 1913.   From 1913-15 Portuguese Captain Teixeira Pinto, known for his brutality and
destruction, was able to use Mandingo auxiliaries equipped
with modern arms in "pacification" campaigns elsewhere
in Guinea-Bissau.
   Today the Mandingo people are still concentrated around
Gabu in the north central area, but there are various
clusters throughout the eastern interior region.   The
1950 population indicated that the Mandingos numbered
63,800 or 14 percent of the population. See GABU; MALI;
PINTO.

MANJACO (Mandyako).   Ethnic group of the Senegambian cultural stock, Atlantic subfamily of the Niger-Congo or Nigritic Language group.   The Manjacos show some very
   slight Islamization and some hierarchical organization
   which they may have acquired through contact with the
   Mandingos.   The Manjacos are related to the Brame,
   Mancanha and Papel peoples.   Their economy is based
   on shifting agriculture and rice cultivation and they are
   concentrated mainly in the area south of the Cacheu River
   and north of the Mansoa River.   The Manjacos provided
   stiff and early resistance to Portuguese settlement between
   1878-90 when they were among the first to try to halt the
   Portuguese penetration of the interior.   They also fought
   between 1913-1915 during the campaigns of Teixeira Pinto.
   The 1950 population identified 71,700 Manjacos (14.2 percent of the population); in 1960 their population was put at
   an estimated 80,000.

MANSOA, RIO [Mansoa River]. The fourth longest river of Guinea-Bissau, the Mansoa travels about 120 miles from the coast as is navigable for at least two-thirds of the way. Its course is roughly parallel to that of the Farim-Cacheu which flows to the north. The headwaters of the Mansoa are found to the east of Mansaba in the Farim concelho. The Mansoa was used as a corridor through the coastal swamps for trade in the interior.

MENDES, FRANCISCO (Chico Te) (1939-1978). Prime Minister of the Republic of Guinea-Bissau, Mendes did not complete his formal education because he joined the PAIGC in 1960 at age 21. He was born in southern Guinea-Bissau in the village of Enxude. From 1960-62 Mendes was the political commissioner at the PAIGC training program in Conakry. From 1962-3 he was assigned to underground organizational work in the eastern town of Bafata and from 1963 to 1964 he served as the political commissioner in the North Front. At the time of the First PAIGC Congress in 1964 Mendes became a member of the Political Bureau and in 1965 he was made a member of the War Council in the capacity of political commissioner. From 1970-71 his War Council responsibility was military logistics. In 1972 Mendes was appointed to the CEL and following the independence of Guinea-Bissau he became the Principle Commissioner (Prime Minister) of the Permanent Secretariat of the nation. Mendes was killed in an automobile accident in Bafata in July 1978. See CEL; PAIGC.

MESTIÇOS. Those people of a "mixed" racial heritage and often incorporated into middle administrative and economic strata in Portuguese colonialism.

MILLET. This is one of the more important grains in the Sudanic food complex. There are various common names and a confusing taxonomy but one may distinguish bulrush millet (Pennisetum typhoideum), which is also known as pearl millet, from sorghum (Sorghum vulgare), also known as durra. These are all known as milho in Portuguese with local distinctions in terminology by varying color of the grains. These tall grasses resemble American corn (Zea mays) at a distance but bulrush millet grains grow in densely packed clusters resembling cat-tails. Sorghum grains grow in a tuft formation by contrast. Bulrush millet is very hardy and requires little rainfall while sorghum is more often irrigated but may be grown as a dry-land crop.

MINDELO   see   SAO VINCENTE

MINERALS.   For Guinea-Bissau see COMPANHIA LUSITANA
DE ALUMINIO; ESSO EXPLORATION.
  Cape Verde: Cape Verdean salt has been mined for
centuries as an important element in the slave trade and
other commerce as well as for use in salted meats.
Most salt production has been located on Sal and Maio
Islands. This export item had been irregularly developed
by a Franco-Portuguese firm. The other mineral expo;t
of any consequence for Cape Verde has been pozzolana,
variety of porous volcanic ash used in making cement.
The Champalimaud monopoly owned the Companhia de
Cimento Pozzolana de Cabo Verde which had its chief
operations on Santo Antão. Production has steadily declined and an original staff of 300 was put at less than
70 in the last report.

MORANCA. Extended family grouping within villages in
Guinea-Bissau, especially among the Balantas.

MOUVEMENT DE LIBERATION DE ILES DU CAP VERT
(MLICV). The MLICV formed in 1960 and immediately
joined the FLGC in the same year. Its role was
very minor and represented little more than a paper
organization. The MLICV was based in Dakar and was
led by Mello e Castro. At times the MLICV called for
the liberation of the Cape Verde Islands by armed struggle, but this tactic and goal was only enunciated, not
practiced, in the Islands.

MOUVEMENT DE LIBERATION DE LA GUINEE "PORTUGAISE"
ET DES ILES DU CAP VERT (MLGCV). This Dakar-
based organization was never of much substance except
for the membership of the UPG of Labéry. The UDG
and the UDCV which were the other two members of the
MLGCV were of no significant importance. The MLGCV
joined with the UPA (União das Populaçoẽs de Angola) to
form a paper front in 1962 called the FACCP (Frente Africana Contra O Colonialismo Portugues). While little
is known of the MLGCV it is known that the UPA was
receiving funds from the American CIA at the time and
that the FACCP was set up to rival the more militant
FRAIN founded two years earlier. The MLGCV was a
temporary affiliate of the PAIGC in 1960 and some reports suggest that Amílcar Cabral sought to establish
unity with the MLGCV in 1958 but soon realized it was
impossible.

MOVIMENTO ANTI-COLONIALISTA (MAC).   The MAC was
    formed in Lisbon in 1957 by revolutionary intellectuals
    from the Portuguese African colonies.   MAC was the
    precursor of FRAIN which started in 1960 and the CONCP
    which began in 1961.   The unity spawned in the MAC has
    effectively persisted until today with the common pro-
    grams of the PAIGC, FRELIMO, and the MPLA.

MOVIMENTO DE LIBERTAÇAO DA GUINE (MLG).   The MLG
    was headed by François Mendy Kankoila who based much
    of the organization on the Manjaco ethnic group partly re-
    siding in Senegal.   In July 1961 while Amílcar Cabral
    was trying to develop the FUL, Mendy launched attacks
    at Suzanna and a Varela hotel.   With these isolated acts
    included, the MLG was the most militant member group
    of FLING.   Mendy was anxious about any loss of auton-
    omy within FLING to which he gave hesitating support as
    he had to the FLGC which preceded FLING.   Neither the
    MLG nor FLING had programs relating to the Cape Verde
    Islands.   The MLG joined the RDAG in 1961 forming the
    FLG, which joined FLING in 1962.   As a result of the
    MLG's military efforts in 1961 the Portuguese staged a
    swift counterattack finally concluding with the breaking of
    relations between Senegal and Portugal.   Despite this re-
    sult the government of Senegal was lukewarm to the PAIGC
    at that time and preferred to support the MLG and, more
    broadly, the FLING which had some base with Senegalese
    Manjacos and was anti-PAIGC.   The MLG also sought to
    divide Cape Verdean supporters from the PAIGC and it is
    alleged that it bribed PAIGC members to stimulate deser-
    tion.   The MLG was dissolved in 1964.

MOVIMENTO DE LIBERTAÇAO DA GUINE PORTUGUESE
    (MLGP).   The MLGP was one of the three component
    groups which merged in 1960 to form the FLG later lead-
    ing to FLING.   See FLING.

MOVIMENTO PARA INDEPENDENCIA NACIONAL DA GUINE
    PORTUGUESA (MING).   MING was founded in 1954 but
    soon proved to be ineffective, however MING was the di-
    rect forerunner of the PAIGC which formed in 1956.
    MING was organized by Amílcar Cabral (later founder of
    the PAIGC) and Henri Labéry (later founder of the UPG).
    MING was formed clandestinely in Bissau by commercial
    workers and civil servants.   There was no reference to
    the Cape Verde Islands in name or program.

MUSA MOLO (?-1931).   The son of Alfa Molo, and the last

effective King of the Fula state in Guinea-Bissau. The son of Musa Molo, Cherno Bande (d. 1950's) acted as a Fula King but with no real power. When Alfa Molo died in 1881 he was succeeded by his brother Bakari Demba, but through continuous intrigues and conspiracies Musa Molo became the Fula King in 1893. During his reign Musa Molo sought to consolidate and expand his rule to the northwest into the territory of the south bank of the Gambia then controlled by Fode Kaba, a Muslim warrior cleric. Alfa Molo had killed the father of Fode Kaba so the conflict was inherited to both sons. Fode Kaba proved very intractable to French and British attempts to curb the slave trade and in 1901, through a joint understanding and effort between Musa Molo and the two European powers, Fode Kaba was killed. In attempting to unify and expand the Fula control, Musa Molo suppressed a revolt by his brother Dikori and he frequently eliminated other contenders by assassination. In general his rule was considered ruthless and cruel. In the early 1900's he settled in Gambia where he was awarded a £500 stipend annually by the British. In 1919 he was exiled to Sierra Leone, but returned to Gambia in 1923 where he died in 1931. After the death of Musa Molo the British appointed Cherno Bande (the son of Musa Molo) as the head of the Fula. Bande's real function was to encourage local peanut production as an agent for the British United Africa Company. See GABU; ALFA MOLO; FUTA JALLON.

-N-

NALUS (Bagas). The Nalus are a Senegambian people having petty chiefdoms as a result of notable Mandingo contact. They appeared on the coast in the 15th century and are mainly concentrated in the Susu area near the town of Catio. These rice cultivators are most closely related to the Bissago people. See SUSU; BISSAGOS.

NATO see NORTH ATLANTIC TREATY ORGANIZATION

NIGER-CONGO LANGUAGES. African linguistic terminology is complex and undergoing constant re-evaluation. Earlier the Niger-Congo languages were known as Nigritic languages. More recently the term Congo-Kordofanian languages has gained increased usage which incorporates the large Bantu stock along with the major coastal West African tongues. See SENEGAMBIANS; FULA; MANDING.

NOLI, ANTONIO DE. De Noli was a Genoese navigator in
    Portuguese service. In 1457, at Arquim, de Noli and
    Gonçalo Ferreira traded slaves for horses from Diogo
    Gomes. De Noli and Gomes are considered to have been
    the first Portuguese navigators to have set foot in the
    Cape Verde Islands. In the early 1460's de Noli was in
    charge of one of the captaincies on São Tiago Island.

NORTH ATLANTIC TREATY ORGANIZATION (NATO). At
    the conclusion of World War II the United States proposed
    the creation of a military alliance of the capitalist nations
    on the North Atlantic. The pact came into effect on
    March 18, 1949, the same year in which Portugal joined.
    While areas to the south of the equator were officially
    out of NATO's jurisdiction, Portugal's membership per-
    mitted NATO to contribute very significant military and
    economic aid to Portugal thus directly freeing the Por-
    tuguese to carry on counter insurgency wars in Africa.
        Before 1958 Portugal spent between 3-4 percent of its
    GNP on the military, similar to other western European
    nations. By 1964 Portugal's defense requirements had
    reached 8 percent of the GNP. In 1965 more than half
    of the state revenues went to the military. Portugal was
    supported mainly by West Germany and the United States
    in loans and grants and in their purchase of colonial pro-
    duction. U. S. aid to Portugal through NATO is meas-
    ured in the 100's of millions of U. S. dollars. Between
    1949 and 1968 the United States military aid to Portugal
    officially reached $349 million, but this does not include
    other bilateral agreements which eased Portugal's own
    hard-pressed economy. In 1972 alone the United States
    arranged financial assistance to Portugal of well over
    $400 million. The vast portion of Portugal's NATO com-
    mitted forces were actually in Africa and NATO equip-
    ment, especially heavy artillery, armored vehicles and
    aircraft, not to mention U. S. -trained counter-insurgency
    specialists, all figured importantly in Portugal's prose-
    cution of the African wars from 1961 to 1974.

NOVA LAMEGO. Town in eastern Guinea-Bissau formerly
    known as Gabu before the advent of colonial rule. Nova
    Lamego is located in the Gabu cicunscrição at 12° 17'N,
    14° 13'W. See GABU; MANDE.

-O-

OIL PALM. This oil-bearing palm is a major contributor to

fats in the diet, but in addition palm oil is an important export commodity with various food and commercial purposes. To a large degree the decline of the slave trade is strongly related to the "legitimate" trade of palm oil for industrial, and cosmetic uses. The oil palm (Elaeis quineensis) is native to West Africa and is found especially in the tropics. In areas of less rainfall closer to the savanna regions the oil palm is replaced by the shea-butter tree (Butyrospermum parkii) also known as karite. The oil-bearing fruits easily produce large amounts of oil for use as a foodstuff and body lotion.

ORGANIZATION OF AFRICAN UNITY (OAU). This first modern Pan-African organization was formed on May 25, 1963, by the then independent African nations. The African Liberation Committee of the OAU sought to coordinate political and military support for the liberation movements such as the PAIGC. From 1963 to 1967 the OAU sought to unite FLING with the PAIGC to build a broader and more moderate unity. After 1967 it only gave recognition to the PAIGC as the sole legitimate expression of the people of Guinea-Bissau and Cape Verde. The Republic of Guinea-Bissau became the 42nd member nation of the OAU when it joined in November 1973. The Republic of Cape Verde joined the OAU on July 18, 1975.

-P-

PAIGC see PARTIDO AFRICANO DA INDEPENDENCIA DA GUINE E CABO VERDE

PAJADINCAS (Bajatancas). This Senegambian group is found in isolated pockets in eastern Guinea-Bissau especially to the northeast of Piche and to the northwest of Buruntuma where they are interspersed with the Fula-forros. See BISSAGOS.

PANO. Distinctive shawl or sash made of 6-7" strips (always six in number), worn by Cape Verdean women. They were woven of island-grown cotton and indigo dyes, perfecting the African weaving tradition. They were formerly used as barter items for trade on the African coast. In 1721 the sale of panos was made illegal to curb Cape Verdeans from dealing in slaves.

PAPEIS (sing., PAPEL, PEPEL). This ethnic group belongs

to the Senegambian cultural stock and is relatively closely
related to the Manjaco and Banyun groups.   Their slightly
hierarchical organization is considered to be an inherit-
ance from long-standing Mandingo contact.   The Papeis
are concentrated on Bissau island and related estuaries
on the Geba but some are also found north of the River
Mansoa.   The petty chiefs have limited authority over
these non-Islamic, coastal, rice-cultivators.   Partly because of their coastal location the Papeis suffered more
direct colonial repression than almost any other group in
Guinea-Bissau, although, on the other hand some Papeis
were involved in selling slaves in Bissau.   The instances
of Papeis resistance are particularly numerous at the
time of the Berlin Congress 1884-5, 1886, 1891-1910
(especially in the Cacheu area), 1912-15 (especially in
the Bissau area, during the campaigns of Teixeira Pinto,
1917, 1924, 1925, the early 1930's, and in 1936, before
they were finally considered "pacified. "   In the 1950 census their numbers were put at 36, 000 or about 7. 2 percent of the total population.   In 1960 the Papel population
was estimated to be about 50, 000.

PARCERIA.   Colonial "partnership" sharecropping system,
especially in Cape Verde; 26, 000 parceria contracts were
abolished by the PAIGC.

PARTIDO AFRICANO DA INDEPENDENCIA DA GUINE E CABO
VERDE (PAIGC) [African Independence Party of Guinea and
Cape Verde].   The PAIGC is the victorious nationalist
organization in Guinea-Bissau and Cape Verde which was
founded clandestinely in Bissau on September 19, 1956.
The PAIGC was the organizational descendant of MING
founded in 1954 by Henri Labéry and Amílcar Cabral.
Two main differences between MING and the PAIGC were
the inclusion of the Cape Verde Islands in the PAIGC program of national liberation and more craftsmen and manual workers in the PAIGC organizations.   Labéry later
went on to form FLING, a small, but persistent rival to
the PAIGC while Amílcar Cabral and his associates were
the founders of the PAIGC.   As the PAIGC began to grow
it attracted some port and transport workers who later
helped to organize the National Union of Guinea Workers
(UNTG) in 1961.   In 1958 the PAIGC and these workers
helped to organize a wave of thinly-veiled nationalist
strikes with a PAIGC membership of only about fifty
people.
    The independence of Guinea-Conakry in 1958 aided in

stimulating an effort to hold a nationalist oriented strike
of the Pijiguiti dockworkers in Bissau on August 3, 1959.
To counter the nationalist demands and labor militance
the Portuguese soldiers and armed settlers reacted with
twenty-minutes of gunfire, killing fifty and wounding about
a hundred and subsequently resulting in the conviction of
twenty-one people for subversion. In September 1959 the
PAIGC General Secretariat was moved to Conakry and in
the following year the Portuguese began a more serious
effort at arrests and repression of the PAIGC. The
PAIGC responded in a period from December 1960 to
September 1961 with an agitational program calling for
a peaceful end to colonial rule by distributing some 14,000
tracts and writing two open letters to the Portuguese people as well as sending various documentation to the United
Nations with the same appeal. April 1961 saw the creation of the CONCP in Casablanca with the PAIGC playing
a leading role in this organization which linked the struggle in Guinea and Cape Verde to those in Angola and
Mozambique. Towards the end of 1961 the PAIGC determined that a course of direct armed action would be
the only realistic course to bring national independence.
In order to block this move the Portuguese secret police
arrested Rafael Barbosa in March 1962, the same month
when the PAIGC staged an abortive attack on Praia in the
Cape Verde Islands. In June and July the PAIGC responded again with acts of sabotage inside Guinea-Bissau.
This escalation soon put Bissau under martial law with
upwards of 2,000 suspected activists arrested and the
Portuguese military strength reaching about 10,000 soldiers.

The years from 1959 to 1963 were devoted to carefully
building a hierarchical structure of groups and sections
united into 13 zones and six regions so that all activities
could be closely coordinated. In January 1963 the movement entered a new phase of protracted armed struggle
when it launched a series of attacks in the southern regions of the country. By July 1963 the PAIGC had opened
a second front of military activity in northern Guinea-
Bissau. Towards the end of the year, in November, Portugal made a feeble effort to conceal the colonial status of
Guinea-Bissau and a special decree from Lisbon was issued saying that Guinea-Bissau had become an overseas
province, hence an integral part of metropolitan Portugal.
This was a case of too little, too late, and the PAIGC
continued to consolidate its gains to such a degree that
from February 13-17, 1964, the first Party Congress was

held in the liberated zones in the southern front at Cas-
saca. Some of the notable positions taken at this Congress were: 1) an enlargement of the Central Committee
from 30 to 65 members; 2) the establishment of the following seven departments: armed forces, foreign affairs,
cadre control, training and information, security, economy
and finance, and mass organizations; and 3) the formation
of the Peoples Revolutionary Armed Forces (FARP) as
well as Peoples' Stores, and an expansion of medical and
educational services.

In April 1964 the PAIGC engaged the Portuguese in an
intensive military confrontation on the large southern,
coastal island of Como. This 65-day offensive forced the
Portuguese to withdraw 3,000 troops after losing hundreds.
By 1965 approximately 50 percent of the countryside was
under PAIGC control even though the Portuguese soldiers
now numbered about 25,000. From 1965 to 1966 there
was something of a military standoff until, in the later
part of 1966, the PAIGC intensified its efforts to regain
the initiative particularly in the newly opened eastern
front which included parts of the former northern and
southern regions. The December 1966 reorganization
of FARP helped to restore momentum to the struggle.
The military headway accounted for political gains at the
OAU which gave its full support to the PAIGC in 1967
thus abandoning efforts to reconcile FLING with the PAIGC.
Other accomplishments of the Party in that year included the
start of the Party's Radio Libertação and the restructuring
of the original seven departments of the Central Committee by reducing them to the following five: control, security, foreign relations, national reconstruction, and
internal organization and orientation. In 1968 the main
thrust was consolidation of the political organization and
strengthening of the infrastructure in the liberated zones
although the February 19, 1968, attack on the Bissalanca
International Airport at Bissau stunned the Portuguese occupation forces. By February 1969 the Portuguese were
forced out of Medina Boe in the south, thus giving the
FARP units of the PAIGC broader points of entry. Throughout 1969 and 1970 more notable military and political re-
verses fell against the Portuguese despite their claims of
614 PAIGC dead in 1969 and 895 killed in 1970.

In Rome, Italy on July 1, 1970, Amílcar Cabral, and
leaders of FRELIMO from Mozambique and the MPLA
from Angola were given an audience with the Pope. As
a strongly Catholic nation the Portuguese ruling class was
enraged at this diplomatic victory for the liberation forces.

In a futile and frustrated gesture on November 22, 1970,
a Portuguese raiding party from Bissau invaded the neighboring capital city of Conakry with the intention of over-
throwing Sekou Toure's government and killing the leading
members of the PAIGC who then had offices based in that
city.   The abortive invasion failed after bloody fighting
but served to underscore the frantic efforts to halt the
spread of PAIGC control and influence.   The Portuguese
made another effort in the early 1970's to halt the PAIGC
with the introduction of General Spinola's "Better Guinea"
program which proclaimed certain minimal reforms.   The
PAIGC response in 1971 was even bolder attacks with
rockets and light artillery against the main towns of
Farim, Bafata, and Bissau.   The Portuguese claim for
PAIGC dead in 1971 reached 1,257, the highest such statistic for the war and served to indicate the heightened
intensity of the fighting.   Formal revisions of the Portuguese Constitution in 1971 and the Overseas Organic Law
of 1972 gave still more formal autonomy to the "overseas
province" of "Portuguese" Guinea, but the pace set by the
PAIGC was now running out of the grasp of the Lisbon
authorities.

New anti-aircraft guns and small but effective Surface-
to-Air-Missiles from the Soviet Union permitted the PAIGC
to open competition for the airspace over Guinea-Bissau
which had formerly been the exclusive domain of Portuguese helicopter gunships, and deadly napalm and white
phosphorus dropped by fighter-bombers.   As a rule, the
PAIGC was beginning to bring down two or three enemy
aircraft each month by this time.   In April 1972 a unique
mission of the United Nations actually visited the liberated
zones and the 848th sessions of the UN Decolonization
Committee recognized the PAIGC as the only effective
movement operating inside Guinea-Bissau.   The observa-
tions and recognition of the Special Mission were endorsed
by the 27th session of the United Nations General Assembly
later in the same year as a major diplomatic triumph for
the PAIGC's long effort to isolate and discredit Portuguese
colonial rule.   In August 1972 another first occurred with
the elections in the liberated zones for 273 regional commissioners and for 99 representatives to the PAIGC's
Peoples' National Assembly to be held in late 1973.   In
an address in the United States, Amílcar Cabral announced
that soon the PAIGC would declare that the national independence of Guinea-Bissau had been achieved, but on January 20, 1973, this towering African nationalist and revolutionary philosopher was assassinated in Conakry in an

intricate plot to take over the PAIGC and protect certain
strategic interests of the Portuguese. The conspiracy
had been well organized using PAIGC dissident elements,
FLING partisans, and logistic and intelligence support
from the Portuguese. While the loss was keenly felt,
the organization that Amílcar Cabral had carefully built
went on to greater achievements. In May 1973 "Operation Amílcar Cabral" resulted in the seizure of Guiledge,
a large fortified base on the southern frontier. This was
possible, in part, because of the introduction of the new
anti-aircraft weapons, but especially because of the collective resolve of the PAIGC to redress the loss of the
Secretary General. From July 18-22, 1973, the PAIGC
held its second Party Congress at Boe which elected
Aristides Pereira as the new Secretary General; made
certain revisions in the proposed constitution; enlarged
the Supreme Committee of the Struggle (CSL) from 81 to
85 members; and created a Permanent Commission of the
Executive Committee. This new formation was headed
by A. Pereira with the Deputy Secretary General being
Luis Cabral, and the other two members being Francisco
Mendes and João Vieira. The July Congress applied the
last official touches to the preparations for the September
23-24, 1973 historic meeting of the First Peoples' National Assembly which formally proclaimed the Declaration of State, adopted the constitution, and elected the
executive organs of the state including Luis Cabral as
the President of the 15-member Council of State, 8 State
Commissioners (Ministers), and 8 sub-Commissioners
of State (Deputy Ministers). Immediately scores of nations around the world recognized the new Republic and
by early October 1973 diplomatic recognition had been extended by 61 nations even though Portuguese troops still
occupied the major towns.

   Elsewhere in Africa, especially in Mozambique, the
liberation movements were showing comparable gains and
it was increasingly clear that the end was near for Portugal. On April 25, 1974, the Portuguese Armed Forces
Movement (MFA) overthrew the colonial, fascist regime
of Prime Minister Caetano and made General Spinola,
recently returned from Guinea-Bissau, the new President
of Portugal. The leader of the Portuguese Socialist Party,
Mario Soares, met with Aristides Pereira on May 15,
1974, and negotiations for full independence were underway. By July 27, Portugal officially stated it was prepared to grant independence and in accords reached in
meetings held in Algiers in August the final details were

determined.   On September 4, the first representatives
of the Executive Committee of the Struggle (CEL) entered
Bissau and on September 10, Portugal gave de jure recognition to the new Republic of Guinea-Bissau.   Luis Cabral and A. Pereira entered Bissau officially on October
19, 1974.

Meanwhile in Cape Verde matters were more compli-
cated as the PAIGC had had a different history in the Islands and had not engaged in any meaningful armed struggle but had concentrated on clandestine political organizing.   A number of rival Cape Verdean groups emerged
and a climate of uneasiness prevailed through late September and into October until it was made clear in dis-
cussions, negotiations, demonstrations, and a general
strike that the PAIGC was to be the sovereign power in
the Islands.   On December 18, 1974, a transitional government had been formed from members of the PAIGC
and of the MFA.   In early 1975 relations between Portugal and Guinea-Bissau became strained over financial
matters and the PAIGC nationalized the Portuguese Overseas National Bank.   Such instances of instability prompted
the moribund FLING movement to make another attempt
at bringing down the PAIGC in a poorly planned coup
d'etat on March 21.   The apparatus of the new state became more fully engaged with the April 28-May 6 Peoples
National Assembly held in Bissau, the first since the
declaration of State in the southern forests a year earlier.   On June 30, 1975, there was an election for representatives to the Cape Verdean Peoples National Assembly
and with this act, the Islands became the fully independent
Republic of Cape Verde on July 5, 1975.   The PAIGC
program calls for unity between the sister Republics and
there are already many agreements which unite the two
lands in commerce, transport, education, and communication.   The PAIGC is the ruling party in both countries
but, at this point, there are still two separate National
Assemblies.

Notable events of 1976 include the creation of the Guinea peso to replace the Portuguese escudo on February
28 and the Second Session of the Peoples National Assembly from April 22 to May 3 as well as visits to Bissau from President Samora Machel of Mozambique and
President Agostino Neto of Angola.   On November 15-20,
1977, the PAIGC held its Third Party Congress.   After
some delays and about a year of meticulous and widespread preparation the central themes of this major event
were unity between Guinea-Bissau and Cape Verde, eco-

nomic development and political consolidation. The former
Permanent Secretariat of four members was enlarged to
eight; the CSL was increased to 90 members; and the
CEL was expanded from 24 to 26 members. The new
four members of the Permanent Secretariat are Pedro
Pires, Umaro Djalo, Constantino Teixeira, and Abilio
Duarte. The new thrust of the PAIGC will be to form a
vanguard political party which will organize, dynamize,
and mobilize the peoples of Guinea-Bissau and Cape Verde.
See A. CABRAL; L. CABRAL; A. PEREIRA; J. VIEIRA;
MING; FLING; A. SPINOLA; CSL; CEL.

PEANUTS (Groundnuts, Mancarra, Arachid). Peanuts (Arachis hypogaea) are known by a variety of names, but this
New World crop did not become important to Africa until
the 18th century when it began to compete with local crops
and displace African earthnuts. Peanuts are often grown
in association with yams, millet, kidney beans, and cas-
sava. For those peanuts consumed locally they may be
roasted or made into a peanut flour. For Guinea-Bissau,
peanuts have been the major export earner under colonialism. In 1960, for example, 70 percent of all peanut production was exported representing 63 percent of the export revenue. In 1963 about 23 percent of the total GNP
for Guinea-Bissau was derived from peanuts. The entire
export of peanuts usually went exclusively to Portugal for
distribution and processing. About 22 percent of the cultivated land was devoted to peanut production; areas in the
east and northeast of the country were generally best
suited. As with rice cultivation the war caused a general
decline in peanut production and export; also factors such
as inadequate rainfall contributed to irregularities in yield.
The areas of peanut cultivation were more generally those
regions under greater control by the Portuguese and Fulas
so that cultivation was somewhat less affected than in
those coastal areas for rice-growing. Statistics are very
contradictory but evidentally a good pre-war harvest was
about 65,000 tons while late in the war, production fell
to about 28,000 tons. Other reports suggest wider vari-
ations. Peanuts are sometimes grown in Cape Verde,
especially on Fogo Island, but little more than 200 hectares are devoted to this crop. Productivity fluctuates
wildly depending upon rainfall. Even the 1964 high in
production was only a minuscule 164 tons followed by
1970 production of only 14 tons. See AGRICULTURE;
ECONOMICS (TRADE).

PEOPLES' STORES   see   ARMAZENS DO POVO

PEREIRA, ARISTIDES MARIA (1924-). A founder of the
PAIGC, born on Boa Vista Island in the Cape Verde Archipelago where he attended a liceu before receiving specialized training as a radio-telegraph technician. Pereira
was one of the organizers of the Pijiguiti strike in 1959
and he worked in Bissau as the Chief of Telecommunica-
tions until 1960 when he left for security reasons to join
Amílcar Cabral in Conakry. Pereira was a member of
the Political Bureau of the Central Committee who organized in Bissau and other urban areas. In 1964 Pereira
was the joint Secretary General of the PAIGC and a member of the War Council after 1965. Following organizational restructuring in 1970 Pereira became a member of
the Permanent Commission of the Executive Committee
for the struggle (CEL) with Luis Cabral and Amílcar Cabral. In this position his chief responsibilities were security and control, and foreign affairs. Before the death
of Amílcar Cabral, Pereira was the Deputy Secretary
General of the Party, but after Cabral's passing, Pereira
became the top political officer of the PAIGC. Subsequent
to the independence of Cape Verde on July 5, 1975, Pereira also became the President of the Republic of Cape
Verde.

PEREIRA, CARMEN (1937-). Born in Guinea-Bissau as a
lawyer's daughter she joined the PAIGC in 1962. Her
husband Umaru Djallo was a party activist and when he
fled to avoid arrest she stayed in Bissau to work as a
dress-maker and care for her children. In 1964 she
also left Guinea-Bissau to engage in full-time party assignments. In 1965 Pereira headed a nurses training delegation to the Soviet Union. As the liberation war progressed
she became the Political Commissioner for the entire
South Front. She was the only woman in the 24-member
Executive Committee of the struggle (CEL) and was the
head of the Women's Commission. Pereira is the second
Vice-President of the Peoples National Assembly and one
of the 15 members of the Council of State. See also
WOMEN.

PEREIRA, DUARTE PACHECO. Portuguese explorer who
accompanied Azambuja in the founding of El Mina in 1482.
He was at El Mina when Cão sailed south from that fort.
He was rescued by Bartholomeu Dias on returning from
the Cape of Good Hope. Pereira later sailed to India.

Between 1505 and 1508 he wrote Esmeraldo de Sita Orbis,
a book of sea routes, in which he described details of
the West African coast.   He also gave details about coastal
trade and environment.   In 1506 he wrote about active
trade in gold, ivory and slaves at Arquim at a period
when Lisbon eagerly backed slavery.

PERMANENT SECRETARIAT.   Within the CEL and the War
   Council is found the Permanent Secretariat of the PAIGC.
   Until 1973 the Permanent Secretariat was composed of
   Amílcar Cabral, the PAIGC Secretary General in charge
   of political and military affairs, Aristides Pereira, Vice
   Secretary General and Responsable for economy and security, and Luis Cabral, Responsable for national reconstruction, health and education.   After the 1973 death of
   A. Cabral and the Second Party Congress, the Secretariat
   changed its name to the Permanent Commission and expanded by one member to include João Bernardo Vieira
   and Francisco Mendes as Secretaries of the Commission.
   The Commission handles the day-to-day decisions of the
   government and during the war all members were also
   members of the 7-man Conselho de Guerra (War Council).
   Since independence the Commission has expanded again
   to eight members.   See also A. CABRAL; L. CABRAL;
   CEL; CSL; F. MENDES; PAIGC; A. PEREIRA; J. B.
   VIEIRA.

PETROFINA AND SOCIEDADE ANONIMA DE REFINAÇAO DE
   PETROLEOS (SACOR).   These two oil companies have
   been the main suppliers of petrochemical products in Guinea-Bissau and Cape Verde.   Both Petrofina and SACOR
   are affiliated with the Portuguese Overseas National Bank
   (BNU) thus with links to CUF through political alliances
   and interlocking directorates.   See BNU; CUF.

PETROLEUM   see   ESSO EXPLORATION OF GUINEA, INC.;
   PETROFINA.

PIJIGUITI.   Site of the dockyards in Bissau at the broad estuary of the Geba River.   In one of the first tests of
   strength of the PAIGC a dock workers' strike was organized to express labor grievances and nationalist senti-
   ments.   On August 3, 1959, the colonial government responded with gun fire killing 50 and wounding 180.   The
   Pijiguiti Massacre was the turning point for the PAIGC
   which soon determined that a course of armed struggle
   would be the only way to achieve independence.

PINTO, MAJOR TEIXEIRA (1876-1917). Pinto is best known
    for a series of four brutal "pacification" campaigns in
    Guinea-Bissau between 1913-15, during which he used
    field action, sea coverage, collaboration, and modern
    arms to destroy villages of the Bijagos, Papeis, Balantas,
    Felupes, Manjacos, and Oincas. His military force was
    commanded by six European officers and about 400 Afri-
    cans, especially Fulas and Mandingas who had long made
    war on the coastal peoples. Before the campaigns, Pinto
    traveled in the Oio River area disguised as a French
    trader to spy on some Mandinga groups, he was aided in
    this intelligence work by the Oio chief and adventurer,
    Abdul Indjai. At the conclusion of the campaigns the
    town of Canchungo was named Teixeira Pinto, but the
    former name was restored after independence in 1974.
    In 1915 a public outcry against the excesses of Pinto
    forced an inquiry into his brutal administration. In World
    War I Pinto was stationed in Mozambique where he was
    killed in combat.

PIONEERS OF THE PARTY (PP). The youth organ of the
    PAIGC during the period of armed struggle sought to ed-
    ucate children under the leadership of the party. The PP
    acted as the political branch of the education policy in the
    liberated areas and at the Pilot School especially after
    1972. Children from 10-15 were eligible to join and par-
    ticipate under the slogan of "Study, Work, Struggle."
    While there were not many children involved in the total
    program the PP was very active at PAIGC boarding
    schools (semi-internatos) and carefully cultivated youth
    leadership qualities within Guinea and in youth contacts
    at international youth forums and festivals. The organ
    of the PP was called "Blufo" which was published more
    or less quarterly and featured educational, cultural, and
    political articles and puzzles. Since September 12, 1974,
    the main work of youth organizing is channeled through
    Juventude Africana Amílcar Cabral (JAAC, Amílcar Ca-
    bral African Youth) which has chapters in most schools
    or neighborhoods. JAAC has concentrated its efforts on
    national reconstruction projects such as drug eradication,
    literacy campaigns, and general youth improvement. It
    is particularly targeted for work with urban youth who
    had not been integrated into the structures of the liberated
    zones during the war.

PIRES, MAJOR PEDRO. During the war (1963-1974) Pires
    was the Commander of the southern frontier region and

member of the War Council.   Pires is also a leading
member of the Executive Committee for the struggle
(CEL).   After the independence of Cape Verde, Pires
became the first PAIGC Prime Minister and he is the
chairman of the Cape Verde National Committee of the
PAIGC.

POLICIA INTERNACIONAL E DE DEFESA DO ESTADO
    (PIDE).   The major Portuguese fascist secret police or-
ganization.   As early as 1957 PIDE arrived in Guinea-
Bissau to assist in intelligence and counter-insurgency
operations, especially widespread arrests of suspected
nationalists.   In 1961 an additional organ, the Polícia de
Segurança Pública (PSP) was introduced to curb the anti-
fascist and anti-colonial movements in Portugal and in
the African colonies.   In the early 1970's PIDE had received such notoriety that it changed its name to the Di-
reção Geral Segurança (DGS).   In 1971 a contingent of
105 PIDE agents arrived in Cape Verde to infiltrate and
break up underground operatives of the PAIGC.   See
TARRAFAL.

POPULATIONS.   The demographic data for Guinea-Bissau and
Cape Verde are generally quite limited.   Under the best
of conditions, unknown numbers of people avoided the census takers for fear of paying higher taxes or for fear of
military conscription.   As a result of large scale emigration from the Cape Verdean drought and from the nationalist war in Guinea-Bissau the data are distorted still
further.   All of these data must be considered as approx-
imate.
    Guinea-Bissau: A census in 1926 put the population of
RGB at 343,000.   The 1950 census in Guinea-Bissau was
one of the better demographic studies undertaken in this
nation.   The census showed a total population of 510,777
of which 502,457 (98.3 percent) were "uncivilized natives"
or basically the peasant population; 4,568 (0.8 percent)
were "mestiços" especially involved in small scale commerce and local government administration; 2,263 (0.4
percent) Europeans; 1,478 (0.2 percent) "assimilados" and
finally 11 Indians.   In the following years the population
statistics show great variation for the same period and
cannot be considered precise, but one may assume that
the population breakdown would remain relatively similar.
Estimates of the population have ranged as high as 800,000
but this figure seems unlikely.   Most statistics do not include the 25,000-30,000 Portuguese soldiers stationed in

Guinea-Bissau and it was only in 1976 that some 70,000 refugees from Senegal and Guinea-Conakry returned to Guinea-Bissau.   By the mid-1960's the population had probably reached about 530,000.   The major effect of the war (1963-74) was population relocation although combatant deaths were perhaps something less than a thousand per year.   A realistic population projection for 1978 for Guinea-Bissau would probably be in the vicinity of 640,000.

The infant death rate in Guinea-Bissau is now at 47.1/ 1,000 which is very high by European standards but there are many African nations with much higher rates.   In 1966 the IDR for RGB was 80.2/1,000.   For the period between 1970 and 1975 the overall crude birth rate is 25.1/1,000 resulting in a rate of natural increase of 1.5 percent/year which is relatively low for the underdeveloped nations.   Health conditions have been extremely poor and consequently the life expectancy for men is 37.0 years and for women it is 40.1 years.   The most densely populated areas of Guinea-Bissau are in the east along the Bafata-Gabu axis and in the vicinity of Cacheu.   The capital city of Bissau has the largest urban population but this probably does not exceed much more than 8 percent of the total populations of the country thus making Guinea-Bissau rather lightly urbanized.   The least populated concelhos are to be found in Bolama and in the Bijagos islands.   The overall population density for Guinea-Bissau is about 45.8/sq. mi. (17.7/km.).

Cape Verde: The census data for Cape Verde are generally more accurate given the more limited nature of inhabitable areas.   Some statistics go back as far as 200 years and indicate the pronounced population fluctuations caused by drought and emigration.   In 1850 the island population was put at 76,685, at the turn of the century the census showed 147,424 persons.   Fifty years later the population was only 150,000 thus demonstrating the powerful effects of emigration and mortality.   In 1960 the population reached 201,549 and reasonable projections for 1978 suggest a population of about 285,000.   The health conditions on the islands are quite poor and the infant death rate is now placed at 79/1,000 due largely to poor maternal nutrition and various protein deficiencies which are more severe in the islands than in Guinea-Bissau. In 1968 the infant death rate for the RCV was 91.7/1,000. After the critical period of infancy has passed, the life expectancy in Cape Verde is 48.3 years for males and 51.7 years for females.   While the infant death rate is high in Cape Verde the absence of a wet tropical climate

results in a general healthier environment for juven-
iles and adults who do not have to face a wide variety
of tropical diseases. The crude birth rate is 29. 2/1,000,
but the crude death rate is only 8. 8/1,000 or only a
third of that in Guinea-Bissau. The rate of natural increase in Cape Verde is about 2. 25 percent/year and
is thus significantly higher than its sister nation. The
limited areas suitable for human occupation cause a relatively high population density of 182. 9/sq. mi. (45. 8/sq. km.)
which is almost five times that of Guinea-Bissau. The
population is distributed very unequally on the various
islands with São Tiago (300. 6 sq. mi.) having 44. 0 percent of the total population, next is Santo Antão with
17. 3 percent, Fogo with 12. 4 percent and São Vincente
and Santa Luzia at 10. 3 percent. The other islands have
between one and 5 percent of the population. There are
three larger towns in the islands. Praia on São Tiago
with about 13,000 people, Mindelo on São Vincente with
19,500, and São Filipe on Fogo with about 3,500. The
population is considered to be 71 percent "Creole" or
"mestiço," 28 percent "African" and one percent "European. "

PORTUGAL. In 1143 Portugal broke from the Spanish monarchy and established its own King under Dom Henriques.
From 1384 to 1910 the House of Aviz (Knights of Cala-
trava) was the royal ruling lineage. Between 1420 and
1470 Portugal was absolute master of the seas and under
the influence of João II, Prince Henry's significant navigational achievements and exploration of Africa took place.
The coast of Guinea was reached in the 1440's and the
Cape Verde Islands discovered in the 1460's. In West
Africa, Portugal's dominance declined rather quickly to
the French, English and Dutch through the following centuries, but Portugal continued to be a major supplier of
slaves to the New World, especially to Brazil until the
late 19th century. From 1580 to 1640 Portugal was returned to the Spanish crown but this had relatively little
effect on the African territories with Portuguese links.
    In 1656 the private Cape Verdean tax collection was
eliminated and a direct officer to the Portuguese Crown
was approved to strengthen Portugal's hold on the Islands
and influence along the African coast. Throughout the
17th and 18th centuries Guinea-Bissau and Cape Verde
continued to supply slaves to the New World through the
services of Luso-African traders on the coast. In 1836

Portugal officially ended the slave trade, but it continued
for several more decades. In 1868 England yielded
its claims on Bolama to Portugal and following the
1884-5 Berlin Congress, Portugal and France agreed
on the southern and northern borders of Guinea-Bissau.
At the close of the 19th century Portugal was virtually
bankrupt and the monarchy sought dictatorial powers to
make certain reforms. Following the assassination of
the King and Crown Prince in 1908 and a popular revolt in 1910 the monarchy was abolished and the House
of Bragança was banished. The republican government
prevailed from 1911 until May 28, 1926, when a military putsch overthrew the democratic republican government. The period of instability in Lisbon had its
effects in Guinea-Bissau in a 1931 revolt of deported
politicians who held out for a month. From 1886 to
the 1930's the Portuguese conducted military expeditions of "pacification" against most of the coastal peoples of Guinea-Bissau.

In 1963 the nationalist movement in Guinea, led by the
PAIGC, began a protracted aimed struggle which paralleled
those in Angola and Mozambique. As a result of these
wars and domestic contradictions in policy and economy,
an Armed Forces Movement ended Portuguese fascism on
April 25, 1974, and restored a multi-party democracy.
The change in power in Lisbon led directly to the independence of Guinea-Bissau on September 24, 1974, and
of Cape Verde on July 5, 1975. See CAETANO; SALA-
ZAR.

PRAIA   see   SAO TIAGO

-R-

RASO   see   BRANCO AND RASO ISLETS

RASSEMBLEMENT DEMOCRATIQUE AFRICAIN DE LA GUINEE
(RDAG).   This Malinke oriented, Senegalese based or
ganization led to the formation of the FLG when it merged
with the MLG in 1961. In 1962 the FLG joined with
FLING.

REGULO.   Paramount African chief, often incorporated into
the system of colonial administration (regimen do indi-
genato).   To a limited extent, regulos were inherited po-

sitions, but they were usually appointed by the colonial administration as former civil servants, soldiers, police or interpreters and were paid token salaries. They did the dirty work of tax collection and labor recruitment and were assisted by brutal armed police.

RESISTANCE. In terms of Luso-African relations the first known example of resistance to European encroachment in Guinea-Bissau took place in 1447 in the Bissagos islands with the death of Nuño Tristão and several of his crew. Since the Portuguese had already begun slaving further up the western coast we may assume that this may have been part of Tristão's mission. One may date the first African resistance to the first arrival of hostile European forces. The second period of resistance was that against the slave system which left little middle ground between those who were enslaved and those who did the slaving. Slavery instigated competition between regions and peoples in order to obtain firearms, economic goods, and power which generally benefited European mercantile and industrial interests. Since no slave went willingly one may easily conclude that this was a period of intense resistance against the slave wars between African peoples which were inspired by the lançados and the Portuguese. Previous forms of African slavery in the region lacked both the scale and qualitative content of the European plantation and chattel slave systems.

After slavery ended slowly in the 19th century, territorial conquest was launched by the Portuguese and their local allies, although before this period they had no regular control of the interior. Some of the first serious challenges to this incursion were in the 1825 and 1826 mutinies at Cacheu. In 1843 the Portuguese began to initiate a program of writing coercive treaties with the people of Guinea-Bissau since slavery and slave wars had become obsolete, and increasing amounts of labor were required for palm oil, coconut oil, rice, and peanut production. Treaties were signed with the Mandingo at Badora, the Banhun and Cobianas. From 1844 to 1845 numerous local uprisings took place as the Portuguese encroachment increased and resulted in treaties with other Banhun sections and some of the peoples in the vicinity of Cacheu. Relative peace prevailed until the Bissau mutiny and the Geba trader revolt of 1853. In 1860 risings against the Portuguese were reported throughout the country while some neighboring Dyulas and Balantas submitted to French rule. However the heroic and protracted

guerrilla war of Samori Toure from 1860 to 1870 in Guinea-Conakry presented the neighboring French with an extremely effective opposition to their authority. Some Bissagos leaders relented to colonial authority in 1861 and
the state of Gabu fell in 1867 to the Fula who were not
opposed by the Portuguese since Portugal's authority did
not yet reach the interior at that time. When the Fulas
had finally destroyed the Mandingo state of Gabu it was
only a matter of time before they, themselves were
brought under colonial rule.

In January 1871 the Portuguese governor of Guinea-
Bissau was assassinated by an African grumetta and an
uprising in the following month had to be vigorously suppressed. The year of 1874 saw the offensive of the Mandingo, Foday Kabba in the Casamance region and provoked
considerable anxiety in colonial ruling circles. From
1878 to 1880 the Portuguese organized a series of attacks
against the Felupes and Manjacos, and from 1880 to 1882
military expeditions were waged against the Beafadas and
some Fula sections. The campaigns were followed by
two years (1883-5) of war against the Balantas and against
the Papeis in 1884, and in 1886 when attacks were made
against both Papeis and Beafadas. These data reflect the
intensification of warfare against African peoples just before and especially after the infamous Berlin Congress of
1884-5 which arranged for the European powers of the day
to partition the entire African continent for open colonial
rule. European claims were accepted on the basis of
their demonstration of effected control of the territories
which they called their own. Thus the "scramble" for
Africa was an episode of frenetic military activity and
oppression. The acephalous Balantas fell under a Portuguese military campaign in 1891 and from that date until 1894 there were virtually continuous revolts of Papeis
who blocked the Cacheu river. In November of 1894 a
rising in Bissau shook the colonial government. In fact,
from 1891 to 1910 rebellions of other Papeis, Balantas
and Malinkes were quite frequent. At the close of the
century in 1897 the colonial troops were dispatched against
the Oincas section of the Mandingo stock.

A number of Fula chiefs formally submitted to colonial
rule in 1900 but a 1907-8 revolt required two reinforced
Portuguese columns to put down these Fula insurgents.
After this period the cephalous Fula remained effectively
controlled by placing the Fula chiefs on colonial retainers.
At the turn of the century expeditions in the interior were
again waged against the Mandingos and Beafadas while

fierce resistance continued among coastal peoples especially
on Canhabaque island and in the Bissagos archipelago. In
1901 and 1903 forces returned to the Felupes and in 1902
against the Oincas. The Cacheu Papeis resumed their
river blockade in 1904 which demanded several Portuguese
counter-attacks. In 1906 the Bissagos people on Formosa
island revolted and were put down. The Beafada chief
Infali Sonco revolted in the Geba region in 1907 thus cut-
ting off Bafata and Gabu in the interior from Bissau on
the coast. This year also had strong Fula revolts and
a rising in the Cuor region. The unending nature of these
revolts and resistance provoked the brutal military "pacification" campaigns of 1912-15 led by Major Teixeira Pinto
which met opposition of the Balantas, Oincas, the Papeis
of the Bissau region, the Manjacos of Xuro-Caixo and
again in the Bissagos islands. Supposed "submission"
of the Balantas of Mansoa was achieved in 1914 and of
the Bissau Papeis in 1915. Other Balanta, Felupe, and
Papel groups were also attacked in 1915. By the end of
that year the colonial government underwent reorganization and Major Pinto's crimes were investigated and ex-
posed by a colonial commission which admitted his ex-
cesses.

Another form of colonial oppression came in the form
of a myriad of taxes such as those for houses, burials,
palm trees, livestock, censuses, and a host of fines for
various infractions of colonial law. Consequently tax revolts broke out among the Bissagos and Papeis in 1917
who were declared defeated in 1918 yet organized other
tax revolts in 1924 and 1925. Another wave of widespread
tax resistance re-emerged in the 1930's especially with
the 1936 revolt of the Papeis. In short, the earliest hostility shown to Guineans by Tristão in 1447 ended with his death
by the Bissagos people. Throughout the intervening centuries between "discovery" and the Berlin Congress, African resistance consisted of fighting the slave-raiders,
either African or European and from 1825 to 1936 a decade did not go by without revolts, uprisings, mutinies,
or other acts of resistance. In 1956 the multi-ethnic and
tightly disciplined PAIGC nationalist movement was organized and continued the heritage of opposition to colonial
rule. The 1959 workers' strike at the Pijiguiti docks in
Bissau was reminiscent of the Papeis revolts in that region in decades gone by and the savage repression of the
strike recalled the campaigns of Major Pinto. Subsequently the PAIGC leadership determined that a well-or-
ganized, protracted, armed guerrilla struggle would be

the only course which would lead to national independence.
During the war (1963-1974) the various ethnic groups were
unified behind basic goals rather than divided and suscep-
tible to the divide-and-rule tactics of the colonial military
force.   Much still needs to be written and discovered about
African resistance movements, but these data attest to a
long history of opposition.   See BISSAU; CACHEU; GABU;
PAIGC; PIJIGUITI; PINTO, T.; SLAVERY; TRISTÃO; and
specific ethnic groups.

RIBIERA GRANDE   see   SAO TIAGO

RICE (Arroz, Mancarra).   Rice (Oryza sp.) has long been an
important staple in the Sudanic regions after millet and
sorghum.   Both wild and cultivated forms may be found.
Oryza breviligulata is considered to be the wild ancestor
of Oryza glaberrima which is cultivated on the Middle
Niger by Mande peoples and by the coastal Senegambians.
O. glaberrima may have been cultivated as early as
1500 B.C.   Oryza sativa is a much later Asiatic species
which is widely cultivated today.   Although regions as far
north as Tekrur grew rice in the Middle Ages it is grown
more extensively as one moves south and toward the
coastal wetlands inhabited by Mandingos, Balantas, or
Susus.   In these wetter areas rice is the only suitable
starch crop.   Approximately 30 percent of the total cultivated acreage in Guinea-Bissau is devoted to rice farming.   Rice is generally not grown in Cape Verde because
of inadequate water and inappropriate soils.
   Before the war the colonial economy exported over
100,000 tons of rice annually.   In the mid 1960's rice
production fell to about 30,000 tons per year and by 1967
production reached only 19,000 tons.   As the liberated
zones expanded the Portuguese were finally forced to begin to import rice.   Just before independence in 1974 the
colonial imports to Guinea-Bissau reached 35,000 tons.
By 1976 a small rice surplus was already being generated.
This tall grass is grown as a grain crop in flooded paddies
with extensive irrigation canals throughout much of coastal
Guinea-Bissau.   In some wet delta areas rice may grow
wild and other species of upland rice will grow on dry
land like other grains.   Commonly rice is served with
chicken or fish and with a palm oil sauce.   Rice is known
as malu in Balanta, malo in the Mande languages, maro
in Fula, and as umane in Manjaco or Brame.   See AR-
MAZENS DO POVO; AGRICULTURE; ECONOMICS (TRADE);
MILLET; SORGHUM.

ROMBOS (or SECOS) ISLETS (14° 58'N, 20° 40'W). The small
islets of Grande, Luis Carneiro, Sapado and Cima constitute the main members of the Rombos Islets in the Sotavento (southern, leeward) group in the Cape Verde archipelago. These lie to the north of Brava and are unin-
habited.

-S-

SAL (16° 45'N, 22° 55'W). The third smallest (83. 5 sq. mi.)
island of the Barlavento group of the Cape Verde archipelago. Sal is generally a low, sandy island with its maximum altitude of only 1,332 feet. Its current population
is about 7,500 people with the largest number at the Es-
pargos-Preguça market town of about 5,000. The village
of Palmeira lies on the west coast, Santa Maria is found
on the extreme south of this narrow island. At Santa
Maria there is a fish processing factory and salt works.
Sal, as well as other members of the archipelago, may
have been known to salt-seeking "Moors" before Portuguese "discovery." The first settlement was by slaves
from Boa Vista but this was not significant until the late
17th century when the demand for salt and livestock had
been intensified by coastal slaving at this time and into
the 18th century. The island was a common stop for
ships in the area to get a cargo of salt for ballast and
trade at little or no cost. In the early 1970's the airport at Sal was expanded to be the largest in the archipelago and can accommodate the 747 type of commercial
aircraft. Tourism was boosted at this time by the Bel-
gian-Portuguese firm DETOSAL which has 70 beds in
beach hotels. Water supply remains a serious problem
for health and hygiene but a desalinization plant is now
under development. The main sources of wage work on
the island would be related to the airport, tourism, the
salinas (salt pans), or at the petroleum storage facility.

SALAZAR, DR. ANTONIO DE OLIVEIRA (1889-July 27, 1970).
Prime Minister of Portugal from 1932 to 1968 when he
was incapacitated by a stroke. Following the overthrow
of the Portuguese Crown and instability of the Republican
government, Salazar came to be the Prime Minister of
Portugal in 1932. In 1933, Salazar and Dr. Marcelo
Caetano were the chief architects of the absolutist Portuguese constitution and of the "Estado Novo" policy which
maintained fascist authority of industry, labor, and press

in Portugal and in their African colonies.   See CAETANO;
PORTUGAL.

SALUM (Saloum)   see   FUTA TORO; GABU.

SAMA KOLI (Kelemankoto Baa Saane).   The first king of the
Mandingo state of Gabu, Sama Koli was either the son or
grandson of Tiramakhan Traore, a general of Sundiata of
Mali.   Sama Koli married Nyaaling of Bonje and continued
the matrilineal line of Gabu kings with their son Saarafa
Nyaaling Jeenung, his son Kuntinka Sira Bula Jeenung, and
his son, Saamanka Dala Jeenung.

SANTA LUZIA (16° 45'N, 24° 45'W).   The smallest (135 sq.
mi.) of the Barlavento (windward, northern) group of the
Cape Verde archipelago.   Santa Luzia is rather low (maximum altitude 1,296 feet) and lies to the southeast of
São Vincente.   The island was not inhabited until the late
17th century and has functioned mainly for livestock raising when rains have been sufficiently favorable.

SANTO ANTAO (17° 5'N, 25° 10'W).   The second largest
(300. 6 sq. mi.) and northernmost island in the Cape Verde
archipelago and largest member of the Barlavento (northern, windward) group.   Santo Antão is rocky and mountainous with its two principal peaks reaching 6,493 feet
and 5,197 feet.   There are permanent sources of water
for São Vincente lying nearby to the southeast.   The main
town and port is Porto Novo; other towns include Vila
Maria Pia, Pombas, and the two villages of Ribeira da
Cruz and Tarrafal.   Santo Antão was first settled in the
early 1500's especially with families from Madeira.   More
significant settlers arrived in the late 17th and again in
the late 18th centuries, but these were mainly from the
other islands.   Exports from Santo Antão have included
rum, slaves, livestock and pozzolana for making cement.
Approximately 17 percent of the population of the archipelago resides in Santo Antão, which now has 47,000 inhabitants.   Since independence the PAIGC has built new
roads, irrigation canals, and other water conservation
projects as well as planting 30,000 coffee plants as a
cash crop and 50,000 new trees.   See also MINERALS.

SAO NICOLAU (16° 35'N, 24° 15'W).   The fifth largest island
in the Cape Verde archipelago and central member of the
Barlavento (windward, northern) group.   Being of average
size (132. 4 sq. mi.), its terrain is rocky but not excep-

tionally high, with its two main peaks at 4,278 feet and
2,175 feet. The narrow shape of the island has caused
the main villages such as Prequica, Castilhano and Car-
riçal and its 1,400-meter airport to be located on the
immediate coast, although the main town, Vila da Ribeira
Brava is located in an interior valley. Several relatively
permanent streams attracted settlement in the early 16th
century especially by families from Madeira and their
slaves especially from Guinea. The European population
of today is quite small. Relatively productive agriculture
and livestock raising attracted further settlement in the
late 17th century. For a brief period in the late 19th and
early 20th centuries a seminary functioned on the island
and was something of a center of scholarly life. Today
the PAIGC has built a new water works, constructed new
rural service centers and has created some 400 new jobs.

SAO TIAGO (15° 5'N, 23° 38'W). The largest (328. 5 sq. mi.)
    of the Cape Verdean archipelago and member of the So-
    tavento (leeward) group. This island is rocky and moun-
    tainous with some permanent sources of fresh water flow-
    ing from the mountains rising to a maximum altitude of
    4,507 feet. The current capital is Praia (25,000 popula-
    tion) on the southern tip of the island. The former capi-
    tal was at Ribeira Grande now known as Cidade Velha.
    Other towns include Tarrafal, Gouveia, Assomada, and
    Santa Catarina   São Tiago, also known as St. James or
    São Jacobo, was first noted by the Portuguese in May
    1460 with the ships of Antonio da Noli and Diogo Gomes.
    Within a few years da Noli, a Genoan serving the Portu-
    guese Crown, brought the first settlers from the Algarve
    to São Tiago and founded Ribeira Grande as the first cap-
    ital. At this time São Tiago was divided into two cap-
    taincies which belonged to Prince Fernando, brother of
    the king. A commerce in slaves grew rapidly to develop
    the island and become a very significant export. By 1466
    settlers and lançados traded freely in African products
    and slaves soon resulting in the mixed population of the
    islands, however São Tiago is considered to have the
    most African population. As an example of the scale of
    the trade, between 1514 and 1516 almost 3,000 slaves
    were landed at Ribeira Grande. The town was elevated
    to the status of a city in 1533 when the official residence
    of the Cape Verdean bishop was begun. The bishop rep-
    resented religious (and Crown) authority in the island and
    on the coast from Morocco to Guinea.
    The relative prosperity and autonomy of the captaincies

on São Tiago resulted, in 1564, in the rule reverted to
the crown for a fuller monopolization of island and coastal
trade.   Ribeira Grande reached a permanent population of
1,500 by 1572 although the interior town of Santa Catarina
was already larger by this time.   The slave plantation
system was deeply entrenched with a population of 5-10
percent of whites and "mestiços" in full authority using
a small group of "free" Africans as overseers regulating
some 90 percent of the population of African slaves.   Not
only was the Portuguese crown interested in gaining this
wealth, but the English under Captain Drake wanted the
benefits.   In 1585 Drake landed at Praia with some 2,000
men and marched quickly overland to attack the poorly
defended rear area of Ribeira Grande, looting and sack-
ing at will.   Drake's forces remained very briefly and the
Portuguese returned to fortify the city and institute new
defenses and governmental reforms.   For example a new
captaincy general system was introduced as the representative of the crown.   This royal appointee oversaw the administration of the islands and the coast.   This change
was made to consolidate the slave monopoly against European encroachment on the Portuguese trade.   Nevertheless
French, English and Dutch forces all attacked the islands
in the late 16th and early 17th centuries stealing livestock,
robbing the people, and destroying property.   Despite
these attacks São Tiago continued its relative prosperity
although the other islands had entered a long decline into
stagnation.   By 1612 neighboring Praia was better defended,
although with a poorer port, than Ribeira Grande.   The
bishop and governors of the region began to rotate their
residence between the two cities.   Slave rivalries on the
coast continued with a Dutch attack on Cacheu in 1624 but
slave trade to and from São Tiago continued and even began to add customers from New England in the 1640's.
Praia became the effective capital by the mid 17th century and Ribeira Grande began its decline.   In 1712 the
French repeated Drake's strategy and attacked Praia and
then assaulted the weak Ribeira Grande making off with
much loot.   The capital was officially moved to Praia in
1769 and Ribeira Grande gained a new identity, Cidade
Velha (old city) as it is now known with its deserted ca-
thedral, dominating fortress and general collapse.
   Aside from the central role of slavery in the economy
São Tiago was also a common stopping place for fresh
water for ships going to South America or down the West
African coast.   Local production of livestock and plant
dyes (urzella) was sometimes important and São Tiago

horses were much prized for riding and in slave exchange.
It is ironic that Matthew Perry's anti-slavery "Africa
Squadron" was based in São Tiago in 1842. Today there
is a 1,200-meter airport in Praia and the port facilities
have been improved, but have no comparison to those of
Mindelo. The island's population has reached about 132,000
or some 46 percent of the people of the whole archipelago.
The PAIGC has introduced an energetic program of dike-
building and water conservation as well as developing new
public service facilities.

SAO VINCENTE (16° 52'N, 24° 58'W). The island in the Barlavento (northern, windward) group in the Cape Verde archipelago ranked seventh in size (87.6 sq. mi.). While
there are rocky mountains they are not of exceptional
height (2,539 feet) for the islands. There is virtually
no regular water supply in São Vincente and its settlement was retarded for this reason. Water was brought
from Santo Antão for cooking and washing needs until the
desalinization plant in Mindelo began its operation in January 1972. The island has about 10 percent of the population of the archipelago and the town of Mindelo itself
is the largest urban area of all of the islands. By 1970
Mindelo's inhabitants numbered about 28,800 while total
population for the island is 34,500. There are few natural resources in São Vincente except for its excellent
harbor at Mindelo (Porto Grande) facing Santo Antão. Another village is São Pedro where the 1,200-meter airport is located.
     The mid 18th century saw the period of the first set-
tlement of São Vincente as its port economy was stimulated by intense slaving on the Guinea coast. In about
1790 the British established a consulate and coal depot
at Porto Grande to strengthen their naval dominance. With
these developments substantial numbers of settlers were
attracted to Mindelo from other Cape Verde islands to
work as longshoremen or to join ship crews. In the mid
19th century British ships on route to Brazil made regular stops at Mindelo. A submarine communications cable
reached Mindelo in 1875. By 1880 the Portuguese firm
Empresa Nacional de Navegação established regular service from Portugal to São Vincente and Guinea-Bissau.
In the early 20th century Mindelo handled about five million tons of shipping annually and had become the main
port for the whole archipelago. Aside from extensive
storage and bunkering facilities there is now an oil re-
finery and attractive hotel. PAIGC development programs

have already initiated a fiber glass boat-building factory
at Mindelo with a fish-processing factory soon to be expanded. Other activities since independence include new
road construction, hospital expansion, new social service
and health centers, and the development and promotion of
horticulture.

SARACOTES (Saracole). This very small group of the Soninke
branch of the Mande stock may be found in small clusters
between Gabu (Nova Lamego) and Bafata.

SENEGAMBIANS. This large cluster of the coastal, Atlantic
stock of the Niger-Congo (or Nigritic) peoples includes
virtually all of those people of Guinea-Bissau who are of
neither Fula nor Manding (Mande) stocks. The Senegambians include the Balantas, Banyuns, Biafadas, Bijagos,
Diolas, Nalus, Papeis, Brams, Manjacos, Serer, Wolof
and Mankanyas. Senegambian peoples were found as far
north as Mauretania until the 11th-century expansion of
the Berbers when they were pushed back southward. They
extended eastward through most of present Guinea-Bissau
until the creation of Gabu and the secondary Mande kingdoms pushed them westward toward the coast. The southward spread of the Senegambians was similarly checked
by the consolidation of power in the Guinea highlands at
Futa Jallon and with the expansion of the Susu kingdom.
At an early date the Senegambians incorporated the Sun-
danic food complex and added rice farming as a local
specialty. The numerous small Senegambian groups represent the shattering effect from the pressure on all sides
by more powerful centralized hierarchies against the Senegambians who are either acephalous or only slightly centralized and who are mostly animist except by more recent Islamization. Sometimes Senegambians are known
as "Semi-Bantu" peoples of the Guinea Littoral.

SERER. This Senegambian group is mainly located in southeastern Senegal but is related to the Diola of Guinea-Bissau and to the small, stratified Sine and Salum kingdoms
which were tributary states of Mali between the 13th and
15th centuries. See TEKRUR; MALI (Mande).

SILLA, ERNESTINA (? -1973). This exemplary woman militant and CSL member of the PAIGC was born in the Tom-
bali region of Guinea-Bissau. In 1962 she contacted the
Party as a teenager and then left home to dedicate herself
to the nationalist struggle. Her main assignment was Public

Health work in the liberated zones of the northern region.
Her active work did not prevent her from marrying and
raising children. On January 31, 1973, she was killed
in combat on the Farim River on the way to the funeral
for Amílcar Cabral in neighboring Guinea-Conakry. In
March of 1977 the "Titina" Silla Juice Factory was opened
in Bolama in her memory. See also WOMEN.

SIN (Sine) see FUTA TORO; GABU.

SINTRA, PEDRO DA. Portuguese navigator who sailed off the
   coast of Guinea-Bissau in 1460 to reach Sierra Leone.

SLAVERY. The Portuguese first captured African slaves in
   the early 1440's on the Moroccan coast. Until the discovery of the New World, slaves were used as domestic
   servants in Europe and on sugar plantations in the various
   Atlantic islands. Slavery in Cape Verde was at its height
   between 1475 and 1575. Guinea-Bissau itself did not use
   the slave plantation system to any degree, but was chiefly
   an exporter. During the 15th century the export of slaves
   from Africa did not exceed 1,000 annually, but this was
   a uniquely Portuguese enterprise and only on the upper
   reaches of the West African coast. The slave trade in
   the 16th century was still monopolized by Portugal, but
   Spanish and English slavers began to erode the monopoly
   in the late 16th century. Cape Verdeans and lançados
   (coastal middlemen) were directly involved in the trade
   along the coast which depended upon slave wars waged
   in the interior. Cape Verdean paños (textiles), horses,
   and salt were brought from the islands to trade along the
   coast. The majority of African slaves were coming from
   Guinea and Senegambia in general. The pace of slaving
   increased through the century reaching a height of some
   5,000 slaves annually by the 1570's. Most of these
   slaves went to the New World, especially to the Caribbean
   and to Brazil although a small trickle still went to the
   Cape Verde Islands and to Europe.
       Throughout the 17th century the Portuguese slave trade
   in Senegambia and Guinea-Bissau declined in both absolute and relative terms. On the one hand more European
   powers were involved and Portuguese slavers became
   more active in Angola and Mozambique. In the first
   half of the 17th century the portion of slaves from Guinea
   and Senegambia fell to about 6 percent of the total number
   of slaves from Africa where it had been as much as 75
   percent in the century before. Likewise the numbers of

slaves fell from previous highs of about 5,000 per year
to an average of 650 per year. The earlier figures related to the various wars of the autonomous state of Gabu
in Guinea-Bissau which generated large numbers of slaves
for trade and export. In the 17th century Gabu became
less dynamic and more stable thus slowing the production
of slave captives. The early 17th century saw renewed
efforts by other European powers to engage in West African slavery; the real heyday of competitive and aggressive slaving had begun. The English Royal African Company averaged some 10,000 slaves each year in the area
between Senegal and Sierra Leone in the late 17th century,
but this large figure represented only 12 percent of their
total slave trade from Africa at the time. At about the
same period two Cape Verdean companies were established
as slave trade monopolies at Cacheu in Guinea-Bissau.
With a marked growth in the New World plantation system the demand was high and insecurity prevailed among
peoples of the coast and the interior as all of the major
Sudanic states in the West African savanna had come to
an end. The portion of slaving done by Portuguese vessels or with Portuguese traders continued to fall. Indeed,
the coastal lançados and Dyula traders had almost free
reign on trading in the context of virtual anarchy of slave
commerce at this time. Slaves were being drawn from
peoples further to the interior as the various Fula wars
maintained a high degree of insecurity in the 18th century.
In 1753 a Brazilian slave trade company was given monopoly rights at Bissau to acquire slaves for the Brazilian
states of Maranhão and Grão Pará. This accounted for
a resurgence in slaving in Guinea-Bissau as slave exports
rose to average some 700 per year in the late 18th century. Many of these slaves were generated from the in-
cessant wars between the Mandingo state of Gabu and the
Fula people of Labé Province of Futa Jallon.
    The early 19th century saw the start of European abo-
lition when it was realized that a cash economy (rather
than slave barter) and industrial exports on a massive
scale would be served better by "free labor" which could
purchase European goods and enter a system of colonial
taxation in which unpaid slaves could not "participate."
The wage-slave system began to cut away at the older
system of chattel slavery. As a poor European nation,
Portugal was slow to make this transition and slavery
lingered on into the 19th century. To a limited extent
there was even some slight increase in the slave trade
at this time in Guinea-Bissau as the abolition and anti-

slavery patrols had resulted in a relative scarcity of the
slave supply thus forcing a temporary increased demand.
At this point the decentralized coastal peoples were again
raided, but as the century wore on there were larger
numbers of slaves from the Mandingo-related peoples
when the Fulas continued to press their attacks on Gabu
in eastern Guinea-Bissau. The Brazilian slave company
still kept its monopoly in Bissau from which they took
the vast portion of their slaves, but the annual numbers
had fallen to only a few hundred per year. Despite the
rather rapid spread of the abolition movement, Portugal
was more often in violation of the restrictions and agreements to limit the trade.

The independence of Brazil from Portugal in 1822 and
the Emancipation Proclamation in the United States in
1863 gave a formal basis for the sharp decline and ultimate extinction of the trade in Guinea-Bissau by the third
quarter of the 19th century. At the close of the 19th century and into most of the 20th century of open Portuguese
colonialism a system of contract labor replaced slavery
although the life of a "contratado" was only a slight im-
provement, as wages were pitiful and the conditions of
employment were most oppressive. The contract labor
system was particularly important to the economy of Cape
Verde which has long had great difficulty in supporting
its own population by island agriculture because of prolonged droughts, gross colonial mismanagement, and backward systems of land ownership. Some Africans had short-
term, personal benefit from the slave trade, but the protracted brutality associated with this commerce in human
beings certainly stands as one of the most exploitative
and inhuman epochs in human history. Also, most Europeans in Europe or in the New World did not benefit
either; not only was there chronic insecurity and anxiety
under the slave system, but only the small European
class of slave owners and traders were the true "bene-
ficiaries" of this launching of the great African diaspora.
See HAWKINS, J.; TRISTAO; GOMES, D.; GONÇALVES,
A.; CACHEU; LANÇADOS; BISSAU; SAO TIAGO.

SONGHAI. Songhai was a major Sudanic state to become
dominant on the Middle Niger after the slow disintegra-
tion of Mali, however Songhai was first established as a
small Niger River state in 1504. Sonni Ali Ber (b. 1443?,
d. 1492) is considered to be the founder of the Empire of
Songhai as a result of his military campaigns in the 1460's
which led to the capture of Timbuktu in 1469. Timbuktu

had already fallen away from Mali in 1433 when it was
seized by Tuareg invaders.   After a long siege at Jenne
this also fell to Songhai in 1473.   The reign of Songhai
was punctuated with military conflict with the Fula who
put up strong resistance.   In 1492 Sunni Ali was replaced
by his Soninke general, Askia Muhammad, who had a
colorful reign until 1528.   In 1496-8 Askia Muhammad
undertook a celebrated pilgrimage (haji) to Mecca and in
1512 he carried out military expeditions against Coli Tenguella (I).   Niani, a capital town of Mali fell to Songhai
in 1546, but in 1591 the Askia dynasty of Songhai came
to an end with the conquest by Moroccan troops.   The
influence of Songhai was not as directly felt in Guinea-
Bissau as Mali but it did have the effect of pushing various ethnic groups toward the coast and disrupting those
already living along the coastal areas.   See TENGEULLA;
MALI; TEKRUR.

SONINKE.   The Soninke are members of the Nuclear Mande
    stock of the Niger-Congo language family, but they speak
    a distinct Manding language.   While the Soninke are found
    in eastern Senegal and Western Mali they are related to
    the Susu and Dyula of Guinea-Bissau.   The most notable
    achievement of the Soninke people is their founding of
    the Sudanic empire of Ghana (literally, in Soninke, "war
    chief").   The Soninke include admixture from the Malinke,
    Fulani, Bambara and especially the Berber people.
    From the neighboring Tukulor the Soninke received Islam.
    The Soninke have both class stratification and traditional
    hierarchies of nobility.   In A.D. 990 the Empire of Ghana
    seized Awdoghast and established its maximum control
    of trans-Saharan trade.   By 1054 the Almoravids captured
    Awdoghast from Ghana and in 1076 the sometime capital
    of Ghana at Kumbi Saleh also fell to the Almoravids.
    The Dyula branch of the Soninke was central in the trade
    and Islamization of the Upper and Middle Niger which led
    to the formation of the state of Mali.   During the rule of
    Askia Mohammad (1493-1529) in the Empire of Songhai the
    Soninke scholar, Mohammad Kati, lived in Timbuktu and
    wrote the important, Tarikh al-Fettash.   See SUSU;
    DYULA; TEKRUR; MALI.

SPINOLA, GENERAL ANTONIO SEBASTIAO RIBEIRO DE
    (b. April 11, 1910-).   Born in Estremoz, Portugal,
    Spinola received a strict military education and was a
    noted horseman.   With his family close to the ruling
    circles of the Portuguese government and the powerful

Champalimand banking group he was long a prominent military officer. In the Second World War, Spinola was invited by Hitler to inspect conquered areas of the Soviet Union and is reported to have visited the German Sixth Army during its unsuccessful attempt to seize Stalingrad. After 1961 he was appointed as a colonial military officer once commanding some 40,000 men in northern Angola. Spinola was assigned as Governor General of Guinea-Bissau in late 1967 when the former Governor Arnaldo Schultz failed to halt the PAIGC military initiative with a fortified hamlet program. In 1968 General Spinola introduced a modest "Better Guinea" program of reforms in addition to commanding about 30,000 troops in counter-insurgency warfare. In 1972 he began a second term in Guinea-Bissau but he continued to fail to curb the PAIGC. In August 1973 he was forced to retire for advocating a new African policy and was replaced by General Jose Bettencourt Rodrigues, 55 years old, compared to Spinola's 63 years. Rodrigues had been Portuguese Chief of Staff in Angola. In September 1973 Spinola returned to Lisbon soon to be appointed Deputy Chief of Staff of the entire Portuguese Armed Forces. On February 22, 1974, Spinola published a book called Portugal and the Future in which he declared that military victory in Africa was impossible and a program of autonomy with federation with Portugal would represent the only possible solution which would favor Portugal and block revolutionary nationalism in the colonies. The book hit a sensitive nerve and Spinola was dismissed on March 12, 1974. However, the Portuguese Armed Forces Movement seized power from Caetano on April 25, 1974, and made Spinola President of the New Republic for several months to reward him for his opposition to Caetano. Spinola was removed from his position and he now plays a behind-the-scenes role in Portuguese politics. As military Governor General of Guinea-Bissau he helped to organize the abortive invasion of Guinea-Conakry in 1970 and supplied backing to the attempted coup against the PAIGC and assassination of Amílcar Cabral in 1973.

SUMAGURU see SUSU

SUNNI ALI. Ruler of Songhai who reasserted Songhai's dominance in 1465 with his control of the Middle Niger from his capital at Gao. See SONGHAI.

SUSUS (Sossos; Sosos). This Mande derived group is found

in the extreme south of Guinea-Bissau's coastal areas
and in adjacent Guinea-Conakry. In Guinea-Bissau they
are concentrated around Catio and Cacine. The Susus
are related to the Dyulas and Soninke, who were the chief
founders of the Empire of Ghana. With the fall of Kumbi
Saleh (the capital of Ghana near Walata) in 1076, the Susu
branch of the Soninke fled to the south, away from the
Almoravids. In the flight to the south, the Susus spread
the main crops of the Sudanic agricultural complex to new
areas. Later, on the coast and in the coastal interior
of today's Guinea-Conakry the Islamized paramount chiefs
blocked further southward expansion of the Senegambians.
In about 1200 one Susu state called Kaniaga emerged and was
able to gain enough strength to reconquer Kumbi Saleh in
1203, thus ruling southern Soninke group and northern
Malinkes. The head of this Susu state was Sumaguru
(Soumaora, Sumawuru) Kante (Konteh) of a Tekrur dynasty.
Sumaguru's rule at Kumbi Saleh was considered harsh and
oppressive and helped to precipitate the final decline of
ancient Ghana. In 1230 Sumaguru extended his empire
with the conquest of Kangaba near the important Wangara
gold mines which he ruled along, with Diara, as Susu
states. During the rule of Sumaguru, he killed eleven
of the local Mandingo kings sparing the life of only one,
a cripple named Sundiata Keita, who was later to become
the powerful founder of the major state of Mali. Even
before the actual defeat of Sumaguru the growing trade at
Walata had already eclipsed that of Kumbi Saleh. Further
expansion of the Susa states was halted by the growth of
Mali under Sundiata. At the battle of Kirina in 1235 Sundiata's forces defeated the army of Sumaguru. By 1240
Sundiata occupied the remaining remnants of Ghana and
founded the Keita dynasty of Mali. The Susu moved back
south to Futa Jallon where they stayed until the period of
Fula jihads in the late 18th century which reduced them
to slaves or drove them to the coast of Guinea-Conakry
and southern Guinea-Bissau. On the coast the Susus acquired local customs and, to a certain extent, brought
the Islam they got from Futa Jallon. Today the coastal
Susu play an important role in commerce. See MALI;
FUTA JALLON.

                            -T-

TANDAS. This tiny concentration of Senegambian people is
    found to the northeast of Gadamael near the southern fron-
    tier with Guinea-Conakry.

TANGOMAUS. Meaning "tattooed men," they were African
slavers who were middlemen for the Portuguese and acculturated to the lançado life-style.

TARRAFAL. A notorious political prison located on the northern end of São Tiago in the Cape Verdean archipelago.
This prison camp was begun during the Portuguese fascist era in 1936 to house Communist Party members and
their sympathizers who were opposed to the rule of Salazar. As the nationalist wars began, the camp was filled
with Africans as well. Tarrafal had a particularly nasty
reputation for torture, brutality and death. Its extremely
isolated location made escape virtually impossible. In
1971 more than 100 PIDE agents arrived in Cape Verde
to infiltrate and arrest the PAIGC. Nationalists were
confined at the Tarrafal concelho prison or the work camp
of Chão Bom. Although politically important the overall
prison staff was about a dozen guards and administrators.
See POLICIA INTERNACIONAL.

TEKRUR. One of the earliest Islamized states of the western
Sudan from which the Fulas of Guinea-Bissau have originated. Tekrur appeared at, or about, the time of ancient
Ghana as early as the 3rd century A.D. and certainly no
later than the 6th century. The Tukulor peoples of Tekrur (Senegal) actively competed with Ghana for control of
the trans-Saharan trade. The Tukulor and the Fula, to
whom they are related, are members of the Atlantic sub-
family of the Niger-Congo language stock. Tekrur was
based on a trading and bureaucratic superstructure built
from traditional settled village political systems and subsistence agriculture. In the 8th and 9th centuries Tekrur
experienced significant growth and until the end of the
10th century Tekrur was a fully autonomous state on the
middle Senegal River valley and was about the equal of
Ghana, however in A.D. 990 Ghana conquered the Berber
trade center at Awdoghast and then forced Tekrur into a
tributary status. Between the late 10th century and the
mid 11th century Islamized Berber traders entered Tekrur
where they settled, married local women, and acquired
slaves. The admixture of Berber and Tukulor elements
resulted in the emergence of the Fula peoples who spread
throughout most of the sub-Saharan Sahel and savanna regions. The sedentary farmers and traders of Tukulor
stock became devout Muslims while the cattle-herding
Fula resulting from the Berber-Tukulor merger were
somewhat less Islamized yet they had a more North Af-

rican appearance. When the Almoravids sought to restore
their control of the trade lost to Ghana and avenge their
loss of Awdoghast, the leaders of Tekrur made an alliance with them in order to aid in the defeat of Ghana in
1076 thus permitting Tekrur to return to its independent
status until the late 13th century when it became a tributary state of expanding Mali. The Islamic traveler and
historian, Al-Idrisi visited Tekrur in 1153-54 and described it as a place of active trade. During its height,
Tekrur was linked to Marrakesh by an overland trade
route about 200 miles inland from the Atlantic Coast.

Although the first Moslems of Tekrur were the traders
and their slaves, the 11th century saw the incorporation
of Islam as the court religion of the Tekrur ruling class.
Many neighboring and subordinated peoples remained animists and even anti-Islamic including some of the early
cattle-herding Fulas. The formative empire of Mali was
first converted to Islam at a later period than Tekrur
usually considered to be 1050 when Barmandana of Mali
accepted this faith and established the Keita dynasty.   In
fact, Islam was spread to and through Mali by Dyula peoples (a Soninke group) who conducted east-west trade from
Tekrur under the Denianke dynastic line.   This east-west
trade became especially important in the 12th and 13th
centuries when the Empire of Mali (1230-1546) experienced
its greatest growth. A new Soninke ruling class came to
power in Tekrur in about 1250 briefly permitting Tekrur
to control Senegal until 1285 when it was brought under
the authority of the Malian ruler Sakura. Tekrur was
only under the direct control of Mali until 1350 when the
Malian representatives were deposed by the Wolof, thus
taking this state beyond the frontiers of Mali once again.
Tekrur, or more properly, Futa Toro, regained an independent status in 1520 at the time of Coli Tenguella (II)
and the line he established until 1893 when it was subju-
gated by the French. See FULA; COLI TENGUELLA;
MALI; FUTA JALLON; DIALONKE; DYULAS; FULA TORO;
SENEGAMBIANS.

TENGUELLA, COLI or KOOLI (Teengala, Tengela, Temala).
Fula leaders of the same name who led the Fula occupation of Futa Toro and Futa Jallon in the late 15th and
early portions of the 16th centuries. Apparently the sen-
ior Coli Tenguella came from Termes, Mauretania at the
end of an early period of Fula migration. In the 1490's
he defeated most Senegalese Wolof and portions of western Mali thereby establishing the Denianke (Denaanke)

dynasty (1490's-1775) in the Futa Toro plateau of Senegal.
Once he and his followers occupied the fertile flood plain
of the Senegal River he was proclaimed as the Sitatigui
(leader of the way) of the Futa Toro Denianke.   The existence of Futa Toro cut the western trade and communication links of the Empire of Mali which had become
important to the Portuguese as a source of gold and
slaves.

The visit of a Portuguese emissary of King João II in
about 1494 prompted Mali's Mansa (Emperor) Mamudi I
to complain about the attacks of Tenguella.   Conflict was
inevitable over such a strategic piece of territory and
Coli Tenguella was finally forced out of Futa Toro and
retreated to the southern plateau region of Futa Jallon
in Guinea Conakry which was also part of a generally declining Malian Empire.   Futa Jallon had been occupied by
Dialonke, Susu, and various Manding peoples as well as
some Fula before Coli Tenguella arrived, but it was he
who merged these various peoples into a new state which
was opposed to the rule of Mali, although one of his several wives was from the Malian ruling class.   Tenguella
organized local resistance to Mali in the late 15th century and in 1510 he and his followers returned to Futa
Toro.   In 1512 Coli Tenguella was killed in a battle at
Diara in trying to expand Futa Toro.   His assailant was
Amar, a general of Askia Muhammad of Songhai.   The
Fula warrior bands had acculturated and assimilated sufficient Manding (Malinke) peoples including some from
Guinea-Bissau that the Denianke dynasty continued until
1775.

Tenguella's son, Coli Tenguella (II), led the army after his father's death and continued to re-establish and
expand Futa Toro rule at the expense of the neighboring
Soninke and Wolof of Senegal, although an effort to expand in Guinea-Bissau was successfully resisted by the
Beafadas.   An attempt to take over the Bambuk goldfields
failed in 1534 and three years later Tenguella (II) was
killed.   The Denianke followers, however, proceeded to
enlarge their control in an area between the Sahel and
Futa Jallon.   The lineage of Coli Tenguella has not yet
been fully unraveled by historians who offer varied inter-
pretations of this man and his successors.   There may
have been a Coli Tenguella (III), who in alliance with
Manding fragments overthrew the Soninke chiefs of Futa
Toro in 1559 to perpetuate the Denianke line.   In any
case this early Denianke period saw the emergence of
sedentary Fula who began to dominante the Fula who remain as pastoralists.

During the Tenguella periods the Fula followers often
crossed over portions of eastern Guinea-Bissau and brought
in new Fula people. Under the influence of the Tenguellas
the Fulas were stimulated to make more permanent set-
tlements. As a result of these movements of the Fula,
a population of Fulacundas, or non-Muslim, semi-seden-
tary cattle herders, was generated from Fula and Manding
peoples already living in the Gabu kingdom of Guinea-
Bissau. In the 18th and 19th centuries the Fulacunda
population of Guinea-Bissau increased even more considerably. See also FULA; FUTA TORO; FUTA JALLON;
DIALONKES; GABU; SONGHAI; MALI.

TIMENES. This very small Senegambian group is located
south of Gabu and was isolated from other Senegambians
after Mandingo expansion.

TIRAMAKHAN (TIRAMANG) TRAORE. A general of Sundiata
Keita (d. 1255 A. D.) of Mali. Tiramakhan entered the
Senegambian region to crush the revolt of a Wolof king
against Sundiata and to strengthen the control of Mali after
it defeated the Susu people under Sumanguru in 1235.
Thus, at some time in the mid 13th century Tiramakhan's
control was consolidated and he married Nyaaling, who
was perhaps a Mandingo of the local area before the arrival of Tiramakhan's forces. His presence laid the
foundation for the Mandingo state of Gabu (ca. 1250-1867).
Sources are unclear as to the exact genealogical relationship between Tiramakhan and the first Gabu king, Sama
Koli (Kelemankoto Baa Saane) but it appears that he was
either the son or grandson of Tiramakhan in a royal line
of matrilineal descent. See GABU; MALI; MANDING.

TOMAS. This very small Senegambian group is located just
east of Gabu. See SENEGAMBIAN.

TRISTAO, NUNO. Portuguese navigator and captain of an
armed caravel who, along with Antão Gonçalves, captured
a dozen Africans (Moors) at Cape Blanc (north coast of
Maoretania) in 1441 and returned to Portugal with them
and a cargo of gold dust. Tristão directly, personally,
engaged in slave capturing, killing those who resisted.
One of the twelve captives was of noble birth. In 1443-
44 Tristão reached Arquim, seizing 29 men and women.
Merchants soon grasped the idea of large and easy profits.
In 1444 Tristão decided to outfit a major raiding expedition of six ships under Lançarote and Gil Eannes thus

initiating one of the earliest European-inspired slave raids
on the African coast.   In 1444 Tristão was the first European beyond the Mauretanian desert reaching the mouths
of the Senegal, Gambia, and Salum rivers thinking they
were branches of the Nile.   In 1446 Tristão reached the
area of Bissau and Bolama but in the following year he
was killed in the Bissagos islands while trying to claim
them for Portugal.   See G. EANNES; A. GONÇALVES.

-U-

UNIAO DAS POPULAÇOES DAS ISLAS DO CABO VERDE
    (UPICV).   The UPICV was led by Jose Leitão da Graca
    and his wife Maria Querido Leitão da Graca who is termed
    the Secretary General.   The UPICV sought to preserve
    the Cape Verdean "personality" in its program of limited
    social transformation.   Apparently the UPICV was first
    formed in 1959 in the United States.   Following the Lis-
    bon coup the UPICV supported the UDCV position of a
    referendum on unity with Guinea-Bissau charging that the
    PAIGC would make Cape Verde "a Soviet military base."
    In the mid 1970's the UPICV sprouted certain Maoist
    terminology and on May 23, 1975, renamed itself the
    Peoples Liberation Front of Cape Verde.   Following the
    independence of Cape Verde on July 5, 1975, the central
    leaders of the UPICV were exiled to Portugal although the
    UPICV claimed responsibility for a small anti-PAIGC dis-
    turbance in São Vincente in August 1975.

UNIAO DEMOCRATICA DA GUINE (UDG).   This small group
    emerged in the late 1950's and merged with the UDCV
    and the UPG to form the MLGCV of Dakar in 1959.   It
    was from such groups as the UDG that FLING emerged
    in 1962.   See FLING.

UNIAO DEMOCRATICA DAS MULHERES (DA GUINE E CABO
    VERDE) (UDEMU).   UDEMU joined the PAIGC in mid-
    1960.   See WOMEN.

UNIAO DEMOCRATICA DE CABO VERDE (UDCV or UDC).
    The UDCV emerged in the late 1950's to join with the
    UDG and the UPG in 1959 to form the MLGCV which ul-
    timately led to the formation of FLING in 1962.   Through
    most of the 1960's the UDCV essentially did not exist.
    In 1974, following the Lisbon coup d'etat some former
    UDCV members supported the idea of General Spinola for

a referendum of the question of unity with Guinea-Bissau and on the possibility of a separate independence for Cape Verde and a possible federation with Portugal in order to prevent PAIGC control of the Islands. The most prominent leaders of the UDCV were João Baptista Monteiro, a leading Cape Verdean lawyer and rich merchant, and Jorge Fonseca also with extensive financial interests in the Islands. Monteiro and Fonseca helped to organize some anti-PAIGC activities mainly in São Vincente. Both were exiled after July 5, 1975. There are some American supporters of the UDCV under the banner of the Juridicial Congress whose leaders, Aguinaldo Veiga, a Cape Verdean lawyer who served colonialism in Angola and Roy Teixeira and his son. Some American Cape Verdeans declared independence in Cape Verde for the UDCV and called for an overthrow of the PAIGC from a Boston hotel rally in 1975.

UNIAO DOS NATURAIS DA GUINE PORTUGUESA (UNGP). Sought independence without revolution. UNGP leader Benjamin Pinto Bull went to Lisbon in July 1963 for negotiations which failed and prompted UNGP unity with FLING a year after its formation. Benjamin Pinto Bull's brother, Jaime, was made Vice-President of the UNGP and was made FLING President after 1966. See BULL, B.; BULL, J.

UNIAO GERAL DOS ESTUDANTES DA AFRICA NEGRA (SOB DOMINAÇAO PORTUGUESA) (UGEAN). UGEAN was formed in Europe for militant nationalist students by the PAIGC and the MPLA of Angola.

UNIAO GERAL DOS TRABALHADORES DA GUINE-BISSAU (UGTGB). UGTGB emerged in 1963 in association with FLING and a rival of the PAIGC's workers' affiliate the UNTG which had been formed in 1959.

UNIAO NACIONAL DOS TRABALHADORES DA GUINE (UNTG). Founded in 1959 and was affiliated with the PAIGC. In 1961 its first statutes were drafted with Luis Cabral acting as the Secretary General. The UNTG is currently headed by Jose Pereira and the organization functions to unify the small Guinean working class. Until the end of the war the UNTG functioned in clandestinity. However, the UNTG growth is slowed by limited industrialization and low working class consciousness. On May 1, 1976 (May Day), the Comissão Organizadora dos Sindicatos

Caboverdeanos (COSC) or the Organizing Commission of
Cape Verdean Unionists was formed as a complement to
the UNTG.

UNIAO POPULAR PARA LIBERTAÇAO DA GUINE (UPLG).
The UPLG was formed in 1961 and then merged with
FLING in 1962.

UNION DES RESSORTISSANTS DE LA GUINEE PORTUGAISE
(URGP). The URGP was formed in 1963 and became
aligned with FLING in 1964.

UNITED NATIONS. International organization formed in 1945
for humanitarian and peace-keeping purposes. On December
14, 1960, the 1514th meeting of the General Assembly
passed a resolution on global decolonization which gave
great support to the anti-colonial and nationalist movements in Africa. In 1961 the PAIGC submitted considerable documentation to the United Nations regarding the
effects of Portuguese colonialism. On April 2-8, 1972,
a special United Nations team entered Guinea-Bissau as
guests of the PAIGC. As a consequence of this trip the
special committee on decolonization announced, on April
13, 1972, that the PAIGC "is the only and authentic representative" of the people of Guinea. Subsequent resolu-
tions in the U.N. General Assembly and U.N. Security
Council reaffirmed the "right of self-determination and
independence" in November 1972 thus isolating Portugal's
position and strengthening the PAIGC. After the PAIGC
declared the independence of Guinea in September 1973
the United Nations General Assembly adopted a resolution
on October 22, 1973, condemning Portugal's continued occupation and then gave its recognition to the new Republic
of Guinea-Bissau on November 2, 1973. The Republic
was admitted to the United Nations as a full member on
September 17, 1974. Just prior to the negotiated independence for Cape Verde, the United Nations Special Committee on Decolonization undertook a fact-finding mission
of the Islands to determine its health, financial, educational, and developmental needs. The Republic of Cape
Verde officially joined the U.N. on September 17, 1975.

URZELLA. This plant dye (Litmus roccella) has frequently
been an export of Cape Verde. Urzella and indigo (In-
digofera sp.) were cultivated to revive the stagnant economy but the commerce in these plant dyes was controlled
by the British. While urzella and indigo were used to

dye Cape Verdean textiles, they never were of great significance as a cash crop and were essentially replaced
by coffee production.

USODIMARE   see   CADAMOSTA; MALFANTE

-V-

VIEIRA, JOAO BERNARDO "NINO" (1939-   ). President of
the Peoples National Assembly, Commander in Chief of
the Armed Forces.   Vieira was born in Bissau and was
an electrician by trade.   Vieira joined the PAIGC in 1960
and in the following year he attended the Party school in
Conakry led by Amílcar Cabral.   From 1961 to 1964
Vieira was the political Commissioner in the Catio region
in southern Guinea-Bissau.   Having received advanced
military training in Nanking, China, Vieira was made
military head of the entire south front in 1964 when he
was also made a member of the PAIGC Political Bureau
as a result of the First Party Congress in that year.   In
1965 he became the Vice-President of the War Council
and he continued his work as military head of the entire
south front.   From 1967 to 1970 he was the ranking member of the Political Bureau assigned to the south front and
after 1970 he held the full national responsibility for military operations on the War Council.   In 1971 he became
a member of CEL and subsequently the Secretary for the
PAIGC Permanent Secretariat.   Following independence
he became the Commander in Chief of all of the Armed
Forces as well as presiding over the Peoples National
Assembly.   In August 1978, Vieira was appointed Prime
Minister of Guinea Bissau following the accidental death
of Francisco Mendes in July of that year.

VIEIRA, OSVALDO "AMBROSIO DJASSI" (1938-1973). Vieira
joined the PAIGC in 1959, a few years after it was
founded.   He received advanced military training in both
Nanking, China and in the Soviet Union and became an
important military commander in the northern region of
Guinea-Bissau.   He was also head of the PAIGC military
training program which was first based in Algeria.   Later
he was a member of the PAIGC War Council and Inspec-
tor General of its military.   After his early death of
cancer in 1973 he became an established national hero.
Vieira has no relation to João Vieira.

-W-

WEST AFRICAN CROPS. Most of the rise of the Sudanic
    states may be attributed to the varied and abundant plants
    native to that region. Grains include fonio, sorghum and
    millet; some areas grow the small root tuber known as
    Guinea yam, and a common leafy vegetable element of
    the diet is okra. Watermelons and calabash gourds are
    widespread. Sudanic crops with important commercial
    usages are cotton, oil palm, and sesame. The condi-
    ment, kola, is also of some regional significance as a
    trade item. See MILLET; FONIO; OIL PALM.

WOMEN. Women were quite active in the liberation struggle
    and are now represented in the post-independence govern-
    ment. There are no restrictions for women being in the
    PAIGC, except neither a woman nor a man in a polygy-
    nous union is permitted, as the institution of plural mar-
    riages is not favored by the PAIGC. During the growth
    of the PAIGC's liberated zones, divorce was made easier
    for women, especially those of Muslim union who had no
    right to divorce. Marriages are only permitted by joint
    consent and forced marriage or child marriage is opposed.
    The institution of bridewealth is also curbed. In general
    the position of women has been greatly improved given
    the predominant traditions which were widely based on
    male supremacy. Now the rights of women are protected
    by law. For example, children born out of wedlock must
    be supported by their father under penalty by law and the
    status of "illegitimacy" has been legally abolished. The
    numbers of women in industry are increasing and this
    also adds to their freedom. Since independence, March
    8, is now observed as International Women's Day. With-
    in the PAIGC about 12 percent of the regular members
    are women and there is one woman member on the Exec-
    utive Committee of the Struggle and there are many wo-
    men members of the Supreme Committee of the Struggle
    and in the Peoples National Assembly. Women are com-
    monly found in the health and education services where
    such possibilities barely existed during colonial rule.
    During the armed struggle UDEMA (Democratic Union of
    Guinean Women) was created to assist in the liberation
    and mobilization of women. UDEMA was replaced by the
    Commissão Feminina (Women's Commission) toward the
    close of the war, but the preoccupation with military af-
    fairs and resistance to change by male chauvinists ulti-
    mately resulted in the failure of the Commissão Feminina

under the leadership of Carmen Pereira.   Since independence efforts to organize women have resumed under COM
(Commissão da Organização das Mulheres) to address
special needs of women and to incorporate them more
fully into national reconstruction.   A number of women
made distinguished contributions during the nationalist
war, of them are Dr. Maria Boal director of the Pilot
School and Friendship Institute, Carmen Pereira, the
highest ranking women in the PAIGC, and Ernestina Silla,
exemplary heroine.   Articles 13, 16, and 25 of the Constitution of the Republic of Guinea-Bissau provide for
legal, social, and electoral equality of men and women.
See C. PEREIRA; E. SILLA; CONSTITUTION.

BIBLIOGRAPHY

Introduction

The preparation of any bibliography is always a challenge for it is difficult to determine what to exclude without losing a vital or unique reference, and it is hard to know what to include without being repetitious. These questions are more difficult when the bulk of the literature on a given topic is in a foreign language and when one comprehensive bibliography already exists. Consequently I refer the reader to the excellent bibliography by McCarthy for one of the most comprehensive sources of works on Guinea-Bissau and Cape Verde. A number of other bibliographies will assist the researcher in probing other areas. With these basic references included I have taken some license in reducing some of the overall volume of possible sources. Thus I make no claim to have compiled an all-inclusive collection of bibliographic references. Instead my orientation was to include the bulk of what has been written in English as this would be most likely to be acquired and read by English-speaking researchers. However, there are numerous and important aspects of Guinea-Bissau and Cape Verde which have only been discussed or recorded in Portuguese or other languages. While there are significant numbers of citations in languages other than English I felt this justified by the sparsity of English sources.

The relatively small sizes of Guinea-Bissau and Cape Verde as well as the colonial monopoly on trade and information are, in part, responsible for the deficiency in reports in languages other than Portuguese. The main exceptions to this are those areas where the two nations were in relation to the wider world, specifically in slavery, foreign trade, and with the recent nationalist war and its leader, Amílcar Cabral so that sources in English are rather numerous on these topics. The outline of the bibliographic materials is as follows:

1 Bibliographies

2 Periodicals Relating to Guinea-Bissau and Cape Verde

3 General References: Statistical

4 General References: Historical/Legal/Political

5 History of Guinea-Bissau and Cape Verde

6 Physical Features, Geography, Flora and Fauna

7 Anthropology and Ethnology

8 Language, Literature, and Crioulo Culture

9 Health and Education

10 Agriculture, Economics, and Development

11 By and About Amílcar Cabral

12 On National Liberation: Including PAIGC and United
   Nations Documents

1 BIBLIOGRAPHIES

Bell, Aubrey F. G. Portuguese Bibliography, New York, 1922.

Berman, Sanford. "African Liberation Movements: A Preliminary Bibliography," Ufahamu, III, 1 (Spring), 1972.

Bibliográfia científica da Junta de Investigações do Ultramar. Lisbon, 1960.

Boletim de bibliografia portuguesa. Biblioteca Nacional, Lisbon.

Chilcote, Ronald H. "Amílcar Cabral: A Bio-Bibliography of His Life and Thought, 1925-1973," Africana Journal, V. 4 (1974): 289-307.

_____. Emerging Nationalism in Portuguese Africa: A Bibliography of Documentary Ephemera Through 1965, Stanford, CA: Hoover Institution, 1969.

Duignan, Peter (ed.). Guide to Research and Reference Works on Sub-Saharan Africa, Hoover Institution Press: Stanford, 1972.

_____, and Gann, L. H. Colonialism in Africa 1870-1960, vol. 5: A bibliographical guide to colonialism in sub-Saharan Africa. London: Cambridge University Press, 1973.

Figueiredo, Jaime de. "Bibliografia caboverdeana: subsidios para uma ordenação sistematica," Cabo Verde: Boletim de Propaganda e Informação. V (49)31; (50)31; (54)31; (56)37; 1953-4.

Flores, Michel. "A Bibliographic Contribution to the Study of Portuguese Africa (1965-1972)," Current Bibliography on African Affairs, VII, 2 (1974): 116-37.

123

Gibson, Mary Jane. Portuguese Africa: A Guide to Official
     Publications, Library of Congress, Reference Department,
     Washington, D. C. , 1967.

Gonçalves, José Júlio. "Bibliográfia antropológica do ultra-
     mar português," Boletim Geral das Colónias, (1961):
     281-90, 335-41, 431-71, 483-501.

Kornegay, Francis A. , Jr. "A Bibliographic Memorial to
     Amílcar Cabral: Selected Survey of Resources on the
     Struggle in Guinea-Bissau," Ufahamu, III, 3 (Winter
     1973): 152-59.

McCarthy, Joseph M. Guinea-Bissau and Cape Verde Islands:
     A Comprehensive Bibliography, Garland: New York,
     1977.

Matthews, Daniel G. "African Bibliography Today: Selected
     and Current Bibliographical Tools for African Studies,
     1967-1968," Current Bibliography on African Affairs (No-
     vember 1968).

Rogers, Francis Millet and David T. Haberly. Brazil, Por-
     tugal and Other Portuguese-Speaking Lands: A List of
     Books Primarily in English, Cambridge, MA: Harvard
     University Press, 1968.

Ryder, A. F. C. Materials for West African History in
     Portuguese Archives, London: Athlone Press, 1965.

Rydings, H. A. The Bibliographies of West Africa, Ibadan:
     Ibadan University Press, 1961.

Tenreiro, Francisco. "Bibliografia geografica da Guiné,"
     Garcia de Orta, II, 1(1954): 97-134.

U. S. Library of Congress. A List of References on the Por-
     tuguese Colonies in Africa (Angola, Cape Verde Islands,
     Mozambique, Portuguese Guinea, São Thome and Prin-
     cipe), Washington, D. C. , 1942.

2 PERIODICALS RELATING TO
GUINEA-BISSAU AND CAPE VERDE

Africa News. A Twice-Weekly Service for Broadcast and
     Print. Durham, N. C.

Afrique-Asie.   Paris.

O Arquipélago; jornal semanário.   Praia, 1962+.

Blufo.   Mimeographed journal for the liberated areas.   Conakry: Partido Africano da Independência da Guiné e Cabo
Verde.

Boletim Cultural da Guiné Portuguesa.   Organ of the Centro
de Estudos da Guiné Portuguesa, Lisbon, 1946+.

Boletim da Sociedade de Geographia de Lisbõa.   Lisbon.

Boletim Geral das Colónias.   Lisbon.

Boletim oficial da Guiné Portuguesa.   Bolama & Bissau:
weekly, 1880+.

Boletim oficial de Cabo Verde.   Praia: weekly, 1842+.

Boletim trissemanal da Agencia Noticiosa da Guine-Bissau
(A. N. G.).

Cabo Verde; Boletim de propaganda e informação.   Praia:
monthly, 1949-1964.

Cape Verdean News.   New Bedford, Mass. , formerly the
Cape Verdean of Lynn, Mass.

Ecos da Guiné: Boletim de informação e de estatística.
Bissau, 1951+.

Facts and Reports.   Press cuttings on Angola, Mozambique,
Guinea-Bissau, Portugal, and Southern Africa, edited by
the Angola Comité, Amsterdam.

Libertação.   Mimeographed journal for the liberated areas.
Conakry: Partido Africano da Independência da Guiné e
Cabo Verde.

Mundo Português.   Lisbon.

Nõ Pintcha.   Official PAIGC publication in Guinea-Bissau
since independence; three times weekly.

Nôs Luta.   Orgão de Informação da Radio Voz de S. Vincente.

Novo Jornal de Cabo Verde. Orgão do Departmento de
   Comunicação Social, Praia.

Objective: Justice. Quarterly magazine covering United Na-
   tions activity against Apartheid, Racial Discrimination and
   Colonialism, published by the United Nations Office of
   Public Information in furtherance of that objective.

PAIGC (Partido Africano da Independência da Guiné e Cabo
   Verde). Ediçao dos Servicos Cultarais do Conselho Superior da Luta.

PAIGC Actualités. Bulletin d'Information édité par la Commission d'Information et Propagande du Comité Central
   du PAIGC, Conakry; monthly, 1969-1974.

PAIGC Actualités. LSM Information Center, Richmond, B.C.,
   Canada; quarterly English edition.

PAIGC Actualités: La vie et la lutte en Guinée et Cap-Vert.
   Monthly; Nos. 21-36, 38 (17 numbers in all); Conakry:
   September, 1970-February, 1972.

Portugal. Anglo-Portuguese Publications.

Portugal em Africa. Lisbon.

Portuguese and Colonial Bulletin. Anti-colonial bulletin published
   by K. Shingler, London, Eng. (during the colonial wars).

Tchuba Newsletter. The American Committee for Cape Verde,
   Inc., Boston.

Terra Nova. Orgão Cristão de Cabo Verde, Composto e im-
   presso nas oficinas da Imprensa Nacional de Cabo Verde.

Tricontinental Bulletin. Published in Spanish, English and
   French by the Executive Secretariat of the Organization
   of Solidarity of the Peoples of Africa, Asia and Latin
   America, Habana, Cuba.

Unidade e Luta. Orgão de Informação da Comissão Nacional
   de Cabo Verde do P. A. I. G. C.

3 GENERAL REFERENCE WORKS: STATISTICAL

Agência Geral do Ultramar. Portugal Overseas Provinces:

Facts and Figures, Lisbon, 1965.

_____. Províncias ultramarinas portuguesas: dados infor-
mativos, Lisbon, 1962-66.

Anuário da Guiné Portuguesa. Lisbon: Sociedade Industrial
de Tipografia, 1946+.

Anuário estatístico. Annuaire statistique. Lisbon: Tipografia Portuguesa, 1947+.

Anuário estatístico. II. Províncias ultramarinas, 1969.
Lisbon: Instituto Nacional de Estatistica, 1971.

Brito, Eduíno. "Guiné Portuguesa--Censo da população não
civilizada de 1950," Boletim Cultural da Guiné Portuguesa, VII, 28 (October 1952): 725-56.

Cape Verde Islands. Secção de Estatistua Geral. Trimestral;
Lisbon.

Correa, Antonio A. Mendes. Aspectos demográficos do Ar-
quipelago do Cabo Verde, Garcia de Orta, I, 1(1953):
3-15.

Curtin, Philip D. The Atlantic Slave Trade: A Census,
Madison, Wis. : University of Wisconsin Press, 1969.

Heisel, Donald Francis. "The Demography of the Portuguese
Territories: Angola, Mozambique and Portuguese Gui-
nea," In W. I. Brass et al. (eds.), The Demography of
Tropical Africa, Princeton University Press, Princeton,
N. J. , 1968. pp. 440-465.

Lima, José Joaquim Lopes de. Prospecto estatístico-econo-
mico da Provincia de Cabo Verde, Lisbon, 1875.

_____. "Sobre a statistica das ilahs de Cabo Verde e
suas dependencias na Guiné Portuguesa," In his Ensaios
sobre a statistica das possessões portuguesas, vol. 1,
Lisbon, 1844.

PAIGC. "La Republique de Guinée-Bissau en chiffres,"
Commissariat d'Etat a l'Economie et aux Finances, Conakry, 1974.

PAIGC. "Sur la création de l'Assemblée Nationale Populaire

en Guinée (Bissau). Résultats et bases des élections générales réalisés dans les regions libérées en 1972, Conakry. " 1973.

Provincia da Guiné--Censo da população de 1950. 2 vols., Imprensa Nacional, Bissau, 1951.

Servicos Aduaneiros. Setimo recenseamento geral da população da Colónia de Cabo Verde em 1940, 3 vols., Imprensa Nacional, Praia, 1945-48.

Tyack, David B. "Cape Verdean Immigration to the United States. " Unpublished bachelor's thesis, Harvard College, 1952.

Vieira, Ruy Alvaro. "Alguns aspectos demográficos dos Bijagós da Guiné," Boletim Cultural da Guiné Portuguesa, X(1955): 23-34.

4 GENERAL REFERENCES:
HISTORICAL/LEGAL/POLITICAL

Abshire, David M. and Michael A. Samuels (eds.). Portuguese Africa: A Handbook, New York: Praeger, 1969.

Agência Geral do Ultramar. Cabo Verde: pequena monografia. Lisbon, 1961.

_____. Guiné. Lisbon, 1967.

_____. Guiné: pequena monografia. Lisbon, 1961.

_____. Les Îles de Cap Vert. Lisbon, 1927.

Angola Comite. Portugal and NATO, 3rd edition, Amsterdam, 1972.

Anon. Liberation Struggle in Portuguese Colonies. New Delhi: Peoples Publishing House, 1970.

Anon. "Portugal's African Wars," Conflict Studies 34(March 1973).

Anon. War on Three Fronts: The Fight Against Portuguese Colonialism. Committee for freedom in Mozambique, Angola, and Guinea, 1971.

Axelson, Eric. Congo to Cape: Early Portuguese Explorers,
    New York: Barnes and Noble, 1973.

_____ . Portugal and the Scramble for Africa, 1875-1891,
    Johannesberg: Witwatersrand University Press, 1967.

Barbosa, Honorio Jose. O processo criminal e civil no
    Julgado Instructor e no Tribunal Privativo dos Indígenas,
    Bissau: Imprensa Nacional, 1947.

Beazley, Charles Raymond. Prince Henry the Navigator,
    (1394-1460). G. P. Putnam, New York, 1895.

Blake, J. W. (ed.). Europeans in West Africa 1460-1560,
    2 vols. 1942.

Boxer, C[harles] R. Four Centuries of Portuguese Expan-
    sion, 1415-1825, Berkeley and Los Angeles: University
    of California Press, 1972.

_____ . Portuguese Society in the Tropics, Madison and
    Milwaukee: University of Wisconsin Press, 1965.

_____ . Race Relations in the Portuguese Colonial Empire
    1415-1825, Oxford, 1963.

Caetano, Marcello. Colonizing Traditions, Principles and
    Methods of the Portuguese, Lisbon: Agência Geral do
    Ultramar, 1951.

_____ . Portugal's Reasons for Remaining in the Over-
    seas Provinces, Lisbon, 1970.

Caroço, Jorge F. Velez. Relatório anual do governador da
    Guine, 1921-1922, Coimbra, 1923.

Carreira, António Augusto Peixoto. Cabo Verde. 1972.

_____ . Guiné Portuguesa. (2 vols.) Lisbon, 1954.

Carson, Patricia. Materials for West African History in the
    Archives of Belgium and Holland, London: Athlone
    Press, 1962.

Chilcote, Ronald H. Emerging Nationalism in Portuguese
    Africa: Documents, Stanford, CA: Hoover Institution,
    1972.

_____. Portuguese Africa, Englewood Cliffs, N. J. : Prentice-Hall, 1967.

Cipolla, C. M. Guns and Sails in the Early Phase of European Expansion (1400-1700). London, 1965.

Conselho de Inspeccão de Produtos de Exportação. Regulamento. Aprovado por Portaria numero 139, de 23 de dezembro de 1935. Bolama: Imprensa Nacional, 1936.

Conselho do Govêrno da Guiné Portuguesa. Acta. Bissau, 1919+.

Conselho do Govêrno das Ilhas de Cabo Verde. Acta. Praia: Imprensa Nacional, 1917+.

Conselho Legislativo. Actas do sessões. Bissau, 1925+.

Corpo de Policia de Segurança Publica. Regulamento, 1956 maio 12. Praia: Imprensa Nacional, 1956.

Corrêa, António A. Mendes. Ultramar Portuguès. II. Ilhas de Cabo Verde. Lisbon: Agência Geral do Ultramar, 1954.

Cortesão, Jaime. Os portugueses em Africa. Lisbon: Portugália Editora, 1968.

Duarte, Fausto Castilho. Anuario da Guiné Portuguesa, 1946-1948. Lisbon: Agência Geral das Colonias, 1948.

_____. "A libertação de Guiné Portuguesa pela carta de lei de 1879," Boletim Cultural da Guiné Portuguesa, VII, 28 (October 1952): 789-832.

Duffy, James. Portugal in Africa. Penguin Books, Baltimore, 1962.

_____. Portuguese Africa. Cambridge, Mass. , 1961.

Duncan, T. Bentley. Atlantic Islands: Madeira, the Azores, and the Cape Verdes in Seventeenth-Century Commerce and Navigation, Chicago: University of Chicago, 1972.

Ellis, Alfred Burdon. West African Islands. London: Chapman and Hall, 1885.

Ermitão, Marcial Pemental.   "As Ilhas de Cabo Verde,"
    Boletim da Sociedade Luso-Africana do Rio de Janeiro.
    1934.

Estatuto da Província da Guiné.   Lisbon: Agência Geral do
    Ultramar, 1955.

Estatuto dos indígenas portugueses das províncias da Guiné,
    Angola e Mocambique.   Lisbon, 1954.

Estatuto político-administrativa de Cabo Verde.   Lisbon:
    Agência Geral do Ultramar, 1964.

Estatuto político-administrativa da Guiné.   Lisbon: Agência
    Geral do Ultramar, 1963.

Estatuto político-administrativa da Guiné.   Lisbon: Agência
    Geral do Ultramar, 1964.

Estatuto político-administrativa da Guiné.   Ultramar, II,
    (1973): 120-38.

Estatuto político-administrativa da Província da Guiné,
    542/72.   Lisbon: December 22, 1972.

Fage, J. D.   "Slavery and the Slave Trade in the Context of
    West African History," Journal of African History, # 3
    (1969).

Fargues, G.   "Guinée-Bissao et archipels portugais," In
    Année Africaine, 1968.   Paris: A. Pédone, 1970,
    pp. 259-60.

Ferreira, Eduardo de Sousa.   Portuguese Colonialism from
    South Africa to Europe.   Germany: Druckerei Horst
    Ahlbrecht, 1972.

_____ .   Portuguese Colonialism in Africa: the end of an
    era.   Paris: Unesco Press, 1974.

Ferro, Mário A. Almeida and M. Saldanha.   Programa da
    Colónia de Cabo Verde.   Lisbon: Ministério das Colón-
    ias, 1936.

First, Ruth.   Portugal's Wars in Africa, London: Christian
    Action Publications Ltd. , 1972.

Gibson, Richard. African Liberation Movements. Contemporary Struggles Against White Minority Rule, London: Oxford University Press, 1972.

Great Britain. Foreign Office. Historical Section. Cape Verde Islands. London: His Majesty's Stationery Office, 1920.

_____. Portuguese Guinea. London: His Majesty's Stationery Office, 1920.

Hakluyt, Richard. Voyages and Discoveries. Baltimore: Penguin Books, 1972 (first published in 1589).

Hammond, Richard J. Portugal and Africa, 1815-1910: A Study in Uneconomic Imperialism. Stanford, CA: Stanford University Press, 1966.

_____. "Race Attitudes and Policies in Portuguese Africa in the Nineteenth and Twentieth Centuries," Race. January 1968.

Humbaraci, Arslan and Nicole Muchnik. Portugal's African Wars. N.Y.: Third World Press, 1973.

Lacerda, João Cesário de. Relatório do Governo Geral da Província de Cabo Verde. Lisbon, 1901.

Lança, Joaquim da Graça Correia. Relatório da Provincia da Guiné Portugueza referido no anno economica de 1888-1889, Lisbon: Imprensa Nacional, 1890.

Lavradio, Marques do. Portugal em Africa depois de 1851. Lisbon: Agência Geral das Colonias, 1936.

Lawrence, A. W. Trade Castles and Forts of West Africa. 1963.

Livermore, Harold. A New History of Portugal, Cambridge, 1966.

Luttrel, A. "Slavery and Slaving in the Portuguese Atlantic to about 1500," In The Trans-Atlantic Slave Trade from West Africa. Edinburgh: Centre of African Studies, University of Edinburgh, 1965.

Markov, P. "West African History in German Archives,"

Journal of the Historical Society of Nigeria. (December 1963).

Marques, A. H. de Oliveira. History of Portugal, New York (2 vols.), 1972-3.

Mello, Guedes Brandão de. Relatório do Governo Geral da Província de Cabo Verde, 1890, Lisbon: Imprensa Nacional, 1891.

Minter, William. Portuguese Africa and the West. Baltimore: Penguin Books, 1972.

Miranda, Nuno de. Compreensão de Cabo Verde. Lisbon, 1963.

Moreira, Adriano. Portugal's Stand in Africa, New York: University Publishers, 1962.

Mota, Avelino Teixeira da. Guiné Portuguesa. 2 vols. ; Lisbon: Agência Geral do Ultramar, 1954.

Nielson, Waldemar A. African Battleline: American Policy Choices in Southern Africa. New York: Harper and Row, 1965.

Nogueira, Franco. The United Nations and Portugal. A Study of Anti-Colonialism. London: Tandem, 1964.

Political and Administrative Statute of the Province of Cabo Verde. Lisbon: Agência Geral do Ultramar, 1963.

Prestage, E. The Portuguese Pioneers, New York: Barnes and Noble, 1967.

Reade, Winwood. The African Sketch Book. 2 vols. ; London: Smith, 1873.

Roberts, George. The Four Voyages of Captain George Roberts; Being a Series of Uncommon Events, Which Befell Him in a Voyage to the Islands of the Canaries, Cape de Verde, and Barbadoes, from which He Was Bound to the Coast of Guiney. London: A. Bettenworth, 1726.

Rodney, Walter. A History of the Upper Guinea Coast, 1545-1800, New York: Oxford University Press, 1970.

Rodrigues, M. M. Sarmento. No governo da Guiné. Lisbon, 1954.

Salazar, António de Oliveira. H. E. Professor Oliveira Salazar, Prime Minister of Portugal, Broadcast on 12 August, 1963, Declaration on Overseas Policy, Lisbon: Secreteriado Nacional da Informação, 1960.

_____. "Policy in Africa," Vital Speeches, XXXIV (March 15, 1968): 325-28.

Serrão, Joaquim V. História breve da historiografia portuguesa. Lisbon, 1962.

Serrão, Joel (ed.). Dicionario de Historia de Portugal, Lisbon (4 vols.), 1963-70.

Spínola, António de. Portugal e o futuro. Lisbon: Arcadia, 1974.

Steeber, Horst. "The European Slave Trade and the Feudal Mode of Production on the West African Slave Coast," Ethnographische-Archaeologische Zeitschrift, #4, 1969.

Teixeira da Mota, A. Guiné Portuguesa. (2 vols.) Lisbon, 1954.

União Nacional de Guiné. Guiné--Ano XVI da revolução nacional, Bissau, 1943.

United States. Department of State. Portuguese Guinea. Washington, D. C., 1966.

Vasconcelos, Ernesto Júlio de Carvalho e. As colónias portuguesas, 2d edition; Lisbon, 1904.

_____. Guiné portuguesa. Lisbon: Tipografia da Cooperativa Militar, 1917.

Venter, Al J. Africa at War, Old Greenwich, CT: The Devin-Adair Company, 1974.

Whitaker, Paul M. "The Revolutions of 'Portuguese' Africa," Journal of Modern African Studies, VIII, 1 (April 1970): 15-35.

5 HISTORY OF GUINEA-BISSAU AND CAPE VERDE

Alexis de Saint-Lô.   Relation du voyage au Cap Verd.   Paris,
    1637.

Almada, André Alvares de.   Relação ou descripção de Guinée,
    Lisbon, 1733.

Almeida, J. B. P.   Exploraçao da Senegambia Portuguesa.
    Lisbon, 1878.

Andrade, António Alberto de.   "História breve da Guiné Por-
    tuguesa," Ultramar, VIII, 4 (April-June 1968):   7-56.

Andrade, Elisa.   The Cape Verde Islands from Slavery to
    Modern Times.   Dakar: U. N. African Institute for Eco-
    nomic Development and Planning, May 1973.

Azurara, Gomes Eannes.   Discovery and Conquest of Guine
    (2 vols.) ed. and trans. E. Porestage and C. R. Beazley.
    London, 1896-99.

Barcellos, Christiano José de Senna.   Subsídios para a his-
    tória de Cabo Verde e Guiné, 7 vols. ; Lisbon, 1899-1913.

Barreto, Honório Pereira.   Memória sobre o estado actual
    de Senegâmbia Portugueza, causas de sua decadencia, e
    meios de a fazer prosperar.   Lisbon, 1843.   Reprint
    edition, Bissau, 1947.

Barreto, João.   História da Guine, 1418-1918.   Lisbon, 1938.

Barros, João de.   Chronicles of the Voyages of Cadamosto.
    Lisbon, 1937.

Barros, Simão.   Origens da Colónia de Cabo Verde.   Lisbon,
    n. d.

Beaver, P.   African memoranda.   Relative to an attempt to
    establish a British settlement on the island of Bulama.
    1805.   New York: Humanities Press, 1968.

Bénézet, A.   Relation de la côte de la Guinée.   4th ed. ,
    London, 1788.

_____.   Some Historical Account of Guinea.   Philadelphia,
    1771.

Brooks, George E. "Bolama as a Prospective Site for American Colonization in the 1820's and 1830's," Boletim Cultural da Guiné Portuguesa, XXVIII (January 1973): 5-22.

Carreira, António Augusto Peixoto. "Alguns aspectos da ad-
ministração publica em Cabo Verde no século XVIII,"
Boletim Cultural da Guiné Portuguesa, XXVII, 105 (January 1972): 123-204.

_____. "Aspectos históricos da evolução do Islamismo na
Guiné Portuguesa," Boletim Cultural da Guiné Portuguesa,
XXI (1966): 405-56.

_____. As Companhias Pombalinas de Navagação, Lisbon,
1969.

Chagas, C. I. R. das. Descoberta e ocupação da Guiné só
pelos portuguesas, Lisbon, 1840.

Congresso Comemorativo do Quinto Centanário do Descobrimento da Guiné. 2 vols. ; Lisbon, 1946.

Corbeil, R. , R. Mauny and J. Charbonnier. "Préhistoire et
protohistoire de la presqu'île du Cap-Vert et de l'ex-
trême Ouest Africain," Bulletin. Institut Français d'
Afrique Noire, X(1948): 378-460.

Cortesão, Armando Zuzarte. "Subsídios para a história do
descobrimento da Guiné e Cabo Verde," Boletim Geral
das Colónias. LXXVI, 1(1931): 2-39.

Costa, Abel Fontoura da. Cartas das ilhas de Cabo Verde
de Valentim Fernandes, 1506-1508. Lisbon: Agência
Geral do Ultramar, 1939.

Cunha, Amadeu. Quinto centenário da descoberta da Guiné,
1446-1946. Bissau, 1946.

Duarte, Fausto Castilho. "Os caboverdeanos na colonização
da Guine," Cabo Verde: Boletim de Propaganda e Informação. I, 2(1949-50): 13.

_____. "O descobrimento da Guiné--Aires Tinoco--Um
héroi ignorado," Boletim Cultural da Guiné Portuguesa,
VII, 27 (July 1952): 645-56.

_____. "Guiné Portuguesa. A influência política, social

e económica dos regimentos na formação da Colonia,"
Boletim Cultural da Guiné Portuguesa, V, 18 (April 1950):
225-56.

_____. "A influência de Cabo Verde na colonização da
Guiné," Boletim da Sociedade de Geografia de Lisbõa,
(1943): 57-64.

Faro, Jorge. "Duas expedições enviades a Guiné anterior-
mente a 1474 e custeadas pela fazenda de D. Afonso V. ,"
Boletim Cultural da Guiné Portuguesa, XII, 45 (January
1957): 47-104.

_____. "O movimento comercial do porto de Bissau de
1788 a 1794," Boletim Cultural da Guiné Portuguesa,
XIV, 54 (April 1959): 231-60.

_____. "A organização administrativa da Guiné de 1615
a 1676," Boletim Cultural da Guiné Portuguesa, XIV,
53 (January 1959): 97-122.

_____. "Os problemas de Bissau, Cacheu e suas depen-
dencias visitos em 1831 por Manuel Antonio Martins,"
Boletim Cultural da Guiné Portuguesa, XIII, 50 (April
1958): 203-18.

Gomes, Diogo. De la première découverte de la Guinée.
Centro de Estudos da Guiné Portuguesa, publication 21,
Bissau, 1959.

_____. "As relaçoes do descobrimento da Guiné e das
ilhas dos Acores, Madeira e Cabo Verde," Boletim da
Sociedade de Geografia de Lisboa, XIV, 5(1898-9): 267-93.

Hawkins, John. A True Declaration of the Troublesome Voyage to the Parts of Guinea and the West Indies in 1567
and 1568. London, 1569.

Ilha de Canhabaque. Relatorio das operações militares em
1935-36 pelo Governador Major de Cavalaria, Luiz Antonio de Carvalho Viegas. Bolama: Imprensa Nacional,
1937.

Innes, Gordon. Kaabu and Fuladu; Historical Narratives of
the Gambian Mandinka. London: School of Oriental and
African Studies, University of London, 1976.

Keymis, Lawrence. A Relation of the Second Voyage to Guinea, Performed and Written in the Year 1596. London, 1596.

Leite, Carlos Alberto Monteiro. "Subsídios para a historia de Cabo Verde," Cabo Verde: Boletim de Propaganda e Informação. VIII, 89(1956-57): 25.

Leite, Duarte. Acerca da "Crónica dos feitos de Guiné. Lisbon: Bertrand, 1941.

_____. "O Cinco centenario do descobrimento da Guiné Portuguesa à luz da critica histórica," Seara Nova (October 26, 1946): 122-30.

_____. "Um crítico da crónica da Guiné," Revista de Universidade de Coimbra, XIV (1942).

_____. "Do livro inédito: 'Acerca da crónica da Guiné'," O Diabo, III, 142(March 14, 1937).

Lereno, Alvaro de Paiva de Almeida. Subsídios para a história da moeda em Cabo Verde, 1460-1940. Lisbon: Agência Geral das Colonias, 1942.

Lobato, Alexandre. "A expansão ultramarina portuguesa nos séculos XVI e XVII," Ultramar, # 29 (1967).

_____. "As fontes e as formas da reorganização ultramarina portuguesa no seculo XIX," Ultramar, # 30 (1967).

_____. "A politica ultramarina portuguesa no seculo XVIII," Ultramar, # 30 (1967).

Lopes, Edmundo Armenio Correia. A escravatura: Subsídios para a sur história, Lisbon, 1944.

Manding Studies Conference. London, School of Oriental and African Studies, 1972.

Marinho, Joaquim Pereira. Primera Parte do Relatorio de Alguns Accontecimentos Notaveis em Cabo Verde, reposta a Differentes Acusações Feitas Contra O Brigadeiro. Lisbon, 1838, 78 pps.

Mauny, Raymond. "Navigations et découvertes portugaises sur les côtes ouest-africaines," Boletim Cultural da Guiné Portuguesa, VII, 27(July 1952): 515-24.

Mauro, Frédéric. Le Portugal et l'Atlantique au XVIIeme
siècle, 1570-1670. Étude économique. Paris: Ecole
Pratique des Hautes Etudes, 1960.

Mees, Jules. "Les manuscrits de la 'Chronica do descobrimento e conquista de Guine' par Gomes Eannes de Azurara et les sources de João de Barros," Revista portuguesa colonial e maritima. IX, 50(1901): 50-62.

Miller, Basil. Miracle in Cape Verde: The Story of Everett
and Garnet Howard. Kansas City: Beacon Hill Press,
1950.

Monod, T. , Avelino Teixeira da Mota, and R. Mauny. De-
scription de la côte occidentale d'Afrique par Valentim
Fernandes (1506-1510). 1951.

Monteiro, Júlio, Jr. "Achegas para a historia de Cabo
Verde," Cabo Verde: Boletim de Propaganda e Informação, I, 12(1949-50): 23.

Mota, Avelino Teixeira da. "O centenário da morte de Hón-
orio Barreto," Boletim Cultural da Guiné Portuguesa,
XIII, 50(April 1958): 195-202.

_____. "Chronologia e âmbito das viagens portuguesas de
descoberta da Africa Occidental, de 1445 a 1462," Boletim Cultural da Guiné Portuguesa, II, 6(April 1947):
315-41.

_____. "A descoberta da Guiné," Boletim Cultural da
Guiné Portuguesa, I, 1(January 1946): 11-68; 2(April
1946): 273-326; 3(July 1946): 457-509.

_____. "Descoberta de bronzes antigos na Guiné Portu-
guesa," Boletim Cultural da Guiné Portuguesa, XV, 59
(July 1960): 625-34.

_____. "Notas sobre a historiografia da expansão portu-
guesa e as modernas correntes da investigação africana,"
Anais do Clube Militar e Naval, LXXIX, 7-9(July-September 1949): 229-94.

Oliveira, Jose Marques de. "Honorio Barreto e os interesses
portugueses em Africa," Cabo Verde: Boletim de Propaganda e Informação, XI, 123(1959-60): 13.

PAIGC. Historia da Guiné e ilhas de Cabo Verde. Porto, 1974.

Pereira, Pachecho. Esmeraldu de Situ Orbis. 1937.

Pimpão, Alvaro Júlio da Costa. "A 'Cronica da Guiné' de
   Gomes Eannes de Zurara," Biblos, XVII (1926): 374-89,
   595-607, 674-87.

Pinto, João Teixeira da. A ocupação militar da Guiné.
   Lisbon: Agência Geral das Colonias, 1936.

Quinn, Charlotte A. Mandingo Kingdoms of the Senegambia.
   Evanston, Ill. : Northwestern University Press. 1972.

_____. "A 19th Century Fulbe State," Journal of African
   History, XII (1971): 427-40.

Ravenstein, E. G. "The Voyages of Diogo Cão and Bartholomeu Dias, 1482-88," Geographical Journal, (1900): 625-
   55.

Sidibe, Bakar. "The Traditional Story of Kabu. " (paper presented at the University of London, School of Oriental and
   African Studies, Manding Conference) 1972.

Silva, Joaquim Duarte. Honório Pereira Barreto. Lisbon,
   1939.

Silva, Viriato Lopes Ramos da. "Subsídios para a história
   militar da ocupação da Província da Guiné," Boletim da
   Sociedade de Geografia de Lisbõa, XXXIII, 9-10 (September-October 1915): 33-50.

Smith, William. Voyage de Guinée, 2 vols. ; Paris, 1751.

Snelgrave, William. Nouvelle relation de quelques endroits
   de Guinee et du commerce d'esclaves qu'on y fait.
   Amsterdam, 1735.

Teague, Michael. "Bulama in the Eighteenth Century," Boletim Cultural da Guiné Portuguesa, XIII, 50(April 1958):
   175-94.

Teixeira, Cândido da Silva. "Companhia de Cacheu, Rios e
   Comércio da Guiné (Documentos para a sua história),"
   Boletim do Arquivo Histórico Colonial I(1950): 85-521.

Trigo, António B. Morais. "A morte de Nuno Tristão,"
   Boletim Cultural da Guiné Portuguesa, II, 5(January 1947):
   189-92.

Walter, Jaime (ed.). Honorio Pereira Barreto: biografia,
   documentes, Centro de Estudos da Guiné Portuguesa, publication 5, Bissau, 1947.

Wren, Walter. The Voyage of Mr. George Fenner to Guine,
   and the Islands of Cape Verde, in the Years of 1566,
   London: J. M. Dent, 1927.

Zurara, Gomes Eannes. The Chronicle of the Discovery and
   Conquest of Guinea, 2 vols. ; London: Hakluyt Society,
   1896-9 (first published 1452).

_____. Crónica dos feitos de Guiné, 2 vols. ; Lisbon,
   1949.

                    6 PHYSICAL FEATURES,
                 GEOGRAPHY, FLORA AND FAUNA

Amaral, Ilídio do. Santiago de Cabo Verde: a terra e os
   homens. Lisbon: Junta das Missões Geograficas e de
   Investigações do Ultramar, 1964.

Azevedo, Rodolfo. "O problema das chuvas em Cabo Verde,"
   Cabo Verde: Boletim de Propaganda e Informação, I,
   10(1949-50): 15.

Bebiano, José Bacelar. A geologia do Arquipélago de Cabo
   Verde, Lisbon, 1932.

Benrós, Júlio Firmino. "Estrada em Santo Antão," Cabo
   Verde: Boletim de Propaganda e Informação, V, 59
   (1953-54): 38.

Boyd, Alexander. Birds of the Cape Verde Islands. London,
   1898.

Cabral, Rego and J. M. Seguro. "Pequeno estudo sobre os
   pavimentos terreos da Guiné e o endurecimento das ruas
   de Bissau," Boletim Cultural da Guiné Portuguesa, IV,
   14 (April 1949): 265-72.

Cadenat, J. "Lista provisória dos peixes observados nas
   ilhas de Cabo Verde, de primeiro de Maio a vente-quarto
   de Junho de 1950," Cabo Verde: Boletim de Propaganda
   e Informação, II, 19(1950-51): 25.

Cardoso, A. Pereira. "Cabo Verde e o seu problema de

comunicações," Cabo Verde: Boletim de Propaganda e
Informação. IV, 40(152-53): 33.

Carvalho, Jose A. T. and Fernando J. S. de F. P. Nunes.
Contribuição para o estudo do problema florestal da
Guiné Portuguesa. Lisbon: Junta de Investigações do
Ultramar, 1956.

Castel-Branco, Armando J. F. "Entomofauna da Guiné Portuguesa e S. Tomé e Príncipe: Hemípteros e Himenóp-
teros," Boletim Cultural da Guiné Portuguesa, XI, 44
(October 1956): 67-86.

Chevalier, Auguste. Flore de l'Archipel du Cap Vert. Paris,
1935.

_____. Les microclimats des îles de Cap Vert et les
adaptations de la végétation, Paris, 1935.

Costa, João Carrington S. da. Fisiografia e geologia da
Província da Guine. Porto: Imprensa Moderna, 1946.

Crespo, Manuel Pereira. Trabalhos da Missão Geo-Hidro-
gráfica da Guiné, 1948-55. Bissau: Centro de Estudos
da Guiné Portuguesa, publication 18, 1955.

Ferreira, Fernando Simoes da Cruz. "A Guiné--Suas carac-
terísticas e alguns problemas," Boletim Geral das Colónias, XXVI, 306 (December 1950): 9-27.

Fonseca, Humberto Duarte. "Algumas notas sobre as chuvas
em Cabo Verde e a possibilidade de uma interventação
artificial," Cabo Verde: Boletim de Propaganda e Informação, I, 5(1949): 5; 11(1950): 9.

Galvão, Henrique. Outras terras, outras gentes, vol. 1,
Lisbon, 1944.

Guerra, Manuel dos Santos. Terras da Guiné e Cabo Verde,
Lisbon, 1956.

Guimarâes, C. "As chuvas na Guiné Portuguesa," Boletim
Cultural da Guiné Portuguesa, XII, 47(July 1957): 315-
32.

_____. "O clima da Guiné Portuguesa," Boletim Cultural
da Guiné Portuguesa, XIV, 55(July 1959): 295-358.

Henriques, Fernando Pinto de Almeida. "'Secas' e 'crises'
    no Arquipélago de Cabo Verde," Cabo Verde: Boletim de
    Propaganda e Informação, XII, 143(1960-61): 35.

Kerhallet, Philippe Charles M. de and Pierre Alexandre Le-
    Gres. The Cape Verde Islands, Washington, D. C. : U. S.
    Hydrographic Office, 1873.

Levy, Orlando. "Aeroporto do Sal," Cabo Verde: Boletim
    de Propaganda e Informação, II, 24(1950-51): 5.

Mota, Avelino Teixeira da. Cinco séculos de cartografia das
    ilhas de Cabo Verde, Lisbon: Junta de Investigações do
    Ultramar, 1961.

_____. Toponimos de origem portuguesa na costa ocidental
    de África desde o Cabo Bojador ao Cabo de Santa Cater-
    ina. Centro de Estudos da Guiné Portuguesa, publication
    14, Bissau, 1947.

Ribeiro, Orlanda. A ilha do Fogo e as suas erupções, Lis-
    bon, 1960.

Seccao de Estatistica Geral. Meteorologia e climatologia;
    resuma das observações efectuadas nos postos oficiais
    da colónia, Imprensa Nacional, Praia, 1936.

Stallibrass, Edward. "The Bijonga or Bissagos Islands,"
    Proceedings of the Royal Geographical Society, XI(1889):
    595-601.

Teixeira, A. J. da Silva. Os Solos da Guiné Portuguesa,
    Lisbon, 1962.

U. S. Department of the Interior. Army Map Service. Geo-
    graphic Names Division. Portuguese Guinea: Official
    Standard Names Approved by the U. S. Board on Geo-
    graphic Names, Washington, D. C. : U. S. Government
    Printing Office, 1968.

Vasconcelos, Ernesto Júlio de Carvalho e. Archipelago de
    Cabo Verde: Estudo elementar de geographia física,
    economica e politica, 2d edition; Lisbon: Tipografia da
    Cooperativa Militar, 1920.

_____. Colonias portuguesas: Estudo elementar de geo-
    grafia física, economica e politica. Guiné Portuguesa,
    Lisbon, 1917.

Viegas, Luis Antonio de Carvalho. Guiné Portuguesa. (3 vols.) Lisbon: Sociedade de Geographie de Lisboa, 1936-40.

7 ANTHROPOLOGY AND ETHNOLOGY

Almeida, António de. "Antropologia de Cabo Verde," Boletim Geral das Colónias, LIV (1938).

_____. "Das etnonomias da Guiné Portuguesa, do Arquipélago de Cabo Verde e das ilhas de São Tomé e Príncipe," In # 797, n.d., pp. 109-48.

_____. "Sobre e etno-economia da Guiné Portuguesa," Boletim Geral das Colónias, LV, 166-67(1939): 22-32.

Almeida, João de. "População de Cabo Verde," Trabalhos do Premeiro Congresso de Antropologia Colonial, Porto, vol. 2, 1934.

Barbosa, Octávio C. Gomes. "Breve notícia dos caracteres étnicos dos indígenas da tribo Beafada," Boletim Cultural da Guiné Portuguesa, I, 2(April 1946): 205-71.

Barros, Augusto de. "A invasão Fula da Circunscrição de Bafata. Queda dos Beafadas e Mandingas. Tribos 'Gabu ngabé'," Boletim Cultural da Guiné Portuguesa, II, 7 (July 1947): 737-43.

Barros, Luis Frederico de. Senegambia Portuguesa ou notícia descriptiva das diferentes tribus que habitam a Senegambia Meridional, Lisbon: Matos Moreira, 1878.

Bérenger-Féraud, L. J. B. Les peuplades de la Sénégambie. Paris, 1879.

Bernatzik, H. A. Aethiopien des Westens. (2 vols.), Wien, 1933.

Brito, Eduíno. "Aspectos demográficos dos Balantas e Brâmes do Território de Bula," Boletim Cultural da Guiné Portuguesa, VIII, 31(July 1953): 417-70.

_____. "O direito costumeiro e o conceito especial de personalidad," Boletim Cultural da Guiné Portuguesa, XX, 79(July 1968): 213-34.

_____ . "Festas religiosas do islamismo Fula," Boletim Cultural da Guiné Portugesa, XI, 41(January 1956): 91-106.

_____ . "Notas sobre a vida familiar e jurídica da tribo Fula. Instituições civis. I. A família.," Boletim Cultural da Guiné Portuguesa, XII, 47(July 1957): 301-14.

_____ . "Notas sobre a vida familiar e jurídica da tribo Fula. Instituições civis. II. O casamento," Boletim Cultural da Guiné Portuguesa, XIII, 49(January 1958): 7-24.

_____ . "Notas sobre a vida religiosa dos Fulas e Mandingas," Boletim Cultural da Guiné Portuguesa, XII, 46 (April 1957): 149-90.

_____ . "Onomástica Fula e os graus de parentesco," Boletim Cultural da Guiné Portuguesa, X(1955): 599-616.

_____ . "A poligamia e a natalidade entre os grupos étnicos Manjaco, Balanta e Brâme," Boletim Cultural da Guiné Portuguesa, VII, 25 (January 1952): 161-79.

_____ . A população de Cabo Verde no século vigésimo. Lisbon: Agência Geral do Ultramar, 1963.

Bull, Jaime Pinto. "Subsídios para o estudo da circumcisão entre os Balantas," Boletim Cultural da Guiné Portuguesa, VI, 24 (October 1951): 947-54.

Caroço, Jorge F. V. Monjur; o Gabu e a sua história, Centro de Estudos da Guiné Portuguesa, publication 8, Bissau, 1948.

Carreira, António Augusto Peixoto. "Alguns aspectos do regime jurídico da propriedade imobiliária dos Manjocos," Boletim Cultural da Guiné Portuguesa, I, 4(October 1946): 707-12.

_____ . "Aspectos da influência da cultura portuguesa na area compreendide entre o rio Senegal e o norte da Serra Leõa (Subsídio para o seo estudo)," Boletim Cultural da Guiné Portuguesa, XIX (1964): 373-416.

_____ . "A etnonímia dos povos de entre o Gâmbia e o estuario do Geba," Boletim Cultural da Guiné Portuguesa, XIX (1964): 233-76.

_____. Fulas do Gabú, Bissau: Centro de Estudos da
Guiné Portuguesa, 1948.

_____. O fundamento dos etnónimos na Guiné Portuguesa,
Bissau: Centro de Estudos da Guiné Portuguesa, 1962.

_____. "O levirato no grupo étnico Manjaco," Boletim
Cultural da Guiné Portuguesa, VIII, 29 (January 1953):
107-12.

_____. Mandingas da Guiné Portuguesa, Bissau, 1947.

_____. Mutilações corporais e pinturas cutaneas rituais
dos negros da Guiné Portuguesa, 51 pp., Centro de Estudos da Guiné Portuguesa, publication 12, Bissau, 1950.

_____. "Organização social e economica dos povos da
Guiné Portuguesa," Boletim Cultural da Guiné Portuguesa,
XVI, 64 (October 1961): 641-736.

_____. "A poligamia entre os grupos étnicos da Guiné
Portuguesa," Boletim Cultural da Guiné Portuguesa, VI,
24 (October 1951): 924-25.

_____. "As primeiras referencias escritas à excisão cli-
toridiana no Ocidente Africano," Boletim Cultural da
Guiné Portuguesa, XX (1965): 147-50.

_____. "Região dos Manjacos e dos Brâmes," Boletim
Cultural da Guiné Portuguesa, XV, 60 (October 1960):
735-84.

_____. "Social and Economic Organization of the People
of Portuguese Guinea," Translations on Africa (October
5, 1962): 1-99.

_____. Vida, religião e morte dos Mandingos, Lisbon,
1938.

_____. Vida Social dos Manjacos, Bissau, 1947.

_____, and A. Martins de Meireles. "Notas sobre os
movimentos migratorios da população natural da Guiné
Portuguesa," Boletim Cultural da Guiné Portuguesa, XIV,
53 (January 1959): 7-20.

Carroco, J. Vellez. Monjur. Bissau, 1948.

Carvalho, Joaquim Pereira Garcia. "Nota sobre a distrib-
uição e história das populações do Posto de Bedanda,"
Boletim Cultural da Guiné Portuguesa, IV (April 1949):
307-18.

Castro, Armando Augusto Gonçalves de Morais e. "Etnografia da Colónia da Guiné," Mensario administrativo,
VII, (April 1948): 27-30.

Corrêa, António A. Mendes. "Etudes anthropologiques sur
les populations de l'archipel de Cap Vert et de la Guinée
Portugaise," vol. 2, Institut Francais d'Afrique Noire,
Dakar, 1950-51.

_____. Uma jornada científica na Guiné Portuguesa.
Lisbon, Agência Geral das Colonias, 1947.

_____. "Les Metis des Iles du Cap-Vert," Zeitschrift
fur Rassenkunde, V, 1, 1937.

_____. "Movimentos de populações na Guiné Portuguesa,"
Actas y Memorias. Sociedad Española de Anthropologia,
Etnografia y Prehistoria, XXII, 1/4 (1947): 179-96.

_____, and Alfredo Ataíde. "Contribution a l'anthropologie
de la Guinée Portugaise," In Quinzième Congrès International d'Anthropologie et d'Archéologie Prehistorique,
Porto, 1930.

Correia, Carlos Bento. Oamendoim na Guiné Portuguesa,
Lisbon, 1965.

Coutouly, Gustave de. "Les populations de l'archipel des
Bissagos," Revue d'Ethnographie et des Traditions Pop-
ulaires, I (1921): 22-25.

Cunha Taborde, A. de. "Apontamentos ethograficos sobre as
Felupes de Suzana." Boletim Cultural da Guiné Portuguesa, 5 (1950): 187-223.

Diagne, Ahmadou Mapaté. "Contribution à l'étude des Balantes
de Sédhiou," Outre-Mer, V, 1 (March 1933): 16-42.

Dinis, António Joaquim Dias. "As tribos da Guiné Portuguesa
na história," Portugal em Africa, 2 ser., III, 16 (July-
August 1946): 206-15.

_____. "As tribos da Guiné Portuguesa na história (Algumas notas)," Congresso Comemorativo do Quinto Centenário do Descobrimento da Guiné, vol. 1, Lisbon (1946): pp. 241-71.

Ethnological Studies on Portuguese Guinea. Translations on Africa, 137 (December 3, 1964): 1-55.

Fiel, Conde de Castillo. "Geografia humana de la Guinea Portuguesa: impresiones de un viage de estudos a través del Africa occidental," Archivos del Instituto de Estudios Africanos, II, 4 (June 1948).

Fonseca, A. H. Vasconcelos da. "Questionário de inquérito sobre as raças da Guiné e seus caracteres étnicos," Boletim Oficial da Colónia da Guiné, suplemento ao 17 Abril, 1927.

Gomes, Barbosa O. C. "Breve notícia dos characteres étnicos dos indígenas da tribo Biafada," Boletim Cultural da Guiné Portuguesa, 1 (1946): 205-274.

Gonçalves, José Júlio. "A cultura dos Bijagós," Cabo Verde: Boletim de Propaganda e Informação, X, 117 (1958-9): 13.

_____. "O islamismo na Guiné Portuguesa," Boletim Cultural da Guiné Portuguesa, XIII, 52 (October 1958): 397-470.

Lampreia, Jose D. "Etno-história dos Bahuns da Guiné Portuguesa," Garcia de Orta, # 4 (1966).

Leprince, M. "Notes sur les Mancagnes ou Brames," Anthropologie 16(1905):57-65.

Lessa, Amerindo and Ruffié, Jacques. Seroantropologia das Ilhas de Cabo Verde, Junta de Investigações do Ultramar, Lisbon, n.d.

Lima, Augusto J. S. Organização económica e social dos Bijagós, Centro de Estudos da Guiné Portuguesa, publication 2, Bissau, 1947.

Lima, J. A. Peres de and Constâncio Mascarenhas. "Populações indígenas da Guiné Portuguesa," Arquivo de Anatomia e Antropologia, XIII, 4 (1929-30): 595-618.

Lopes, Edmundo Armenio Correia. "Antecedentes da aculturação dos povos da Guiné Portuguesa," Mundo Português, XI, 124 (April 1944): 135.

Lopes, Francisco. A importância dos valores espirituais no panorama cabo-verdiano, Lisbon: Centro de Estudos Políticos e Sociais, 1959.

McCullough, Charles Ross. "The State of Prehistoric Archaeology in Morocco, Spanish Sahara, Mauritania, Mali, Gambia, Portuguese Guinea and Senegal." Unpublished master's thesis, University of Pennsylvania, 1969.

Marques, Jose Eduardo A. da Silva. "A gerontocracia na organização social dos Bijagós," Boletim Cultural da Guiné Portuguesa, X (1955): 293-300.

Mascarenhas, Constâncio and J. A. Pires de Lima. "Populações indígenas da Guiné Portuguesa," Arquivo de Anatomia e Antropologia, XIII (1929-30).

Mateus, Amílcar de Magalhaes. "Acerca da pre-história da Guiné," Boletim Cultural da Guiné Portuguesa, IX, 35 (July 1954): 457-72.

_____. "Estudo da população da Guiné Portuguesa. Relato preliminar da primeira campanha da Missão Etnológica e Antropologica da Guiné," Anais. Junta de Missões Geograficas e de Investigações do Ultramar, I (1946): 243-60.

Meireles, Artur Martins de. "Baiu (Gentes de Kaiu). I. Generalidades," Boletim Cultural da Guiné Portuguesa, III, 11 (July 1948): 607-38.

_____. Mutilações etnicas dos Manjacos, Centro de Estudos da Guiné Portuguesa, publication 22, Bissau, 1960.

Mello, Lopo Vaz Sampayo e. "Esquisso etnográfico da população de Cabo Verde," Anuario do Escola Superior Nacional, Anos XII-XIII, 1931-2.

Moreira, José Mendes. "Breve ensaio etnográfico acerca dos Bijagós," Boletim Cultural da Guiné Portuguesa, I, 1 (January 1946): 69-115.

_____. Fulas do Gabu, Centro de Estudos da Guiné Portuguesa, publication 6, Bissau, 1948.

_____. "Da ergologia dos Fulas da Guiné Portuguesa," Boletim Cultural da Guiné Portuguesa, XXVI, 101-102 (January-April 1971).

Mota, Avelino Teixiera da. "A agricultura de Brâmes e Balantas vista através da fotografia aéra," Boletim Cultural da Guiné Portuguesa, V, 18 (April 1950): 131-72.

_____. "Etnográfica," Boletim Cultural da Guiné Portuguesa, I, 1 (January 1946): 183-90.

_____. Inquérito etnográfico organizado pelo Governo da Colonia no ano de 1946, Bissau: Publicação Comemorativa do Quinto Centenário da Descoberta da Guiné, 1947.

_____. "Notas sobre o povoamento e a agricultura indígena na Guiné Portuguesa," Boletim Cultural da Guiné Portuguesa, VI, 23 (July 1951): 657-80.

_____. "A Secunda Conferencia Internacional dos Africanistas Ocidentais," Boletim Cultural da Guiné Portuguesa, III, 9 (January 1948): 13-74.

_____, and Mario G. Ventim Neves. A Habitação Indígena na Guine Portuguesa, Centro de Estudos da Guiné Portuguesa, publication 7, Bissau, 1948.

Murdock, George Peter. Africa: Its People and Their Culture and History. New York: McGraw-Hill Book Co., 1959.

Nogueira, Amadeu I. P. "Monografia sobre a tribo Banhum," Boletim Cultural da Guiné Portuguesa, II, 8 (October 1947): 973-1008.

Pereira, A. Gomes. "Contos Fulas," Boletim Cultural da Guiné Portuguesa, III, 10 (April 1948): 445-52.

Pereira, F. Alves. "Utensílios da época da pedra na Guiné Portuguesa," O Archéologo Portugueses, XIII (1918).

Quintino, Fernando R. Rogado. "Os povos da Guiné," Boletim Cultural da Guiné Portuguesa, XXII, 85-86, (January-April 1967).

_____. "No segredo das crencas. Das instituições religiosas na Guiné Portuguesa," Boletim Cultural da Guiné

Portuguesa, IV, 15 (July 1949):   419-88; 16 (October
1949):   687-721.

_____ . "Totemism in Portuguese Guinea," Translations
on Africa, # 271 (1965):   20-41.

Ribeiro, Maria Luisa Ferro.   "Apontamento etnográfico sobre
a ilha de Santiago," Cabo Verde: Boletim de Propaganda
e Informação, XIII, 148 (1961):   7; 149 (1962):   10.

Santos, Eduardo dos.   "Catolicismo, protestantismo, e islamismo na Guiné Portuguesa," Ultramar, VIII, 4 (April-
June 1968):   112-24.

Santos Lima, A. J.   "Organização económica e social dos
Bijagós," Centro de Estudos da Guiné Portuguesa, 2
(1947):1-154.

Silva, Artur Augusto da.   "Usos e costumes jurídicos dos
Felupes da Guiné," Boletim Cultural da Guiné Portuguesa,
XV, 57 (January 1960):   7-52.

_____ . Usos e costumes jurídicos dos Fulas da Guiné
Portuguesa, Bissau: Centro de Estudos da Guiné Portuguesa, 1958.

_____ . "Usos e costumes jurídicos dos Mandingas," Boletim Cultural da Guiné Portuguesa, XXIII, 90-91 (April-
July 1968); XXIV, 93 (January 1969).

Taborda, Antonio da Cunha.   "Apontamentos etnográficos sobre os Felupes de Suzana," Boletim Cultural da Guiné
Portuguesa, V, 18 (April 1950):   187-224; 20 (October
1950):   511-61.

Tadeu, Viriato A.   Contos do Caramô, lendas e fabulas mandingas da Guiné Portuguesa, Lisbon: Agência Geral das
Colonias, 1945.

Valoura, Francisco.   "O Balanta e a Bolanha," Boletim Cultural da Guiné Portuguesa, XXV (1970):   561-68.

Viegas, Luis Antonio de Carvalho.   "Os diferentes nucleos
populacionais da Guiné Portuguesa e seu estado de civilização na vida familiar," Conferéncia Internacional dos Africanistas Ocidentais, vol. 5, Bissau (1947):   333-46.

8 LANGUAGE, LITERATURE, AND CRIOULO CULTURE

LANGUAGE

Barbosa, Jorge Morais. "Cabo Verde, Guiné e São Tomé e
Príncipe: Situação linguística," Instituto Superior de Ciencias
Socias e Politica Ultramarina, Lisbon, 1966.

_____. Crioulos: Estudos linguísticos, Lisbon: Academia
Internacional da Cultura Portuguesa, 1967.

Bella, L. de Sousa. "Apontamentos sobre a língua dos Balantas de Jabadá," Boletim Cultural da Guiné Portuguesa,
I, 4 (October 1946): 729-65.

Bocandé, Bertrand de. "De la langue creole de la Guinée
Portugaise. Notes sur la Guinée portugaise ou Sénégambie meridionale," Bulletin de la Société de Géographie
de Paris, ser. III, XI (1849): 265-350; XII, 57-93.

Cardoso, Henrique Lopes. "Pequeno vocabulário do dialecto
'Pepel'," Boletim da Sociedade de Geografia de Lisbôa,
XX, 10 (1902): 121-28.

Carreira, António Augusto Peixoto. "Alguns aspectos da in-
fluêcia da língua Mandinga na Pajadinca," Boletim Cultural da Guiné Portuguesa, XVIII, 71 (July 1963): 345-84.

_____, and João Basso Marques. Subsídios para o estudo
da língua Manjaca, Bissau: Centro de Estudos da Guiné
Portuguesa, 1947.

Costa, Joaquim Vieira Botelho da and Custodio Jose Duarte.
"O creolo de Cabo Verde," Boletim da Sociedade de
Geografia de Lisbôa, IV (1866): 6.

Klingenheben, August. "Die Permutationen des Biafada und
des Ful," Zeitschrift fur Eingebornen-Sprachen, XV 3
(1924): 180-213; 4 (1925): 266-72.

Lopes, Edmundo Armenio Correia. "O dinheiro nas línguas
da Guiné," Mundo Português, XII (1945): 139.

_____. "Manjacos. Língua," Mundo Português, X (1943):
113-114.

Marques, João Basso. "Aspectos do problema da semelhança

da língua dos Papéis, Manjacos e Brâmes," Boletim Cultural da Guiné Portuguesa, II, 5 (January 1947): 77-109.

Meintel, D. "The Creole dialect of the Island of Brava, in Valdhoff, M. F. ," et al. , Miscelanea Luso-Africana: colectanea de estudos coligidos, Lisbõa, 1975.

Quintino, Fernando R. Rogado. "Algumas notas sobre a gramática Balanta," Boletim Cultural da Guiné Portuguesa, VI, 21 (January 1951): 1-52.

_____. "Conhecimento da língua Balanta, através da sua estrutura vocabular," Boletim Cultural da Guiné Portuguesa, XVI, 64 (October 1961): 737-68.

Silva, Baltazar Lopes da. O dialecto crioulo de Cabo Verde. Lisbon: Junta de Investigações do Ultramar, 1957.

Silva, Viriato Lopes Ramos da. "Pequeno vocabulário Portugues-Mandinga," Boletim da Sociedade de Geografia de Lisbõa, XLVII, 3-4 (March-April 1929): 98-108; 5-6 (May-June 1929): 142-51.

Westermann, Diedrich and M. A. Bryan. Languages of West Africa, Oxford University Press, 1952.

Wilson, William Andre Auquier. The Crioulo of Guine, Johannesburg: Witwatersrand University Press, 1962.

LITERATURE

Almada, Maria Dulce de Oliveira (ed.). Poètes des îles du Cap-Vert: 1) Osvald Alcântara, 2) Jorge Barbosa, 3) Gabriel Mariano. Conakry: Partido Africano da Independencia da Guiné e Cabo Verde, 1962.

Andrade, M. de. Antologia de poesia negra de expressão portuguesa, Lisbon, 1956.

_____. Literatura africana de expressão portuguesa, Lisbon, 1967.

Araújo, Norman. A Study of Cape Verdean Literature, Chestnut Hill, MA: Boston College, 1966.

Barbosa, Alexandre. Guinéus: contos, narrativas, crónicas, Lisbon: Agência Geral do Ultramar, 1967.

Barbosa, Jorge Vera-Cruz. "O ambiente literário cabover-
diano e a influência brasileira," Cabo Verde: Boletim
de Propaganda e Informação, VI, 61 (1956-57): 9.

Becari, Gilberto. Danza di cuori al Capo Verde (Romanzo
coloniale), Firenze, 1935.

Belchior, Manuel Dias. Contos mandingas, Porto: Portuca-
lense Editora, 1968.

_____. Grandeza africana: Lendas da Guine Portuguesa.
1963.

Boletim Cultural da Guiné Portuguesa. (Published African
oral literature).

Boletim dos Alunos do Liceu Gil Eannes. (Cape Verdean literary journal first published in 1959, then very sporadically.)

Cardoso, Pedro Monteiro. Folclore caboverdeano, Porto:
Edição Maranus, 1933.

Certeza. (Cape Verdean literary and cultural journal appear-
ing between 1937 and 1947, featuring Portuguese neo-real-
ism with a progressive tone.)

Cesar, Amandio. Contos portugueses do ultramar. I. Cabo
Verde, Guiné e S. Tomé e Príncipe, Porto: Portuca-
lense Editora, 1969.

Conduto, Joao Eleuterio. "Contos Bijagós," Boletim Cultural
da Guiné Portuguesa, X (1955): 489-506.

Claridade. (Cape Verde literary and cultural journal published from March 1936 until 1960, featuring modernistic
outlook, appeared sporadically from São Vincente.)

De Sousa, P. Jose Maria, C. S. SP. Hora di bai, Cape-
verdean-American Federation, East Providence, R. I.
(Vols. 1 and 2) 1973.

Dickinson, Margaret. When Bullets Begin to Flower: Poems
of Resistance from Angola, Mozambique and Guiné, Nai-
robi: East Africa Publishing House, 1973.

Ferreira, Manuel. "Introdução a ficção cabo-verdiana contemporânea," Cabo Verde: Boletim de Propaganda e Informação, XI, 129 (1959-60): 27.

_____. Morabeza, contos de Cabo Verde, Lisbon: Agência Geral do Ultramar, 1958.

Figueiredo, Jaime de. Modernos poetas caboverdianos: antologia, Praia: Edições Henriquinas, 1961.

Filipe, Daniel. O manuscrito na garrafa, Lisbon: Guimaraes, 1960.

Gérard, Albert S. "The Literature of Cape Verde," African Arts/Arts d'Afrique, I, 2 (Winter 1968): 62-64.

Gomes, A. "Notas sobre a música indígena da Guiné," Boletim Cultural da Guiné Portuguesa, V, 19 (July 1950): 411-24.

Hamilton, Russell G. Voices From an Empire: A History of Afro-Portuguese Literature, Minneapolis: University of Minnesota Press, 1975.

Lopes, Baltazar, M. Ferreira, and A. A. Gonçalves. Antologia da ficção cabo-verdiana contemporânea, Praia: Imprensa Nacional, 1960.

Lopes, Manuel António. "A literatura cabo-verdiana," Cabo Verde: Boletim de Propaganda e Informação, XI (October 1, 1959): 8.

Lopes, Norberto. Terra ardentes: narrativas da Guiné, Lisbon: Editora Maritimo Colonial, 1947.

Margarido, Alfredo. "Estruturas poéticas cabo-verdianas," Cabo Verde: Boletim de Propaganda e Informação, XIV, 162 (1962-63): 18.

Mariano, Jose Gabriele Lopes da Silva. Poetas de Cabo Verde, Lisbon: Casa dos Estudantes do Império, 1960.

Miranda, Nuno de. "Literatura e insularidade," Cabo Verde: Boletim de Propaganda e Informação, XIII, 145 (1961-62): 1.

Moser, Gerald M. A Tentative Portuguese-African Bibliography: Portuguese Literature in Africa and African Literature in the Portuguese Language, University Park, PA: Pennsylvania State University Press, 1970.

Moura, Jacinto José Nascimento. "Crioulos e folclore de Cabo Verde," Trabalhos do Primeiro Congresso de Antropologia Colonial, vol. 2. 1934.

Neves, João Alves das. "Poesia em Cabo Verde," Cabo Verde: Boletim de Propaganda e Informação, XIII, 156 (1961-62): 39.

Oliveira, José Osório de. Poesia de Cabo Verde, Lisbon: Agência Geral das Colonias, 1944.

Parsons, Elsie Clews. Folclore do Arquipélago de Cabo Verde, Lisbon: Agência Geral do Ultramar, 1968.

_____. "Ten Folk-Tales from the Cape Verde Islands," Journal of American Folk-Lore, XXX (April 1917): 230-38.

_____. "Folk-lore from the Cape Verde Islands," Memoirs of the American Folklore Society, 15 (1923): 1-2.

Quintino, Fernando R. Rogado. "Música e dança na Guiné Portuguesa," Boletim Cultural da Guiné Portuguesa, XVIII, 72 (October 1963): 551-70.

_____. "A pintura e a escultura na Guiné Portuguesa," Boletim Cultural da Guiné Portuguesa, XIX (1964): 277-88.

Saraiva, Arnaldo. "Modernos poetas caboverdianos," Cabo Verde: Boletim de Propaganda e Informação, XIII, 100 (1961-62): 20.

Silveira, Onesimo. Consciencialização no literatura caboverdiana, Lisbon: Casa dos Estudiantes do Império, 1963.

_____. Hora grande: Poesia caboverdiana, Nova Lisbõa: Publicações Bailundo, 1962.

Silveira, Pedro da. "Relance da literatura caboverdeana," Cabo Verde: Boletim de Propaganda e Informação, V, 58 (1953): 26; 59 (1954): 26.

Simoes, João Gaspar. "A antologia da ficção cabo-verdiana," Diário de Noticias (January 1, 1961): 13-15.

_____ . "Modernos poetas caboverdianos," Cabo Verde: Boletim de Propaganda e Informação, XIII, 143 (1961-62): 11.

Virgínio, Teobaldo. Poemas de Cabo Verde. Cabo Verde, 1960.

CRIOULO CULTURE

Almeida, Manuel Ribeiro de. "Aspectos sociais do povo cabo-verdiano," Cabo Verde: Boletim de Propaganda e Infor-mação, IX, 108 (1957-58): 30.

Araújo, Norman. "Civilação em Cabo Verde," Cabo Verde: Boletim de Propaganda e Informação, XII, 141 (1960-61): 31.

Levy, Bento. "Ao povo de Cabo Verde," Cabo Verde: Bo-letim de Propaganda e Informação, XIII, 146 (1961-62): 1.

Lyall, Archibald. Black and White Make Brown: An Account of a Journey to the Cape Verde Islands and Portuguese Guinea, W. Heineman, London, 1938.

Marupa, M. A. Portuguese Africa in Perspective: The Making of a Multi-Racial State, 1973.

Melo, Luis Romano Madeira de. Cabo Verde: renascensa de uma civilização no Atlantico Medio, Ocidente, Lisbon, 1967.

Mota, Avelino Teixeira da. "Contactos culturais luso-afri-canos na 'Guiné do Cabo Verde'," Boletim da Sociedade de Geografia de Lisbõa, LXIX, 11-12 (November-Decem-ber 1951): 659.

Pattee, Richard. "Portuguese Guinea: A Microcosm of a Plural Society in Africa," Plural Societies, IV, 4 (Win-ter 1973): 57-64.

Sousa, Henrique Teixeira da. "Cabo Verde e a sua gente," Cabo Verde: Boletim de Propaganda e Informação, VI, 63 (1954-55): 21; IX, 108 (1957-58): 2; X, 109 (1958-59): 7.

Tenreiro, Francisco. "Acerca de arquipélagos crioulos,"

Cabo Verde: Boletim de Propaganda e Informação, XII, 137 (1960-61): 31.

9 HEALTH AND EDUCATION

Almeida, Fernando C. M. Tavares "Serviços de Saúde e Assistência na Guiné Portuguesa," Ultramar, VIII, 4 (April-June 1968): 165-75.

Brandao, J. da Costa. "O ensino na Guiné Portuguesa," Ultramar, VII, 4 (April-June 1968): 146-64.

Brooks, George E. "Notes on Research Facilities in Lisbon and the Cape Verde Islands," International Journal of African Historical Studies, VI, 2 (1973): 304-14.

Cabral, Tomaz Antonio. "Serviços de Saúde e Assistência de Cabo Verde," Ultramar, VIII, 2 (1967): 165-72.

Costa, Damasceno Isac de. Relatório do Servico da Delegação de Saúde da vila de Bissau, respectivo ao ano de 1884, Lisbon: Typografia Guineense, 1887.

Ferreira, Fernando S. da C. As tripanosomiases nos territorios africanos portugueses, Centro de Estudos da Guiné Portuguesa, publication 9, 1948.

Figuerido, Jaime de. "O ensino nas ilhas de Cabo Verde," Cabo Verde: Boletim de Propaganda e Informação, V, 57 (1953-54): 27.

Lopes, José. "Instrução publica," Cabo Verde: Boletim de Propaganda e Informação, IV, 41 (1952-53): 29.

Miranda, Nuno de. "Sobre educação e desenvolvimento em Cabo Verde," Cabo Verde: Boletim de Propaganda e Informação, XI, 127 (1959-60): 9.

Monteiro, Manuel da Costa. "Os Servicos de Saúde em Cabo Verde," Cabo Verde: Boletim de Propaganda e Informação, VIII, 91 (1956-57): 27.

Mota, Avelino Teixeira da. "O Centro de Estudos da Guiné Portuguesa," Boletim Cultural da Guiné Portuguesa, VIII (1953): 609-50; X (1955): 641-55.

Programa do ensino para as escolas das regioes libertadas.
Conakry: Partido Africano da Independência da Guiné e
Cabo Verde, n. d.

Regulamento das escolas do partido.   Conakry: Partido Africano da Independência da Guiné e Cabo Verde, September
19, 1966.

Spencer, Maria Helena.   "Ensinemos o povo," Cabo Verde:
Boletim de Propaganda e Informação, V, 49 (1953):   25;
50 (1954):   13.

Tavares, Estevao.   L'enseignement en Guinée 'Portugaise',
Conakry: Partido Africano da Independência da Guiné e
Cabo Verde, June 1962.

Tendeiro, João.   Actualidade vetermária da Guiné Portuguesa,
Centro de Estudos da Guiné Portuguesa, publication 15,
Bissau, 1951.

_____ .   Tripanosomiases animais da Guiné Portuguesa,
Centro de Estudos da Guiné Portuguesa, publication 110,
Bissau, 1949.

10 AGRICULTURE, ECONOMICS, DEVELOPMENT

Aguiar, Armando de.   "Cabo Verde--A ilha de Santiago,
celeiro da provincia cabo-verdiana vive um fase de grande
desenvolvimento," Cabo Verde: Boletim de Propaganda
e Informação, XIII (1961-62):   155.

Areal, Joaquim A.   "Possibilidades industriais da Guiné,"
Boletim Cultural da Guiné Portuguesa, IX, 36 (October
1954):   707-70.

Baptista, Manuel Martins.   "Agricultura da Colónia da Guiné,"
Boletim Geral das Colónias, L (February 1934):   49-64.

Barros, A. F. Figueiredo de.   Inquerito acerca das indus-
trias de Cabo Verde, Praia, 1917.

Bebiano, José Bacelar.   "Alguns aspectos económicos do
Arquipélago de Cabo Verde," Boletim Geral das Colónias,
LXII (1932).

Campos, Ezequiel de.   O desenvolvimento da riqueza do

Arquipélago de Cabo Verde, Lisbon: Agência Geral das Colónias, 1945.

Galvão, Henrique. Informação económica sobre o império: Cabo Verde, Lisbon, 1934.

Harrison, Robert. "Famine and Poverty: The Cape Verde Islands," Africa Today, X (March 1963): 8-9.

Henkes, William C. Mineral Industry of Angola, Mozambique and Portuguese Guinea, Washington: U. S. Bureau of Mines, 1966.

International Labour Office. Portugal, Portuguese Guinea, Legislative Decrees: Native Labour, Geneva, 1938.

Lima, João B. Ferreira. "Estradas, levadas, barragems e arborização," Cabo Verde: Boletim de Propaganda e Informação, VIII, 88 (1956-57): 40.

Loreno, Alvaro de Paiva de Almeida. "Moeda metálica em Cabo Verde," Cabo Verde: Boletim de Propaganda e Informação, I, 12 (1949-50): 2.

Macedo, Zeferino Monteiro de. A estatística ante o movimento comercial da Província no periodo de 1939-1961, Bissau: Repartição Provincial dos Serviços de Economica e Estatística Geral, 1961.

Mendes, José-Luis Morais Ferreira. Problemas e perspectivas do desenvolvimento rural da Guiné, Lisbon, 1968.

Mendonça, Pio Coelho de. "Elevação do nível de vida do trabalhador na Guiné Portuguesa," Boletim Cultural da Guiné Portuguesa, XI, 42 (April 1956): 111-30.

Ministerio do Ultramar. "Missão de Inquérito Agrícolas de Cabo Verde, Guiné, São Tomé e Príncipe," Recenseamento agrícola da Guiné, 1960-61, Lisbon: Imprensa Nacional, 1963.

Projecto do IV Plano de Fomento. II. Ultramar. Lisbon: Imprensa Nacional, Casa de Moeda, 1973.

Provincia de Cabo Verde. Comercio externo, 1949-1955. Lisbon: Tipografia Portuguesa, 1960.

Quintino, Fernando R. Rogado. "Das possibilidades do aumento da produção na Guiné," Boletim Cultural da Guiné Portuguesa, VI, 22 (April 1951): 365-70.

Recenseamento agrícola da Guine, 1960-61. Lisbon: Comissão para os Inquéritos Agrícolas no Ultramar, 1963.

Ribeiro, Maria Luisa Ferro. "Ilha de Santiago--Principais culturas e seu valor económico," Cabo Verde: Boletim de Propaganda e Informação, XIII, 153 (1961-62): 30.

Santareno, José Alberto Lemos Martins. "A agricultura na Guiné Portuguesa," Boletim Cultural da Guiné Portuguesa, XII, 47 (July 1957): 355-84.

Santos, António Lopes dos. Problemas de Cabo Verde: a situação mantém-se controlada, Lisbon: Agencia Geral do Ultramar, 1971.

Santos, Jesus Nunes dos. "Alguns aspectos da economia da Guiné," Boletim da Sociedade de Geografia de Lisbõa, LXV, 1-2 (January-February 1947): 49-71.

Sardhina, Raul M. de Albuquerque and C. A. Picado Horta. "Perspectivas da agricultura, silvicultura e pecuária na Guiné," Boletim Cultural da Guiné Portuguesa, XXI, 81 (January 1966): 24-306.

Seca, Mário. A pesca em Cabo Verde, Praia: Serviço de Estatística, Divisão de Propaganda, 1945.

Silva, Artur Augusto da. "Ensaio de estudo da introdução na Guiné Portuguesa, das cooperatives agrícolas," Boletim Cultural da Guiné Portuguesa, IX, 34 (April 1954): 417-30.

Teixeira, Antonio Jose da Silva and Luís Augusto Grandvaux Barbos. A agricultura do Arquipélago de Cabo Verde, Lisbon: Agência Geral do Ultramar, 1958.

U. S. Bureau of Labor Statistics. Office of Foreign Labor and Trade. Labor Conditions in Portuguese Guinea. Washington, D. C.: Government Printing Office, 1966.

Valdez, Henrique Lapa Travassos. "O desenvolvimento das obras portuárias de Cabo Verde," Cabo Verde: Boletim de Propaganda e Informação, IX, 98 (1957-58): 21.

Veiga, Aguinaldo and L. Patrício Ribas. "Alguns aspectos da estrutura economica da Guiné," Boletim Cultural da Guiné Portuguesa, IV, 14 (April 1949): 289-305.

11 BY AND ABOUT AMILCAR CABRAL

Andelman, David A. "Profile: Amílcar Cabral. Pragmatic Revolutionary Shows How an African Guerilla War Can Be Successful," Africa Report, XV, 5 (May 1970): 18-19.

Andrade, Mário de. "Amílcar Cabral: Profil d'un révolutionnaire africain," Présence Africaine, # 2 (1973): 3-19.

Anon. "L'Assassinat d'Almícar Cabral." Afrique-Asie, February 5-18, 1975, 8-19.

Anon. "Cabral Is Assassinated by Portuguese Agents," African World, (February 3, 1973): 1-16.

Bienen, Henry. "State and Revolution, the work of Amílcar Cabral," Journal of Modern African Studies, 15(1977):4.

Blackey, Robert. "Fanon and Cabral: A Contrast in Theories of Revolution for Africa," Journal of Modern African Studies, XII (June 1974): 191-210.

Bragança, Aquino de. "L'Assassinat de Cabral," Afrique-Asie, XXIV (February 19-March 4, 1973): 8-15.

_____. "The Plot Against Cabral," Southern Africa, (May 1973): 4-8.

Cabral, Amílcar Lopes. "Algumas considerações ácerca das chuvas," Cabo Verde: Boletim de Propaganda e Informação, I, 1 (1949): 15.

_____. "Em defasa da terra," Cabo Verde: Boletim de Propaganda e Informação, I, 2 (1949-50): 2; 6, 15; II, 14 (1950-51): 19; 15, 6; III, 29 (1951-52): 24.

_____. "Apontamentos sobre poesia caboverdeana, Cabo Verde: Boletim de Propaganda e Informação, 28, Praia, 1952.

_____. "Para o conhecimento do problema da erosão do

163   Bibliography

solo na Guiné, I. Sobre o conceito de erosão," Boletim
Cultural da Guiné Portuguesa, IX, 33 (January 1954):
163-94.

_____. "A propósito de mecanização da agricultura na
Guiné Portuguesa," Boletim Cultural da Guiné Portuguesa,
IX, 34 (April 1954): 389-400.

_____. "Acerca da utilização da terra na Africa Negra,"
Boletim Cultural da Guiné Portuguesa, IX, 34 (April
1954): 401-16.

_____. "Queimados e pousios na Circunscrição de Fula-
cunda em 1953," Boletim Cultural da Guiné Portuguesa,
IX, 35 (July 1954): 627-46.

_____. "Acerca da contribuição dos 'povos' guineenses
para a produção agrícola da Guiné," Boletim Cultural da
Guiné Portuguesa, IX, 36 (October 1954): 771-78.

_____. "Recenseamento agrícola da Guiné: estimativa
em 1953," Boletim Cultural da Guiné Portuguesa, XI, 43
(July 1956): 7-243.

_____. "A propos du cycle cultural arachide-mils en
Guinée Portugaise," Boletim Cultural da Guiné Portuguesa, XIII, 50 (April 1958): 146-56.

_____. "Feux be brousse et jachères dans le cycle cul-
tural arachide-mils," Boletim Cultural da Guiné Portuguesa, XIII, 51 (July 1958): 257-68.

_____. Memorandum enviado ao govérno português pelo
Partido Africano da Independência, Conakry: Partido
Africano da Independência da Guiné e Cabo Verde, De-
cember 1, 1960.

_____. Discurso proferido pelo delegado da Guiné 'Por-
tuguesa' e das ilhas de Cabo Verde, Amílcar Cabral, sec-
retário geral do Partido Africano da Independência,
Cairo: Partido Africano da Independência da Guiné e
Cabo Verde. March 25-31, 1961.

_____. "The Death Pangs of Imperialism," In Rapport
général sur la lutte de libération nationale, Conakry,
July 1961.

_____. Memorandum à Assembleia Geral da Organização das Nações Unidas, Conakry: Partido Africano da Independência da Guiné e Cabo Verde, September 26, 1961.

_____. "Une crise de connaissance," Third Conference of African People, (Cairo). 1961.

_____ (under pseudonym Abel Djassi). The Facts About Portugal's African Colonies, Introduction by Basil Davidson, Union of Democratic Control, London, 1961.

_____. Un crime de colonialisme (Fondements juridiques de notre lutte armée de libération nationale). Extrait du rapport présénte par le camarade Amílcar Cabral, au Comité Spécial de l'ONU pour les territoires administrés par le Portugal, Conakry: Partido Africano da Independência da Guiné e Cabo Verde, 1961.

_____. Rapport général sur la lutte de liberation nationale, Conakry: Partido Africano da Independência da Guiné e Cabo Verde, 1961.

_____. Note ouverte au gouvernement portugais, Conakry: Partido Africano da Independência da Guiné e Cabo Verde, 1961.

_____. The Facts About Portugal's African Colonies, London: Union of Democratic Control, 1961.

_____. Déclaration sur la situation actuelle de lutte de libération en Guinée 'Portugaise' et aux îles du Cap Vert, Conakry: Partido Africano da Independência da Guiné e Cabo Verde, January 20, 1962.

_____. "Liberation Movement in Portuguese Guinea," Voice of Africa, II (March 1962): 32.

_____. "La Guinée Portugaise et les îles du Cap-Vert," Voice of Africa, II (May 1962): 37, 39.

_____. Le peuple de la Guinée 'Portugais' devant l'Organisation des Nations Unies: Présentee au Comité Spécial de l'ONU pour les territoires administres par le Portugal, Conakry: Partido Africano da Independência da Guiné e Cabo Verde, June 1962.

_____. "Guinée, Cap-Vert, face au colonialisme portugais," Partisans, II, 7 (November-December 1962): 80-91.

_____. La lutte de libération nationale en Guinée Portugaise et aux îles du Cap-Vert, Conakry: Partido Africano da Independência da Guiné e Cabo Verde, 1962.

_____. Rapport aux Etats-Unis, Conakry: Partido Africano da Independencia da Guiné e Cabo Verde, 1962.

_____. Discours prononcé par chef de la délégation de la Guinée 'Portugaise' et des îles du Cap-Vert, secrétaire générale du PAIGC, Conakry: Partido Africano da Independência da Guiné e Cabo Verde, 1962.

_____. Déclaration faite par M. Amílcar Cabral du Parti Africaine de l'Indépendance de la Guinée et du Cap-Vert (PAIGC) lors de la 1420ème séance de la Quatrième Commission le 12 décembre 1962, N.Y.: Partido Africano da Independência da Guiné e Cabo Verde, 1962.

_____. Déclaration à l'occasion du anniversaire des grèves de Bissao et du massacre de Pigiuiti. Conakry: Partido Africano da Independência da Guiné e Cabo Verde, 1962.

_____. Déclaration du PAIGC sur l'évacuation par les autorités portugaises des civils européens du sud, Paris: Comité de Soutien à l'Angola et aux Peuples des Colonies Portugaises, February, 1963.

_____. "Solução pacifica para Guiné e Cabo Verde," Portugal Democratico, VII (February-March 1963): 6.

_____. Nous avons lutté par des moyens pacifiques. Nous n'avons eu que les massacres et le génocide, Addis Ababa: Partido Africano da Independência da Guiné e Cabo Verde, May 1963.

_____. Pourquoi nous avons pris les armes pour libérer notre pays, Addis Ababa: Partido Africano da Independência da Guiné e Cabo Verde, May 1963.

_____. "The War in Portuguese Guinea," African Revolution, I (June 1963): 103-108.

_____. "A guerra na Guiné," Portugal Democrático, VIII (October 1963): 3.

_____. "O PAIGC pede à ONU auxílio concreto," Portugal Democrático, VIII (December 1963): 4.

_____. "The Struggle in Guinea," International Socialist Journal, I (August 1964): 428-46.

_____. "The Struggle of Portuguese Guinea," Translations on África, # 77 (1964): 29-40.

_____. Le développement de la lutte nationale en Guinée 'Portugaise' et aux îles du Cap Vert en 1964, Conakry: February 1965.

_____. "La lutte du PAIGC," Remarques Africaines, VII (May 26, 1965): 19-22.

_____. "Liberating Portuguese Guinea from Within," The New African, IV (June 1965): 85.

_____. "Contra a guerre colonial: mengagem de Amílcar Cabral ao povo da Guiné e de Cabo Verde," FPLN Boletim (August 1965): 14-15.

_____. Intervention faite à la Première Conférence de la Solidarité des Peuples d'Afrique, d'Asie et d'Amérique Latine, Havana, January 1966.

_____. "The Social Structure of Portuguese Guinea and its Meaning for the Struggle for National Liberation," Translations on Africa, # 420 (August 24, 1966): 37-48.

_____. "Portuguese Colonial Policy," Africa Quarterly, V, 4 (1966): 287-99.

_____. Fondements et objectifs de la libération nationale. Sur la domination impérialiste, Conakry: Partido Africano da Independência da Guiné e Cabo Verde, 1966.

_____. "L'arme de la théorie," Partisans, # 26-27 (1966).

_____. "Combattre et bâtir," La Nouvelle Revue Internationale (February 1967).

_____. "Breve análisis de la estructura social de la Guinea 'Portuguesa'," Pensamiento Crítico, 2-3 (March-April 1967): 24-48.

_____. "Mankind's Path to Progress," World Marxist Review, X (November 1967): 88-89.

_____. "Determined to Resist," Tricontinental Magazine, # 8 (September-October 1968): 114-26.

_____. "National Liberation and Social Structure," in William J. Pomeroy (ed.), Guerilla Warfare and Marxism: A Collection of Writings from Karl Marx to the Present on Armed Struggles for Liberation and Socialism. New York: International Publishers, 1968.

_____. "Guinea (B): Political and Military Situation," Tricontinental, 37 (April 1969): 25-34.

_____. "Guinea: The Power of Arms," Tricontinental Magazine, # 12 (May-June 1969): 5-16.

_____. Revolution in Guinea. An African People's Struggle, London: Stage One, 1969; reprinted by Monthly Review, New York, 1970, 1972.

_____. The Struggle in Guinea, Cambridge: Africa Research Group, 1969.

_____. National Liberation and Culture. (Speech delivered at Syracuse University under the auspices of The Program of Eastern African Studies of the Maxwell School of Citizenship and Public Affairs.) February 20, 1970.

_____. "Report on Portuguese Guinea and the Liberation Movement, Hearing before the Subcommittee on Africa of the Committee on Foreign Affairs, House of Representatives, 91st Congress, second session, Thursday, February 26," Washington: U.S. Government Printing Office, 1970.

_____. "Our Army Is Our Whole People," Newsweek, LXXV (March 9, 1970): 38-39.

_____. "PAIGC: Optimistic and a Fighter," Tricontinental Magazine, # 19/20 (July-October 1970): 167-74.

_____. "Report on Portuguese Guinea and the Liberation Movement," Ufahamu, I, 2 (Fall 1970): 69-103.

_____. Sur les lois portugaises de domination coloniale.

Conakry: Partido Africano da Independência da Guiné e Cabo Verde, 1970.

_____. Sur la situation de notre lutte armée de libération nationale, janvier-septembre 1970. Conakry: Partido Africano da Independência da Guiné e Cabo Verde, 1970.

_____. Libération nationale et culture, Conakry: Partido Africano da Independência da Guiné e Cabo Verde, 1970.

_____. Guinée 'Portugaise': le pouvoir des armes, Paris: Francois Maspero, 1970.

_____. Message to the People on the Occasion of the Fourteenth Anniversary of the Foundation of the PAIGC, Conakry: Partido Africano da Independência da Guiné e Cabo Verde, 1970.

_____. Revolution in Guinea, New York: Monthly Review Press, 1970.

_____. The Eighth Year of Our Armed Struggle for National Liberation, Conakry: Partido Africano da Independência da Guiné e Cabo Verde, 1971.

_____. A Brief Report on the Situation of the Struggle (January-August 1971), Conakry: Partido Africano da Independência da Guiné e Cabo Verde, 1971.

_____. Sobre a situação da luta. Sobre alguns problemas práticos da nossa vida e da nossa luta, Conakry: Partido Africano da Independência da Guiné e Cabo Verde, August 9-16, 1971.

_____. A consciência nova que a luta forjou nos homens e mulheres da nossa terra é a arma mais poderosa do nosso povo contra os criminosos colonialistas portuguesas, Conakry: Partido Africano da Independência da Guiné e Cabo Verde, September 1971.

_____. "PAIGC Attacks," Tricontinental, 68 (November 1971): 38-39.

_____. Our People Are Our Mountains: Amílcar Cabral

on the Guinean Revolution, London: Committee for Freedom in Mozambique, Angola and Guiné, introduction by
Basil Davidson, 1971.

_____ . "New Year's Address to the People of Guinea and
Cape Verde," January 1972.

_____ . "PAIGC's Denunciation," Tricontinental Bulletin,
71 (February 1972):   44.

_____ . "Speech Given at the 1632nd session of the United
Nations Security Council, Addis Ababa," February 1972.

_____ . "Frutos de una lucha," Tricontinental 31 (July-
August 1972):   61-77.

_____ . "The People of Guinea and the Cape Verde Islands
in front of the United Nations, Speech at the 27th session
of the United Nations General Assembly," October 1972.

_____ . "Identity and Dignity in Struggle," Southern Africa,
V, 9 (November 1972):   4-8.

_____ . "Identity and Dignity in the National Liberation
Struggle," Africa Today (Fall 1972):   39-47.

_____ . "A Brief Report on the Situation of the Struggle
(January-August 1971)," Ufahamu, II, 3 (Winter 1972):
5-28.

_____ . "Interview" In NLF: National Liberation Fronts,
1960/1970, edited by Donald C. Hughes and Robert E. A.
Shanab (New York: Morrow), 1972, pp. 156-70.

_____ . Rapport bref sur la lutte en 1971, Conakry: Partido Africano da Independência da Guiné e Cabo Verde,
1972.

_____ . "Establishment of the Peoples National Assembly
and the 1972 Election Results, 8 January," 1972.

_____ . Mensagem do ano novo. Conakry: Partido Africano da Independência da Guiné e Cabo Verde, January
1973.

_____ . "Support for the People's Legitimate Aspirations

to Freedom, Independence and Progress," Objective: Justice, V (January-March 1973): 4-7.

_____. "An Informal Talk by A. Cabral," Southern Africa, VI, 2 (February 1973): 6-9.

_____. "Cinquante ans de lutte pour la libération nationale," Questions Actuelles du Socialisme/Socialist Thought and Practice, (March-April 1973): 98-110.

_____. "The Struggle Has Taken Root," Tricontinental, 84 (1973): 41-49. (Press Conference in Conakry in September 1972.)

_____. "Realidades," Tricontinental, 33 (1973): 97-109. (Interview.)

_____. "Original Writings," Ufahamu, III, 3 (Winter 1973): 31-42.

_____. "On the Utilization of Land in Africa," Ufahamu, III, 3 (Winter 1973): 32-35.

_____. "The Contribution of the Guinean peoples to the Agricultural Production of Guinea, I. Cultivated Area," Ufahamu, III, 3 (Winter 1973), 35-41.

_____. Return to the Sources: Selected Speeches of Amílcar Cabral, New York: African Information Service and Partido Africano da Independência da Guiné e Cabo Verde, 1973.

_____. Cabral on Nkrumah, Newark, N.J.: Partido Africano da Independência da Guiné e Cabo Verde, 1973.

_____. Revolutsiya v Guinee. Moscow: Glavnaya Redaktsiva Vostochnoi Literaturi, 1973.

_____. "National Liberation and Culture," Transition, IX, 45 (1974): 12-17.

_____. Alguns Princípios do Partido, Lisbon: Seara Nova, 1974.

_____. "Culture and Nationalism," Transition, IX, 45 (1974): 12-17.

_____ . Unite e lutte. Paris: Maspéro (Tome I: L'arme de la theorie; Tome II: La pratique revolutionnaire), 1975.

Cabral, Maria H. and Amílcar Lopes Cabral. "Breves notas acerca da razão de ser, objectivos e processo de execução do recenseamento agrícola da Guiné," Boletim Cultural da Guiné Portuguesa, IX, 33 (January 1954): 195-204.

Chaliand, Gérard. "The Legacy of Amílcar Cabral," Ramparts, (April 1973): 17-20.

_____ . "The PAIGC Without Cabral: An Assessment," Ufahamu, III, 3 (Winter 1973): 87-95.

Chilcote, Ronald H. "African Ephemeral Material: Portuguese African Nationalist Movements," Africana Newsletter, I (Winter 1963): 9-17.

_____ . "The Political Thought of Amílcar Cabral," Journal of Modern African Studies, VI, 3 (October 1968): 378-88.

Crimi, Bruno. "Les assassins de Cabral," Jeune Afrique (February 3, 1973): 8-12.

Davidson, Basil. "Amílcar Cabral--Death of an African Educationist," Times Educational Supplement, #3009 (January 26, 1973): 6.

_____ . "Profile of Amílcar Cabral," West Africa, XXVII (April 1964).

Ferreira, Eduardo de Sousa. "Amílcar Cabral: Theory of Revolution and Background to His Assassination," Ufahamu, III, 3 (Winter 1973): 49-68.

Figueiredo, A. de. "Amílcar Cabral," Race Today (February 1973): 40.

Intelligence Report. "Amílcar Cabral: a commentary," Overseas Companies of Portugal, Lisbon, 1973.

Kravcova, T. I. "Amilkar Kabral (1924-1973)," Narodny Azii Afriki, #3, (1974): 76-87.

Magubane, Bernard. "Amílcar Cabral: Evolution of Revolutionary Thought," Ufahamu, II, 2 (Fall 1971): 71-87.

Marcum, John A. "Guinea Bissau: Amílcar Cabral; The Meaning of an Assassination," Africa Report, #18 (March 1973): 21-23.

Morgado, Michael S. "Amílcar Cabral's Theory of Cultural Revolution," Black Images, III, 2 (1974): 3-16.

PAIGC. "Amilcar Cabral: O homen e a sua obra," July 1973.

_____. "Palavras de ordem gerais do camarada Amílcar Cabral aos responsaveis do partido, november de 1965," Conakry, 1969.

Reed, Rick. "A Song of World Revolution: In Tribute to Amílcar Cabral," Institute of the Black World Monthly Report (February 1973).

"Tributes to Amílcar Cabral," Ufahamu, III, 3 (Winter 1973): 11-29.

Vieyra, Justin. Amílcar Cabral: liberté pour 350,000 guinéens, Jeune Afrique, #230 (May 1, 1965): 23.

"Without Cabral," Economist, CXLVI (January 1973): 29+.

12 ON NATIONAL LIBERATION

Afrique-Asie. "Numero special à l'occasion de l'indépendence du Cap Vert," 86, June 23, 1975.

"Allies in Empire: The U.S. and Portugal in Africa," Africa Today, 17, 4 (July-August 1970).

Anderson, P. "Portugal and the End of Ultra-colonialism," New Left Review, nos. 15 and 16, 2 parts, n.d.

Andrade, F. J. H. Rebelo de. "Armed Forces Activities in Portuguese Guinea," Ultramar, VII, 4(April-June 1968): 176-200.

Andrade, Mario de. A guerra do povo na Guiné-Bissau, Lisbōa: Livraria Sa da Costa Editoria, 1975.

Anon. Guiné-Bissau: 3 Anos de Independência, Africa in
     Struggle Series, CIDA-C (Anti-Colonial Center for Infor-
     mation and Documentation), Lisbon, 1976.

Anon. "L'Independance du Cap-Vert: Un nouveau pas vers
     l'unité avec la Guinée-Bissau," Afrique-Asie, No. 86
     (1975).

Anon. "Liberation Movement in Portuguese Guinea (PAIGC)
     Totes Up 1964 Achievements," Translations on Africa,
     220 (1964): 5-10.

Anon. "La politique étrangère de Guinée-Bissau," La Revo-
     lution Africaine, Oct. 1974.

Anon. "Portuguese Guinea: More War Than Most," Africa
     Confidential, 3 (February 2, 1968).

Anon. Profile of PAIGC, World Council of Churches Pro-
     gram to Combat Racism, Geneva, 1970.

Anon. "Report of a visit to the liberated areas of Guinea-
     Bissau," International Union of Students and National
     Union of Finish Students, Helsinki, 1971.

Anon. "The Situation of Portuguese Guinea Refugees in the
     Casamance Region of Senegal," Translations on Africa,
     108 (1964): 17-21.

Beetz, Dietmar. Visite in Guine-Bissau, Berlin: Podium,
     1975.

Bender, Gerald J. "Portugal and Her Colonies Join the
     Twentieth Century," Ufahamu, IV, 3 (1974): 121-62.

Bergersol, J. "Guinea-Bissau Begins to Reconstruct," Afri-
     can Development, (October 1974): 18-19.

Biggs-Davison, John. Portuguese Guinea: Nailing a Lie.
     London: Congo Africa Publications, 1970.

Bosgra, S. J. and C. Van Krimpen. Portugal and Nato,
     Amsterdam: Angola Comité, 1970.

Bragança, Aquino de. "La longue marche d'un révolutionnaire
     africain", Afrique-Asie, XXIII, 5 (February 18, 1973):
     12-20.

Cabral, Vasco. "Foreign Capitalist Interests in the So-Called Portuguese Guinea and the Islands of the Green Cape," In Peace and Socialism--Al Tali'a Seminar: Africa; National and Social Revolution, (Cairo, October 24-29), II, ref. #36 (1966).

_____. "Guinea-Bissau," World Problems of Marxism, Peace and Socialism Review (February 1974): 113-16.

_____. Intervention du camarade Vasco Cabral, membre du Comité Executif de la Lutte de PAIGC, au symposium en mémoire d'Amílcar Cabral, Conakry: Partido Africano da Independencia da Guiné e Cabo Verde, January 1973.

_____. "Speech of the Delegation of 'Portuguese' Guinea," In Peace and Socialism--Al Tali'a Seminar: Africa; National and Social Revolution (Cairo, October 24-29) I, ref # 42 (1966).

"Cape Verde," Objective: Justice (February-March 1973): 1.

"Cape Verde: Agreement Between Portugal and PAIGC," Objective: Justice (April-June 1975): 14-15.

Chaliand, Gérard. Armed Struggle in Africa: With the Guerrillas in "Portuguese Guinea", New York: Monthly Review Press, 1969.

_____. Guinée "Portugaise" et Cap Vert en lutte pour leur indépendance, Paris: Francois Maspero, 1964.

Chilcote, Ronald H. "Development and Nationalism in Brazil and Portuguese Africa," Comparative Political Studies (January 1969).

_____. "Nationalist Documents on Portuguese Guinea and Cape Verde Islands and Mozambique," African Studies Bulletin, X, 1 (April 1967): 22-42.

_____. "Struggle in Guinea-Bissau," Africa Today, # 21 (Winter 1974): 57-62.

Comité de Soutien à l'Angola et aux Peuples des Colonies Portugaises. Guinée "Portugaise" et îles du Cap-Vert, l'an deux de la guerre de Guinée, janvier-décembre, 1964, Paris, 1965.

_____. La lutte continue, janvier-avril, 1964, Paris,
1964.

Cornwall, Barbara. The Bush Rebels: A Personal Account
of Black Revolt in Africa, New York: Holt, Rinehart and
Winston, 1972.

Cruz, Luis Fernando Diaz Correia da. "Alguns aspectos da
subverção na provincia portuguesa da Guiné," Ultramar,
VIII, 4 (April-June 1968): 125-47.

Davidson, Basil. Growing from Grass Roots. The State of
Guinea Bissau, London: Committee for Freedom in Mozambique, Angola and Guiné, n. d.

_____. "Guinea-Bissau and the Cape Verde Islands: The
Transition from War to Independence," Africa Today (Fall
1974): 5-20.

_____. "Guinea-Bissau Builds for Independence," New
World Review, XLI, 2 (1973): 36-42.

_____. "An Independent Guinea-Bissau: Political Founda-
tions," West Africa (January 29, 1973).

_____. The Liberation of Guiné: Aspects of an African
Revolution, Harmondsworth: Penguin, 1969.

_____. "Liberation Struggle in Angola and 'Portuguese'
Guinea," Africa Quarterly, X, 1 (April-June 1970): 25-
31.

_____. "Notes on a Liberation Struggle," Transition, IX,
45 (1974): 10-21.

_____. "The Prospect for Guinea-Bissau," Third World
(April 1973): 3-6.

_____. "Revolt of 'Portuguese' Guinea," Tricontinental
Magazine, #8 (September-October 1968): 88-91.

_____. "Victory and Reconciliation in Guinea-Bissau,"
Africa Today, XXI (Fall 1974): 5-22.

Davis, Jennifer. The Republic of Guinea-Bissau: Triumph
Over Colonialism, New York: The Africa Fund, n. d.

Decisão. Conakry: Partido Africano da Independência da Guiné e Cabo Verde, August 30, 1970.

Dias, H. "'Portuguese' Guinea," Portuguese and Colonial Bulletin, V, 6 (December 1965-January 1966): 300.

Duarte, Abilio Monteiro. "Aiding the Struggle in 'Portuguese' Guinea," Revolution, I (August-September 1963): 44-47.

_____. "On the Question of Territories under Portuguese Domination," United Nations General Assembly Document A/AC.109/PV.966, 29 March, 1974, 53 pps.

_____. "'Portuguese' Guinea," Information Bulletin (World Marxist Review), # 42 (May 13, 1965): 53-54.

Duffy, J. "Portugal in Africa," Foreign Affairs, XXXIX (April 1961): 481-93.

Ehhmark, Anders and Per Wastberg. "Angola and Mozambique: the case against Portugal," New York: Roy Publishers, 1963.

Felgas, Helio. Os movimentos terroristas de Angola, Guiné, Moçambique (Influencia externa), Lisbon, 1966.

Fernandez, Gil. "Talk with a Guinean Revolutionary," Ufahamu, I, 1 (Spring 1970): 6-21.

_____. "We Are Anonymous Soldiers of U.N.," Objective: Justice, IV, 1 (January-March 1972): 48.

Frente de Libertação da Guiné e Cabo Verde, Partido Africano da Independência. Message to the Portuguese Colonists in Guiné and Cape Verde, Conakry: October 1960.

Frente de Luta pela Independência Nacional da Guiné Bissau. Charte préambule. Dakar, 1962.

Galtung, Ingegerd. Reports from so-called liberated Portuguese Guinea-Bissau, Morgenbladet, Oslo, n.d.

"Guerre et paix en Guinée-Bissau: Naissance d'une Nation," Afrique-Asie, 66 (September 23-October 6, 1974).

"Guinea-Bissau: Along the People's Paths," Tricontinental Bulletin, # 70 (January 1972): 43-47.

Guinée et Cap-Vert. Libération des colonies portugaises.
Algiers: Information CONCP (Conférence des Organisations Nationales des Colonies Portugaises), 1970.

"Guinea-Bissau's Liberation Struggle," Race Today, III,
11 (November 1971): 377-75.

Guinea-Bissau: Toward Final Victory. Selected Speeches and
Documents from PAIGC (Partido Africano da Independência
de Guiné e Cabo Verde), LSM Press, Richmond, B. C.,
Canada, 1974.

Guinée, Peter. Portugal and the EEC. Amsterdam: Angola
Comité in co-operation with the Programme to Combat
Racism of the World Council of Churches, Geneva, 1973.

Gupta, Anirudha. "African Liberation Movements: A Bibliographical Survey," Africa Quarterly, X, 1 (April-June
1970): 52-60.

Hadjor, Kofi B. "The Revolution in Guinea-Bissau," Africa,
(April 1974): 12-14.

Hoti, Ukson. "The Liberation Struggle in the Portuguese
Colonies," Review of International Affairs (November 5-
20, 1972): 30-31.

Hubbard, Maryinez L. "Culture and History in a Revolutionary Context: Approaches to Amílcar Cabral," Ufahamu,
III, 3 (Winter 1973): 69-86.

Ignatyev, Oleg Konstantinovich. Along the Paths of War:
War Diaries from Three Fronts of Guinea. Moscow:
Political Literature Publications, 1972.

International Union of Students. Report of a Visit to the
Liberated Areas of Guinea-Bissau, Helsinki: National
Union of Finnish Students, 1971.

Kelani, Haissam. "Conditions in the Cape Verde Islands on
the Eve of Independence," Objective: Justice (April-June
1975): 3-10.

Labéry, Henri. "Le Cabo Verde aussi est africain," Afrique
Nouvelle, # 695 (November 30, 1960): 7.

Lefort, René. "Avec les nationalistes de Guinée portugaise,"
Le Monde, # 6-7 (November 1970).

Liberation Support Movement. "Sowing the First Harvest: national reconstruction in Guinea-Bissau," Oakland, California, 1978.

Lipinska, Suzanne. "Deux semaines dans le maquis de la Guinée-Bissao," Africasia, #16-18 (1970).

Lobban, Richard. "The Cape Verde Islands: Colonialism on the Wane," Southern Africa, VIII (January 1975): 4-7.

_____. "Cape Verde Islands: Portugal's Atlantic Colony," Africa (May 1973): 36-39.

_____. "The Fall of Guiledge," AFRICA Magazine, August 1973, no. 24, Paris.

_____. "Guinea-Bissau: A New Era," New World Review, January-February 1975.

_____. "Guinea-Bissau: 24 September and Beyond," Africa Today 21, 1 (1974): 15-24.

_____. "Interview with President Luis Cabral," Southern Africa, VIII, 9 (1975): 12-14.

_____. "The Progress of the War in Guinea-Bissau," Southern Africa, August 1973.

McCollester, Charles. "The Political Thought of Amílcar Cabral," Monthly Review, XXIV, 10 (March 1973): 10-21.

Marcum, J. "Three Revolutions," Africa Report, 12, 6, November 1967.

Marcum, John A. The Politics of Indifference: Portugal and Africa, A Case Study in American Foreign Policy, Syracuse University: Program of Eastern African Studies, 1972.

Marcus, J. "A New Departure in Luso-America Relations," Africa Today, 16, 1 (February-March 1969).

Margarido, Alfredo. "Guinée et Guinée-Bissau: Bilan provisoire de la tentative d'invasion de novembre," Revue Francaise d'Etudes Politiques Africaines, #63 (March 1971): 18-20.

_____. "Partis politiques africains sous domination por-

tugaise," Revue Francaise d'Eudes Politiques Africaines
(July 1968): 44-68.

_____. "Les partis politiques en Guinée portugaise, en
Angola, et aux îles du Cap Vert," Mois en Afrique,
9 (July 1966).

Maria, Victor. "La Guinée 'portugaise'," Voices of Africa,
II (March 1962): 34-35.

Martelli, George. "Progress in Portuguese Guinea," Geographical Magazine (June 1967): 128-37.

Matteos, Salahudin Omawale. "The Cape Verdeans and the
PAIGC Struggle for National Liberation," Ufahamu, III,
3 (Winter 1973): 43-48.

Mendy, Justin. "The Struggle Goes On," Africa Report
(March-April 1973): 24.

Miranda, Nuno de. "Defesa de Portugal," Cabo Verde: Boletim de Propaganda e Informação, XIII, 147 (1961): 6.

Moolman, J. H. "Portuguese Guinea: The Untenable War,"
Africa Institute Bulletin, XII, 6 (1974): 243-60.

"Movimento de Libertação da Guiné e Cabo Verde." Proclamação. Conakry, November 1960.

"Naissance d'un nouvel état africain: la République de Guinée-
Bissau," Présence Africaine, IV (1973): 248-301.

Neto, Joao Baptista Nunes Pereira. "Movimentos Subver-
sivos da Guiné, Cabo Verde, e São Tome e Princípe,"
Cabo Verde, Guiné, São Tomé e Príncipe, Lisbon, 1966.

Ngwube, Douglas. "Guinea-Bissau: Decisive Phase," Africa
(June 1974): 23-24.

Obichere, Boniface I. "Reconstruction in Guinea-Bissau:
From Revolutionaries and Guerillas to Bureaucrats and
Politicians," Current Bibliography on African Affairs,
XIII (1975).

Ogawa, Tadahiro. Nô Pintcha. Tokyo: Taimatsu-Sha, 1972.

PAIGC. "Estatutos dos Pioneiros do Partido," Conakry, n. d.

_____. "Programa do Partido," Conakry, n. d.

_____. "Statuts et programme," Conakry, 1962.

_____. Communiques: "Le Peuple de la Guinée 'portugaise' devant l'ONU," New York, 1962.

_____. Communiques. Extraits de quelques articles de l'organe du Partido Africano da Independência de la Guinée 'Portugaise' et des îles du Cap-Vert. Conakry, April 1963.

_____. Communiques. Développement de la lutte de libération nationale: l'action du PAIGC. Algiers, 1963.

_____. Communiques. Le développement de la lutte de libération nationale en Guinée 'portugaise' et aux îles du Cap Vert en 1964. Conakry, 1964.

_____. Communiques. Le PAIGC à la conférence des chefs d'état et de gouvernement des pays non-alignés le Caire, octobre 1964. Conakry, 1965.

_____. Lei da justiça militar de 19 de Setembro de 1966, com as modificações introduzidas pelo Bureau Político do Partido, na reunião de 20a 23 de dezembro de 1966. Conakry, 1966.

_____. Statuts de l'Institut Amitié. Conakry, 1969.

_____. O nosso livro, primeira classe. Uppsala, 1970.

_____. Regulamento de disciplina interna. Quembra, 1970.

_____. Regulamento interno dos internatos das regiões libertades, Conakry, September 1971.

_____. Manual Politico. Vol. 1, Conakry, 1972.

_____. O nosso livro, quarta classe, Uppsala, 1972.

_____. Projecto da rivisão de lei da justiça militar, Conakry, 1972.

_____ [and United Nations]. Resolution adoptée par le Comité Special a sa 854ème séance, le 13 avril 1972 à Conakry (Guinée), AF/109/63, 1972.

_____. Message du Comité Exécutif de la Lutte du PAIGC, Conakry, January 1973.

_____. Biographies sommaires des membres du Secré-
tariat Permanent du Comité Exécutif de la Lutte, 24 July,
Conakry, 1973.

_____. Proclamação do Estado da Guiné-Bissau, Adopted
by the Peoples National Assembly, 24 September 1973,
Boé, Guiné-Bissau, 1973.

_____. Sobre a situação em Cabo Verde. Lisbõa, 1974.

Pereira, Aristides. Communiqué, Conakry: Partido Africano da Independência da Guiné e Cabo Verde, October
2, 1972.

Pinto, Cruz. "Guinea-Bissau's Liberation Struggle Against
Portuguese Colonialism," Freedomways, # 3 (1972).

Portuguese Colonies: Victory or Death. Havana, Cuba:
Tricontinental, 1971.

Rodrigues, Manuel M. Sarmento. No Governo da Guiné.
Discursos e afirmacões, Lisbon: Agência Geral do Ultramar, 1949.

Rudebeck, L. Guinea-Bissau: A Study of Political Mobili-
zation, Scandinavian Institute of African Studies, Uppsala
1974.

Rudebeck, Lars. "Political Mobilisation for Development in
Guinea-Bissau," Journal of Modern African Studies, 10,
1 (1972): 1-18.

Sampaio, Mário. "The New Guinea-Bissau: How Will It
Survive?" African Development (March 1974): 11-13.

Schilling, Barbara (ed.). Angola, Guinea, Mozambique.
Dokumente und Materialien des Befreiungskampfes des
Volker Angolas, Guinea und Mozambique. Frankfurt-am-
Main: Verlag Marxistische Blätter, 1971.

Sevilla-Borja, H. et al. "U.N. General Mission to Guinea
(Bissau)," Objective: Justice, # 4 (July-September 1972):
4-15.

Simão, José Veiga. "Cape Verde Islands: Decolonization
and Economic Assistance," Objective: Justice, (April-
June 1975): 11-13.

Spínola, António de. Por uma Guiné melhor. Lisbon:
  Agência Geral do Ultramar, 1970.

_____. Portugal e o futuro. Lisbõa: Arcadia, 1974.

_____. O problema da Guiné. Lisbon: Agência Geral do
  Ultramar, 1970.

Sun of Our Freedom: The Independence of Guinea Bissau.
  Chicago: Chicago Committee for the Liberation of Angola,
  Mozambique and Guinea, 1974.

Tavares, Estevão et al. Déposition des ex-détenus par la
  police politique portugaise (PIDE) à Bissau, en Guinée
  "Portugaise," Conakry: Partido Africano da Independência da Guiné e Cabo Verde, 1962.

United Nations. "Security Council's Attention Drawn to Situation in Portuguese Territories, with resolution," United
  Nations Review, X (April 1963): 9-11.

_____. "Questions Relating to Africa: Communications
  Concerning Portuguese Guinea," Yearbook of the United
  Nations, (1964): 120-21.

_____. "Statement on Territories Under Portuguese Ad-
  ministration," U. N. Monthly Chronicle V (July 1968):
  32-42.

_____. "Adoption of General Assembly Resolution on Ter-
  ritories Under Portuguese Administration," U. N. Monthly
  Chronicle VI (December 1969): 23-33.

_____. "Security Council Condemns Portugal and Demands
  Compensation," U. N. Monthly Chronicle, VII (January
  1971): 3-19.

_____. "Report of the U. N. Special Mission to Guinea
  (Bissau)," Objective: Justice, September 1972.

_____. "Working Paper on Guinea (Bissau) and Cape
  Verde, Special Committee on the Situation with Regard
  to the Implementation of the Declaration on the Granting
  of Independence to Colonial Countries and Peoples,"
  United Nations General Assembly, 24 May 1973.

_____. "Statement of the President of the U. N. General

Assembly on the Implementation of the Declaration on the Granting of Independence to Colonial Countries and Peoples," U. N. General Assembly, 29th session, October 3, 1974.

_____. "Developments in Angola, Cape Verde and São Tome and Principe," Decolonization, II 4 (March 1975).

_____. "Report of Visiting Mission to Cape Verde", U. N. General Assembly, April 17, 1975.

_____. "Working Paper on Cape Verde, Special Committee on the Situation with regard to the Implementation of the Declaration on the Granting of Independence to Colonial Countries and Peoples," U. N. General Assembly, 23 May 1975.

"União Democratica das Mulheres da Guiné e Cabo Verde," Status, Conakry, n. d.

"União Nacional dos Travalhadores da Guiné," 1962 Estatutos, Conakry, August 1962.

United States. Congress. House Committee on Foreign Affairs, Subcommittee on Africa. Report on Portuguese Guinea and the Liberation Movement, Washington, D. C. : Government Printing Office, 1970.

Urdang, Stephanie. A Revolution Within a Revolution: Women in Guinea-Bissau, Somerville, MA: New England Free Press, n. d.

_____. "Towards a Successful Revolution: The Struggle in Guinea-Bissau," Objective: Justice (January-March 1975): 11-17.

Venter, Al J. Portugal's Guerrilla War: The Campaign for Africa, Cape Town: John Malherbe Party, Ltd. , 1973.

_____. "Portugal's War in Guinea-Bissau," Munger Africana Library Notes, #19, California Institute of Technology April 1973, 202 pps.

Wallerstein, Immanuel. "The Lessons of the PAIGC," Africa Today (July 1971): 62-68.

World Council of Churches. Program to Combat Racism.

A Profile of PAIGC, Geneva: World Council of Churches,
    1970.

Zartman, I. William. "Guinea: The Quiet War Goes On,"
    Africa Report, XII, 8 (November 1967): 67-72.

APPENDIX A

THE PAIGC PROGRAMME

I.   Immediate and Total Independence

1.   Immediate winning, by all necessary means of the total and unconditional national independence of the people of Guinea and the Cabo Verde Islands.

2.   Taking over of power, in Guinea by the Guinean people, and in the Cabo Verde Islands by the people of Cabo Verde.

3.   Elimination of all relationships of a colonialist and im erialist nature; ending all Portuguese and foreign prerogatives over the popular masses; revision or revocation of all agreements, treaties, alliances, concessions made by the Portuguese colonialists affecting Guinea and the Cabo Verde Islands.

4.   National and international sovereignty of Guinea and the Cabo Verde Islands.   Economic, political, diplomatic, military and cultural independence.

5.   Permanent vigilance, based on the will of the people, to avoid or destroy all attempts of imperialism and colonialism to re-establish themselves in new forms in Guinea and the Cabo Verde Islands.

II.   Unity of the Nation in Guinea and the Cabo Verde Islands

1.   Equal rights and duties, firm unity and fraternal collaboration between citizens, whether considered as individuals, as social groups or as ethnic groups.   Prohibition and elimination of all attempts to divide the people.

2.   Economic, political, social and cultural unity.   In Guinea this unity will take into consideration the characteristics of the various ethnic groups at the social and cultural levels, regardless of the population in these groups.   In the

Cabo Verde Islands, each island or group of identical and close islands will be able to have certain autonomy at the administrative level, while remaining within the framework of national unity and solidarity.

3. The return to Guinea of all émigrés who wish to return to their country. The return to the Cabo Verde Islands of all émigrés or transported workers who wish to return to their country. Free circulation for citizens throughout the national territory.

III. Unity of the Peoples of Guinea and the Cabo Verde Islands

1. After the winning of national independence in Guinea and the Cabo Verde Islands, unity of the peoples of these countries for the construction of a strong and progressive African nation, on the basis of suitably consulted popular will.

2. The form of unity between these two peoples to be established by their legitimate and freely elected representatives.

3. Equal rights and duties, solid unity and fraternal collaboration between Guineans and Cabo Verdians. Prohibition of all attempts to divide these two peoples.

IV. African Unity

1. After the winning of national independence and on the basis of freely manifested popular will, to struggle for the unity of the African peoples, as a whole or by regions of the continent, always respecting the freedom, dignity and right to political, economic, social and cultural progress of these peoples.

2. To struggle against any attempts at annexation or pressure on the peoples of Guinea and the Cabo Verde Islands, on the part of any country.

3. Defence of the political, economic, social and cultural rights and gains of the popular masses of Guinea and the Cabo Verde Islands is the fundamental condition for the realisation of unity with other African peoples.

V. Democratic, Anti-Colonialist and Anti-Imperialist Government

1. Republican, democratic, lay, anti-colonialist and anti-

imperialist government.

2. Establishment of fundamental freedoms, respect for the rights of man and guarantees for the exercise of these freedoms and rights.

3. Equality of citizens before the law, without distinction of nationality or ethnic group, sex, social origin, cultural level, profession, position, wealth, religious belief or philosophical conviction. Men and women will have the same status with regard to family, work and public activities.

4. All individuals or groups of individuals who by their action or behaviour favour imperialism, colonialism or the destruction of the unity of the people will be deprived by every available means of fundamental freedoms.

5. General and free elections of the organisations in power, based on direct, secret and universal voting.

6. Total elimination of the colonial administrative structure and establishment of a national and democratic structure for the internal administration of the country.

7. Personal protection of all foreigners living and working in Guinea and the Cabo Verde Islands who respect the prevailing laws.

VI. Economic Independence, Structuring the Economy and Developing Production

1. Elimination of all relationships of a colonialist and imperialist nature. Winning of economic independence in Guinea and the Cabo Verde Islands.

2. Planning and harmonious development of the economy. Economic activity will be governed by the principles of democratic socialism.

3. Four types of property: state, co-operative, private and personal. Natural resources, the principal means of production, of communication and social security, radio and other means of dissemination of information and culture will be considered as national property in Guinea and the Cabo Verde Islands, and will be exploited according to the needs of rapid economic development. Co-operative exploitation on the basis of free consent will cover the land and agricultural production, the production of consumer goods and artisan articles. Private exploitation will be allowed to develop according to the needs of progress, on the condition that it is useful in the rapid development of the economy of Guinea and the Cabo Verde Islands. Personal property--in particular individual consumption goods, family houses and savings resulting from work done--will be inviolable.

4.   Development and modernisation of agriculture.   Transformation of the system of cultivating the soil to put an end
to monocultivation and the obligatory nature of the cultivation
of groundnuts in Guinea, and of maize in the Cabo Verde Islands.   Struggle against agricultural crises, drought, glut and
famine.
5.   Agrarian reform in the Cabo Verde Islands.   Limitation of the extension of private rural property in order that
all peasants may have enough land to cultivate.   In Guinea,
taking advantage of the traditional agrarian structures and
creating new structures so that the exploitation of the land
may benefit the maximum number of people.
6.   Both in Guinea and in the Cabo Verde Islands, con-
fiscation of the land and other goods belonging to proven enemies of the freedom of the people and of national independence.
7.   Development of industry and commerce along modern
lines.   Progressive establishment of state commercial and
industrial enterprises.   Development of African crafts.   State
control of foreign commerce and co-ordination of internal
trade.   Adjustment and stabilisation of prices.   Elimination
of speculation and unfair profits.   Harmony between the economic activities of town and countryside.
8.   Budgetary balance.   Creation of a new fiscal system.
Creation of a national currency, stabilised and free from in-
flation.

VII. Justice and Progress for All

a. On the Social Level

1.   Progressive elimination of exploitation of man by
man, of all forms of subordination of the human individual to
degrading interests, to the profit of individuals, groups or
classes.   Elimination of poverty, ignorance, fear, prostitu-
tion and alcoholism.
2.   Protection of the rights of workers and guaranteed
employment for all those capable of work.   Abolition of forced
labour in Guinea and of the exporting of forced or "contract"
labour from the Cabo Verde Islands.
3.   Fair salaries and appointments on the basis of equal
pay for equal work.   Positive emulation in work.   Limitation
of daily working hours according to the needs of progress and
the interests of the workers.   Progressive elimination of the
differences existing between workers in the towns and those
in the countryside.

4. Trade union freedoms and guarantees for their effective exercise. Effective participation and creative initiative of the popular masses at every level of the nation's leadership. Encouragement and support for mass organisations in the countryside and in the towns, mainly those for women, young people and students.

5. Social assistance for all citizens who need it for reasons beyond their control, because of unemployment, disability or sickness. All public health and hygiene organisations will be run or controlled by the state.

6. Creation of welfare organisations connected with productive activity. Protection of pregnant women and children. Protection of old people. Rest, recreation and culture for all workers, manual, intellectual and agricultural.

7. Assistance for victims of the national liberation struggle and their families.

b. On the Level of Education and Culture

1. Teaching centres and technical institutes will be considered as national property and as such run or controlled by the state. Reform of teaching, development of secondary and technical education, creation of university education and scientific and technical institutes.

2. Rapid elimination of illiteracy. Obligatory and free primary education. Urgent training and perfection of technical and professional cadres.

3. Total elimination of the complexes created by colonialism, and of the consequences of colonialist culture and exploitation.

4. In Guinea development of autochthonous languages and of the Creole dialect, creation of a written form for these languages. In Cabo Verde development of a written form for the Creole dialect. Development of the cultures of the various ethnic groups and of the Cabo Verde people. Protection and development of national literature and arts.

5. Utilisation of all the values and advances of human and universal culture in the service of the progress of the peoples of Guinea and Cabo Verde. Contribution by the culture of these peoples to the progress of humanity in general.

6. Support and development of physical education and sport for all citizens of Guinea and the Cabo Verde Islands. Creation of institutions for physical education and sport.

7. Religious freedom: freedom to have or not to have a religion. Protection of churches and mosques, of holy places and objects, of legal religious institutions. National independence for religious professionals.

VIII. Effective National Defence Linked to the People

1. Creation of the necessary means of effective national defence: army, navy and air force, linked to the people and directed by national citizens. Those fighting for independence will form the nucleus of national defence.

2. Democratic government within the armed forces. Discipline. Close collaboration between the armed forces and the political leadership.

3. The whole people will have to participate in vigilance and defence against colonialism, imperialism and the enemies of its unity and progress.

4. Complete ban on foreign military bases on the national territory.

IX. Proper International Policy in the Interests of the Nation, of Africa and of the Peace and Progress of Humanity

1. Peaceful collaboration with all the peoples of the world, on the basis of principles of mutual respect, national sovereignty, territorial integrity, non-aggression and non-interference in internal affairs, equality and reciprocity of advantages, and peaceful co-existence. Development of economic and cultural relations with all peoples whose governments accept and respect these principles.

2. Respect of the principles of the United Nations Charter.

3. Non-adhesion to military blocs.

4. Protection for Guinean and Cabo Verdian nationals resident abroad.

APPENDIX B

COUNCIL OF STATE COMMISSIONERS, REPUBLIC OF CAPE VERDE
(as of January 1977)

President	Aristides Pereira
Prime Minister	Pedro Pires
Commissioner of State for:	
Foreign Affairs	Abilio Duarte
Defense and Social Security	Silvino da Luz
Economics and Finance	Osvaldo Lopes da Silva
Education, Youth, Culture, Sports	Carlos Reis
Transport and Telecommunication	Herculano Vieira
Rural Development	João Pereira da Silva
Public Works	Silvino Lima
Justice	David Hopffer Almada
Health and Social Affairs	Manuel Faustino

COUNCIL OF STATE COMMISSIONERS, REPUBLIC OF GUINEA-BISSAU
(as of June 1978)

President, Council of State	Luis Cabral
Vice-President, Council of State	Umaro Djalo
Secretary, Council of State	Lucio Soares
Prime Minister	Francisco Mendes

191

Commissioner of State for:

Armed Forces	João Bernardo Vieira
National Security and Public Order	Constantino Teixeira
Economic Planning and Development	Vasco Cabral
Foreign Affairs	Victor Saúde Maria
Communication and Transportation	Rui Barreto
The Fighters of Freedom	Paulo Correia
Justice	Fidélis Cabral d'Almada
Commerce and Handcraft	Armando Ramos
Industry, Energy, and Natural Resources	Filinto Vaz Martins
Health and Social Affairs	João da Costa
Post and Telecommunication	Fernando Fortes
Information and Tourism	Manuel dos Santos
National Education and Culture	Mário Cabral
Agriculture and Animal Husbandry	Samba Lamine Mané

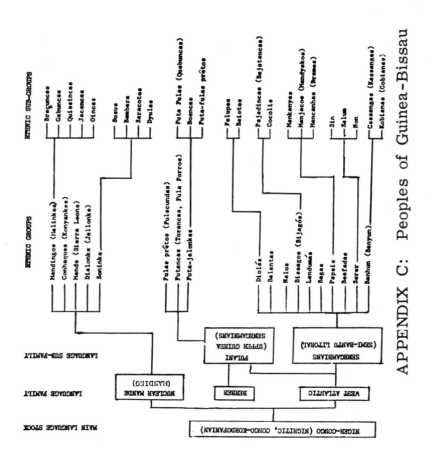

APPENDIX C: Peoples of Guinea-Bissau